Sybaritic
Sex Drive & Success
Genius

Excellence comes from a driven personality!

Landrum says, "Get excited about something and success will follow. Leadership eminence is born of lust for life and the enthusiastic pursuit of a dream." He feels strongly that excellence in any field is a function of ardor, and any life without passion is akin to having wine without cheese. For him passion is just another word for Productivity, Persistence, Persuasion, Possibilities, Performance, and Philandering. He draws on the research of Napoleon Hill "Sex energy is the creative energy of all geniuses" and Freud "unsatisfied libido is responsible for producing all art and literature" to validate his thesis. Landrum says passion is not emotion nor romance, it is something else, and that something can propel the average person to unlikely heights, and the exceptional to eminence. He uses fourteen creative visionaries from disparate disciplines to authenticate his work – men like psychotherapist Carl Jung, Nobel Prize winners Bertrand Russell and Albert Camus, entertainers Charlie Chaplin, Isadora Duncan, Colette, and Madonna, inventor Bucky Fuller, artist Picasso, athlete Babe Ruth, dramatist Oscar Wilde, business tycoons Howard Hughes and Larry Ellison, and President John F. Kennedy. Passion fueled their trek to the top. With it they became rich and famous. Without it they would have been lost in the muddle of mediocrity.

Genie-Vision Books
Naples, Florida
E-Mail: genelandrum@CS.com

Published by Genie-Vision Books
Naples, Florida
E-mail: **genelandrum@cs.com**

1st edition

Copyright 2001
Library of Congress Cataloging-in-Publication Data

Cover by Tammy Hildreth
nfn11322@naples.net

Sybaritic Genius – Sex Drive & Success by Gene N. Landrum.
    p.   cm

ISBN# 0-9659355-1-5

1. SELF-HELP, 2. SEXUALITY 3. CREATIVITY
4. BIOGRAPHY, 5. EDUCATION, 6. PSYCHOLOGY

ATTENTION: BOOK CLUBS, NON-PROFITS & EDUCATORS

COPIES OF THIS BOOK ARE AVAILABLE AT DISCOUNT FOR FUND RAISERS, BULK PURCHASES, SALES MEETINGS & PROMOTIONS.

**CONTACT
GENIE-VISION BOOKS % GENE N. LANDRUM
941-597-9545 – FAX 941-597-7347
E-MAIL: genelandrum@cs.com
WEB SITE: genelandrum.com**

Printed in the United States of America

DEDICATED TO

My Loving Wife Diedra
Who understands the nuances of passion in people

"Any organism in equilibrium is a dead organism"
Fritjof Capra, *The Web of Life* (1996)

"The process of sexual pleasure is the life process *per se*"
Wilhelm Reich, Psychotherapist

**"Mad passion or passionate madness is the reason
why psychopathic personalities are often creators and why their
productions are perfectly sane"**
Jaques Barzun, *The Paradoxes of creativity* (1990)

ACKNOWLEDGEMENTS

Many people contributed to this book including International College and Collier County, Florida librarians, tennis and golf buddies, and especially past business associates whose passion set them apart from the pack. But the book was initially spawned by the passionate subjects researched for my other books – men like Napoleon and Frank Lloyd Wright and women like Catherine the Great and Golda Meir. These subjects were passion incarnate to such a degree it motivated a further look into the relationship between passion and productivity and seduction personally and professionally. Unrequited drive was at the core of these individuals and it undoubtedly had a major bearing on their ultimate fame and fortune. When they faced catastrophe ardor came to the rescue and when they found doors closed their zeal knocked them down. Nothing could deter them, not adversity, or rejection, and that is the genesis of this work.

The book cover was designed and illustrated by free-lance artist Tammy Hildreth with special inputs from bankers Mike Surgeon and Bradley Towle. Tim Quillen offered valuable insight into the passion of San Francisco creative wunderkinds and Barbie Brill of Naples offered insight into Colette as a woman with passion. A wealth of important research data was provided on Babe Ruth by California stand-up comedian, and strong supporter of my writing, a Mr. Rockne Skyberg. Friend and fellow educator Tim Jones helped with computer software enhancements, as did Gay Aryros, who also provided valuable data on trait-anxiety. Ex-student Becky Quimby contributed valuable research data on the sex lives of the rich and famous and my wife Diedra provided scrupulous editing services.

About the Author

Dr. Gene Landrum is a high-tech start-up executive turned educator and writer. He originated the Chuck E. Cheese concept of family entertainment among other entrepreneurial ventures. His doctoral thesis was on the *Innovator Personality.* He lectures extensively and teaches in the graduate and undergraduate programs at International College in Naples, Florida. His books look into what makes the great tick, and can be found in most bookstores or on the author's website - genelandrum.com. Titles are as follows:

Sybaritic Genius – Sex Drive & Success **(2001)**

Literary Genius – A Cathartic Inspiration **(2000)**

Eight Keys to Greatness **(1999)**

Prometheus 2000: Truth - Vision - Power **(1997)**

Profiles of Black Success – 13 Creative Geniuses **(1997)**

Profiles of Power & Success - 14 Geniuses Who Broke the Rules **(1996)**

Profiles of Female Genius - 13 Women Who Changed the World **(1994)**

Profiles of Male Genius - 13 Males Who Changed the World **(1993)**

Gene N. Landrum, PhD
Fax: 941-597-7347
Web Page: genelandrum.com

CONTENTS

TABLES ON PASSION

PREFACE

Why do passionate people achieve at a higher rate than those less driven? They have no choice. They must be the best or lose self-worth. Why is it that so many individuals born with so much natural talent allow it to go fallow? Why do so many of the gifted children end up in mediocre jobs or careers? This anomaly is the focus of this work. In writing seven other books it became obvious that the eminent individuals in the world were not only different they were passion incarnate. And that was the genesis of this work, to show the relationship between passion and performance. To show how talented people without passion go wanting, and why many with mediocre talent end up rich and famous.

Is this book about sex? No! Is it about sex drive (passion) and its relationship to success? Yes! And the relationship will be explored in both the positive and negative sense. Our greatest strengths are always our greatest weaknesses, and passion is no exception. Ardor can lead us to the penthouse, but our families are often left in the guesthouse. This book will show the importance of using passion as the fuel to the top. It will also explore all those bodies left in the wake of the driven individual.

PASSION & PERFORMANCE. Why are passion and success inextricably intertwined? Because success is not a by-product of some mystical innate talent, it is born of inner drive and psychic energy. A prime example is the Mistress of Shock, Madonna, a woman with limited talent who has been eminently successful as a song writer, dancer, recording artist, actress, and rock concert performer. Madonna has parlayed limited ability into a net worth of $200 million. Her secret? Passion! It was not natural ability, and it was not genetic talent. It came from unparalleled zeal! Thousands of women with more talent than Madonna are on welfare. But when Madonna came to a closed door, she knocked it down. When she found someone who could help her move up, she tripped them and beat them to the ground. She had few inhibitions. The goal was godly and no rule was beyond breaking. Passion made her because she had little talent. She just wanted it more than others.

Conversely, NBA basketball player Shawn Bradley is blessed with incomparable physical size and skills. Here is a man 7' 6" with the ability to move like a man 5' 9". While in college the pro coaches were drooling. But for whatever reason, a strong commitment to his Mormon religion, lack of passionate. These individuals were passionate to a fault, despite not marrying or having sexual liaisons. Similarly, Socrates was very passionate, but his passion targeted truth at any cost. Cleopatra was passionate, but it transcended her reputation as a seductress. Her seduction of Caesar had little to do with the need for sex or even romance. What it was about was wresting control of Egypt from her siblings. She crawled nude out of that carpet and into Caesars arms to use his power to gain her own. It worked! Her passion was similar to that of Napoleon and Karl Marx, men willing to sacrifice family, friends, and fortune for a dream out of a seething psyche.

Is there a relationship between passion and sex drive? Of course there is but it varies by gender, time, place, need, and the motivation. As discussed women equate passion with romance, men with a sexual conquest. In some men libidinal drive even interferes with their ability to make rational decisions. Bill Clinton was elected in part due to charismatic appeal to women voters. But once in office those same women expected him to alter his behavior, which was a bit naïve. Sales managers have long known the high correlation existing between sales success and the ability to leave the lounge with a lady.

Passion has been used in varying contexts over the millenniums. It has been used to depict the Last Supper and the death of Jesus in what have come to be known as "passion plays." Webster describes passion as "emotions as distinguished from reason," or "intense, driving, or over mastering feeling." This comes closest to the definition posed by sports psychology textbooks where passion is "arousal to peak performance." This work will use passion as an *internal drive that enhances performance in the boardroom or bedroom.*

QUESTIONS OF PASSION. *Sybaritic Genius* will look at passion and performance relative to a number of variables. Was *power* a catalyst or a provocateur, especially in the lives of powerbrokers Charlie Chaplin and President Kennedy? And do the insecure overcompensate via passion as Alfred Adler thought? Virtually every male in this book over-compensated for some basic insecurity and seduced to prove their manhood. Billionaire Larry Ellison and existentialist Albert Camus are two men who used self-doubt to drive them. And what about charm? Magnetic sex appeal was found in most but the two personifying this dimension are Oscar Wilde and Madonna. Thrill-seeking is another dimension that is aligned with the passionate. This book will be through the provocative lives and lusts of Bucky Fuller and Picasso. Ego and passion will be explored with Carl Jung and Bertrand Russell.

What chance does a person have if they are passionless? Is there a performance gap between the libertines and the average person? Those are questions to be

6

PREFACE

Why do passionate people achieve at a higher rate than those less driven? They have no choice. They must be the best or lose self-worth. Why is it that so many individuals born with so much natural talent allow it to go fallow? Why do so many of the gifted children end up in mediocre jobs or careers? This anomaly is the focus of this work. In writing seven other books it became obvious that the eminent individuals in the world were not only different they were passion incarnate. And that was the genesis of this work, to show the relationship between passion and performance. To show how talented people without passion go wanting, and why many with mediocre talent end up rich and famous.

Is this book about sex? No! Is it about sex drive (passion) and its relationship to success? Yes! And the relationship will be explored in both the positive and negative sense. Our greatest strengths are always our greatest weaknesses, and passion is no exception. Ardor can lead us to the penthouse, but our families are often left in the guesthouse. This book will show the importance of using passion as the fuel to the top. It will also explore all those bodies left in the wake of the driven individual.

PASSION & PERFORMANCE. Why are passion and success inextricably intertwined? Because success is not a by-product of some mystical innate talent, it is born of inner drive and psychic energy. A prime example is the Mistress of Shock, Madonna, a woman with limited talent who has been eminently successful as a song writer, dancer, recording artist, actress, and rock concert performer. Madonna has parlayed limited ability into a net worth of $200 million. Her secret? Passion! It was not natural ability, and it was not genetic talent. It came from unparalleled zeal! Thousands of women with more talent than Madonna are on welfare. But when Madonna came to a closed door, she knocked it down. When she found someone who could help her move up, she tripped them and beat them to the ground. She had few inhibitions. The goal was godly and no rule was beyond breaking. Passion made her because she had little talent. She just wanted it more than others.

Conversely, NBA basketball player Shawn Bradley is blessed with incomparable physical size and skills. Here is a man 7' 6" with the ability to move like a man 5' 9". While in college the pro coaches were drooling. But for whatever reason, a strong commitment to his Mormon religion, lack of

PREFACE

aggressive behavior, or whatever Mr. Bradley is a journeyman NBA player and is out rebounded every night by players a foot shorter who push him out of the way and take the ball.

DIVERSE SUBJECTS. This work is aimed at looking into what makes a Bradley different from a Madonna. One had talent (Bradley) and has little to show for it. The other (Madonna) had no talent and is rich and famous.

The book will look into the subtle relationships, drives, motivations, needs, and behavior of fourteen eminent people who exhibited libidinal drive beyond the ordinary, and some beyond comprehension. A few of the qualities that make for passion are not necessarily admirable traits; and even those in this book were not always proud of their trek to the top. The passionate are driven. They tend to be maniacs-on-a-mission and god forbid anyone who get in their path. Many are inconsiderate, impatient, intolerant, and even depraved. Sating their need for success and conquest was all-consuming. And the individuals used here to study the process were purposely selected from a wide cross section of nationalities, professions, religions, ethnicities, and cultures. Examples are psychotherapist Carl Jung, philosopher Albert Camus, dancer Isadora Duncan, industrialist, Howard Hughes, mathematician Bertrand Russell, painter Pablo Picasso, computer guru Larry Ellison, and American President John F. Kennedy.

These subjects came from a wide range of cultures - French, Spanish, British, American, and Swiss, and even more diverse professions: athletics, business, science, psychology, entertainment, literature, politics, and the performing arts. Six were European and eight were Americans. Chaplin was born in Europe but made his mark in America, while Duncan was born in San Francisco but made her mark in Europe.

The research uncovered a vast amount of data on that gulf separating the passionate and passionless. The intent of this analysis is to find out why and what were the implications for them and their families. In addition, the book will delve into why the passionate tend to end up a penthouse while their less-driven brethren end up in a poorhouse. Why do many passionate women get labeled emotional while men are labeled lustful. Neither are deserving, but that is the price paid for ardor. Men with it end up in the Boardroom while their less driven peers end up in the poolroom. Women with it can end up as prime minister, their passionless sisters may end up on the street. Why? The book will ask this question and attempt to answer it.

4

LIBIDINAL ENERGY. Passion can move mountains. It can make the mediocre magical and the capable incredible. It can elevate a Forest Gump into a mystical state, and elevate the zealous into a netherland, where money is not the motivation, or glory or titles. It is the inner need to satiate that driving force that Freud labeled the Pleasure Principle and others like George Bernard Shaw called the *Life Force*.

This passion journey will take us into the life, loves, and lusts of the eminent. It is important to recognize passion is not about sexual proclivity or emotions. It is about professional overachieving. It just happens that *libidinal energy*, aka *sex drive*, appears to be a critical agent for success. And even though *sex drive* is the issue, the sex part is but a by-product of the more operative issue of why ordinary people with it (sex drive) are able to regularly out-perform, out-work, out-think, out-run, out-distance, and out-fox their adversaries. As you will find the passionate tend to sleep less – Kennedy slept sparingly, and Fuller only in 20 minute spurts - risk more, compete with ferocity, are renegades, have a propensity for evangelism, seek power, and have many quirks and dysfunctions.

Most people think of arousal as a one-dimensional concept relating to sexual arousal. That is hardly the case from a psychological perspective. Arousal has an emotional component that is not sexual but that certain quantity that differentiates world-class athletes from their less successful peers. The same is true of successful business people, poets, entertainers, artists, and those in the humanities like Maria Montessori or Martin Luther King, Jr. Arousal equates to getting "psyched up," a place where experienced athletes enter "the zone" or a state of "flow."

This author found it interesting that the women interviewed on the subject of passion were prone to relate the word to romance. The men immediately saw it as sexual. This book is not about either *sex* or *romance*. It is about arousal theory, and how such arousal can impact the ability to perform effectively at the professional and personal level. Passion is used here as an "inner drive" to expend more energy on a task. It is that special something that separates Michael Jordan and Tiger Woods from the pack in sports, Bill Gates in business and Oprah in entertainment.

WHAT IS SYBARITIC SUCCESS?

Sybaritic is a four-dollar word for *passion* or external manifestation of an internal desire. And it is important that we recognize that passion is not the same as sex or romance. If it were, Michelangelo, Leonardo da Vinci, Joan of Arc, Nikola Tesla, and Mother Teresa would not have qualified as

passionate. These individuals were passionate to a fault, despite not marrying or having sexual liaisons. Similarly, Socrates was very passionate, but his passion targeted truth at any cost. Cleopatra was passionate, but it transcended her reputation as a seductress. Her seduction of Caesar had little to do with the need for sex or even romance. What it was about was wresting control of Egypt from her siblings. She crawled nude out of that carpet and into Caesars arms to use his power to gain her own. It worked! Her passion was similar to that of Napoleon and Karl Marx, men willing to sacrifice family, friends, and fortune for a dream out of a seething psyche.

Is there a relationship between passion and sex drive? Of course there is but it varies by gender, time, place, need, and the motivation. As discussed women equate passion with romance, men with a sexual conquest. In some men libidinal drive even interferes with their ability to make rational decisions. Bill Clinton was elected in part due to charismatic appeal to women voters. But once in office those same women expected him to alter his behavior, which was a bit naïve. Sales managers have long known the high correlation existing between sales success and the ability to leave the lounge with a lady.

Passion has been used in varying contexts over the millenniums. It has been used to depict the Last Supper and the death of Jesus in what have come to be known as "passion plays." Webster describes passion as "emotions as distinguished from reason," or "intense, driving, or over mastering feeling." This comes closest to the definition posed by sports psychology textbooks where passion is "arousal to peak performance." This work will use passion as an *internal drive that enhances performance in the boardroom or bedroom.*

QUESTIONS OF PASSION. *Sybaritic Genius* will look at passion and performance relative to a number of variables. Was *power* a catalyst or a provocateur, especially in the lives of powerbrokers Charlie Chaplin and President Kennedy? And do the insecure overcompensate via passion as Alfred Adler thought? Virtually every male in this book over-compensated for some basic insecurity and seduced to prove their manhood. Billionaire Larry Ellison and existentialist Albert Camus are two men who used self-doubt to drive them. And what about charm? Magnetic sex appeal was found in most but the two personifying this dimension are Oscar Wilde and Madonna. Thrill-seeking is another dimension that is aligned with the passionate. This book will be through the provocative lives and lusts of Bucky Fuller and Picasso. Ego and passion will be explored with Carl Jung and Bertrand Russell.

What chance does a person have if they are passionless? Is there a performance gap between the libertines and the average person? Those are questions to be

6

answered in the book. Is hyper-sexuality a curse or a blessing? It appears it is a blessing for the individual and a curse for their families. This and other questions are the essence of this study. In other words, is there a linear path between the bedroom and boardroom, and if so, what are the wins and costs of such a perilous journey?

Sybaritic Genius will attempt to understand the underlying motivation in the lives of the overachieving personality. If libidinal energy is important to professional success, then what role does the family play in the life of such individuals? Can a person have two masters, professional and personal? Can a passionate person remain faithful to just one mate? Who are the casualties in the lives of the psychosexually driven? Can a person allow free reign to their passions without leaving a lot of bodies in their wake? Are drive, lust, and love, just more notches on the bedpost? What about the families and children of the hyper-passionate? Do womanizers or seductresses have an ulterior motive? These and other similar questions will be looked at in the following chapters with the intent of identifying the variables in a driven person whether male or female, married or single, moral or amoral.

SCOPE OF STUDY

Fourteen subjects were selected from a wide range of professions including: *art (Picasso), athletics (Babe Ruth), industry (Howard Hughes & Larry Ellison), dance (Isadora Duncan), entertainment (Charlie Chaplin & Madonna), philosophy (Albert Camus), psychoanalysis (Carl Jung), science (Buckminster Fuller), literature (Colette), mathematics (Bertrand Russell) politics (Jack Kennedy) theater (Oscar Wilde).*

The book may be read as an interesting biographical analysis of these powerbrokers or as a self-help guide for using passion to succeed. It may also be helpful for those who have lived outside the box and have been called everything from crazy to maverick. A close look at these subjects, even the revered Carl Jung, Isadora Duncan, Bucky Fuller, Jack Kennedy, or Babe Ruth, will portray individuals on the edge and clearly outside convention.

Sybaritic Genius will also look into the part played by childhood crises, birth-order, parental influences, obsessions, books, formal education, religious training, mentors and heroes on the formation of their character and actions. See Table 1 for a listing of the subjects and their professional background.

TABLE 1
PASSIONATE SUCCESSES
7 AMERICANS & 7 EUROPEANS; 11 MEN & 3 WOMEN

PROFESSION	SUBJECT	PASSION
1. ATHLETE	**BABE RUTH**	INSATIABLE PLAYBOY
2. PHILOSOPHER	**ALBERT CAMUS**	PHILANDERER
3. AUTHOR	**COLETTE**	BISEXUAL SEDUCTRESS
4. ACTOR	**CHARLIE CHAPLIN**	LOLITA SYNDROME
5. MODERN DANCE	**ISADORA DUNCAN**	FREE LOVE ADVOCATE
6. ENTREPRENEUR	**LARRY ELLISON**	LECHEROUS
7. SCIENTIST	**BUCKY FULLER**	PROSTITUTES
8. INDUSTRIALIST	**HOWARD HUGHES**	RANDY BISEXUAL
9. PSYCHOTHERAPIST	**CARL JUNG**	POLYGAMIST
10. POLITICIAN	**JACK KENNEDY**	*MENAGE A TROIS* ADDICT
11. ENTERTAINER	**MADONNA**	MISTRESS OF SHOCK
12. ARTIST	**PABLO PICASSO**	HYPER-SEXUALITY
13. MATHEMATICIAN	**BERTRAND RUSSELL**	LASCIVIOUS
14. PLAYWRIGHT	**OSCAR WILDE**	SCANDALOUS BISEXUAL

PROFILES OF PASSION AND PERFORMANCE (SEX & SUCCESS)

The following Mini-Biographies on these subjects has been provided to give the reader a brief introduction to them before delving into their life stories. It will also allow one to read on a favorite individual or to explore subjects relative to the arts (Duncan or Picasso), business (Hughes or Ellison), politics (Kennedy), sports (Ruth), or literature (Colette or Wilde). It will also allow a teacher or researcher to look at the behavioral characteristics of one individual.

TABLE 2

MINI-BIOGRAPHIES ON PASSIONATE SUBJECTS

BABE RUTH

The Sultan of Swat was energy incarnate, a zealot who destroyed his health by overindulging in food and fornicating. The New York Yankees fined him often for philandering. He regularly went to a Massachusetts farm to dry out after wild drinking binges that were but one of his obsessions. When queried about his nature a roommate told the reporter, "I don't know him. I just sleep with his suitcase." The Babe had an insatiable appetite for women, cigars, food, gambling and drinking. He lived life on the edge, a lifestyle that made him and destroyed him. He was named "Babe" in his first year in the big leagues because he acted like a big kid. He never stopped acting the part until the day he died. Babe's prodigious feats dwarfed those of ordinary men. Who else would have called two strikes in an important game in the World Series and then pointed to the center field stands and then hit the ball there? That takes a combination of nerve and verve. When asked about the possibility of striking out he responded, "Never thought of that." In one year, he not only hit more homeruns than any other individual, he hit more than everyone on any one team, and also more than all the American League teams. If success has anything to do with a comparison to your peers the Babe was in a league of his own. Once, after hitting the winning homer in a game in St. Louis, the Babe walked into a brothel and bought it for himself. He spent the whole night bedding every prostitute, topping off his yeomen effort with an eighteen-egg omelet. The Babe said, "I like to live as big as I can."

ALBERT CAMUS

This Nobel Prize winning French philosopher overcompensated for a deep-seated insecurity. By seducing every female that crossed his path. Passion permeated his very being and dominated his plays and philosophy. Camus was given a death-sentence of TB as a teen and from that point in his life he was on a mission that knew no moderation. Camus' life was one long excursion of dissipation and existential reverie with work and love, or lust, depending on one's perspective. Camus married twice but never allowed such things to interfere with his insatiable lifestyle. His long-suffering wife finally gave up and attempted suicide over his unfaithfulness. In a moment of introspection, the existentialist philosopher admitted, "For a ten minute love affair I would have renounced my parents. It is painful for me to admit that I would have

PREFACE

BUCKMINSTER FULLER

The creator of the Geodesic Dome wrote, "Love is the most important principle in the world." Bucky Fuller was one of the world's truly great visionaries despite dropping out of Harvard, not once, but twice. He would later be named to a poetry chair. Ardor defined him. To him sleep was a waste of valuable time to the point that he developed a whole system aimed at overachieving. His intensity was pure vitality that could destroy lesser men. He was an iconoclast with an innovative flare and wrote, "You have to make sense or make money." Fuller was transformed just before age thirty when he escaped suicide at the 11th hour. From that moment he dedicated his life to altruistic development, but not before going within for two whole years during which he didn't speak to another human being including his wife. Energy and speed became godly leading to a theory he labeled *ephemeralization.* He said, "Any successful society needs to achieve more and more with less and less." Bucky admitted to sleeping with 1000 prostitutes before age thirty, and in a moment of introspection said, "I have an unquenchable need for love." Fuller had a compulsion for fast cars, fast women, and fast thinking.

HOWARD HUGHES

The wacky billionaire was prolific, dysfunctional, manic, and brilliant. All contributed to his success in the movie industry (RKO studios), airline industry (TWA & Hughes Air), Las Vegas real estate (owned 35% of Las Vegas casinos), aerospace (Hughes Aircraft) and a myriad of other operations. He was manic-depressive, obsessive- compulsive, and in the end a drug-addict. Hughes had an insatiable appetite for beautiful women and men and used his power to seduce them on his terms. His Hollywood conquests included such internationally famous stars as Ginger Rogers, Jean Harlow, Katherine Hepburn, Susan Hayward (an aborted pregnancy), Rita Hayworth, Ava Gardner, Betty Davis, and Lana Turner along with male stars like Tyrone Power and Cary Grant. Hughes was in love with control and it dominated his life until he was unable to even control himself. A sad commentary for a man who once said, "I can buy any man or woman in the world." He led a lonely and sad life despite having succeeded at his dream of becoming a tycoon. By the time he could buy anything he wasn't even able to control himself and was little more than a slave locked in a self-imposed prison called the Desert Inn.

SYBARITIC GENIUS

CARL JUNG

Freud's disciple was a mystic visionary and polygamist psychotherapist. Jung had a cult following of devoted female disciples who moved to Switzerland to be near their master. Among his faithful followers was no less than John D. Rockefeller's daughter Edith Rockefeller McCormick, a woman who left her husband and children, moved to Switzerland and refused to return for over ten years. Edith contributed $2 million to the English translation of Jung's works. She was not alone in her devotion to the man who created everyday concepts like Extraversion, Introversion, Collective Unconscious, Archetypes, Synchronicities, and Syzygy. Jung was an advocate of free-love and open marriage and practiced his beliefs freely among his clients, employees and patients. Former patient and associate Toni Wolff actually took residence in the Jung home along with his wife Emma and his five children. He lived by the motto, "Free love will save the world, and sexuality is the *sine quo non* of spirituality." Freud said, "He had a colossal narcissism and god complex. He believes he is an Aryan Christ."

JOHN F. KENNEDY

The 35th President of the United States used power to persuade and seduce. He enticed Jackie with money, Marilyn Monroe with power, female admirers with charm and wit, and American votes with a seductive magnetism that had few equals. There is little question his rise to power was fueled by physical and emotional, not intellectual assets. Most think his father bought him the election, but the facts show otherwise. Kennedy was a charismatic man who was driven by a need to live life on the edge. Jack had an insatiable appetite for women and refused to curtail his needs just because he was an elected politician. He had the temerity to place two women on the FBI payroll for the sole purpose of sating his need for *menage a trois* experiences. When his wife left the White House, Fiddle and Faddle were driven in. Jack felt his migraines were due to not getting laid regularly. On taking office in 1960 he said, "This administration is going to do for sex what the last one did for golf." True to his commitment, according to biographer Sy Hersch (1997), he smuggled Marilyn Monroe aboard Air Force One and had liaisons with the likes of Audrey Hepburn, Lee Remick, Sophie Loren, Joan Crawford, and even his wife's press secretary Pamela Turnure. Florida Senator Smathers said, "Jack has the most active libido of any man I've ever known." Passion made him and in the long run it would destroy him.

PREFACE

MADONNA

Sex was a form of ammunition in the rise to the top for the woman who would become known as the Bimbo of Babylon. Losing her virginity was what she called a "career move." She came on stage at age nine in a skin-colored bikini to the remorse of her conservative father and the nuns at St. Francis. Winning that school talent contest conditioned a girl who would from that moment use shock to succeed and sex to sell. Her videos, concerts, songs, and life are permeated with sensuality. When approaching forty and watching her maternal clock ticking away she seduced her trainer and bore her daughter Lourdes. To Madonna a husband is but excess baggage so the trainer was history. She then moved to London to raise her daughter out of the limelight of America and found another man six years younger to father her son Rocco in 2000. These moves only validate her statement to *Vanity Fair* (1990), "pussy rules the world." The shock-Queen used such comments to sell her work and to open doors that would otherwise be closed. She is the mistress of Machiavellian moves. In her earlier years in Manhattan she and a manager played "elevator games" with unsuspecting young men. One ex manager spoke of her many orgies with members of both sexes. Camille Borbonne told the media, "Madonna seduces men like men seduce women," estimating that the Material Girl slept with over 100 men between 1977 and 1983.

PABLO PICASSO

The father of Cubism and one-time poster boy for Surrealism was a renegade. He had an insatiable passion for painting, seduction, and destruction. He used and abused women like few men in history. An attractive young painter Francoise Gilot was forty years his junior. She was taken with his presence and would bear his last two children. Gilot wrote, "He had an inexhaustible passion for work and sex." Picasso was raised to believe that men were born to spend Sunday mornings in church, Sunday afternoons at the bullfights, and Sunday evenings in a brothel. He lived his fantasy. Prostitutes would dominate many of his masterpieces including the one that launched Cubism in 1907 – *Les Demoiselles d'Avignon*. His liked to say, "I have no true friends, only lovers." Coco Channel offered credence to his power of seduction saying, "I was swept up by a passion for him." Picasso was destructive. He firmly believed that women were either "goddesses or doormats," and unabashedly told friends, "You can't be my friend unless I sleep with your wife." Such a mentality contributed to his wife Olga's and mistress Dora Maar's breakdowns, mistress Maria-Theresa's suicide, wife Jacqueline's suicide, and son Paulo's alcoholism.

14

SYBARITIC GENIUS

BERTRAND RUSSELL

Russell's Paradox was not only a world-famous mathematical concept, it could also could be used to describe the mathematical geniuses iconoclastic nature. This creative eccentric ignored all experts in his quest for a Utopian world. Like Jung he was a vocal advocate of polygamy and free love. He was brilliant visionary but was living and loving in Victorian England, not thrilled with his venturesome ideas on open marriage. His ethical preachments and anti-war pacifism caused him to lose his teaching job at Cambridge and other jobs in America at Harvard, UCLA, and CCNY. Defiance and diffidence defined him. He wrote, "I cannot know a woman until I sleep with her," and he practiced what he preached. He slept with two teachers who worked at his London experimental school, and married both, but kept sleeping with others. Russell was a self-proclaimed radical who was raised in a Puritan household. But he was willing to go to prison for his beliefs and spent many nights incarcerated, the last time at age 89. Russell was awarded the Nobel Prize for *Principia mathematica*, a work achieved in concert with Alfred N. Whitehead. He had the misfortune of falling in love with Whitehead's wife, an experience that altered his life. He admitted to "having abnormally strong sexual urges," and has been described as having "galloping satyriasis" (Wallace 1981).

OSCAR WILDE

The flamboyant Irish wit was arguably England's best 19th century playwright. He was certainly the most topical and infamous. He was insightful and imaginative in his articulation on any subject but never more so than on his analysis of romance and lust. He wrote, "There are only two tragedies. One is not getting what one wants. The other is getting it." Wilde was dashing, erudite, and stylish beyond his peers. Passion pervaded his being to the point it affected his demeanor and behavior. This unique way of thinking and acting found its way into his drama about married men's plight. His words would come to haunt him but when on stage they were magnificent and insightful, no more than in the *The Picture of Dorian Grey*, where a man could envision himself as he was and not as he is. Wilde was married with two children when he submitted to his passions and what had made him soon destroyed him. But when he fell for and seduced the son of the Marquees of Queensberry, one Alfred Lord Douglas, his family, life, and work, came to an abrupt end. During this period he wrote, "Bigamy is having one wife too many. Monogamy is the same," followed by, "When a man has loved a woman he will do anything for her except continue to love her." The Irish wit came up with some real lines to justify his lifestyle such as, "The way to get rid of temptation is to yield to it" and "Nothing succeeds like excess." Wilde's two extraordinary works were the novel *The Picture of Dorian Gray* (1891) and the play *The Importance of Being Ernest* (1895). The latter was about living life as a lie that soon led to one of the world's most notorious trials. He was tried and convicted of sodomy and sent to jail, and never worked again dying young as an exile in France. Uninhibited passion for life led to fame and fortune and then to his demise.

> **The book's chapters will be structured on a subject such as Chapter #1 Dysfunctional Passion or #2 Sex Appeal & Passion with two subjects used in each to validate the points of dysfunctional behavior on that nuance of passion. The two featured subjects in each chapter (#1 features Isadora Duncan and Howard Hughes) will appear at the beginning of the chapter to present a substantive overview prior to beginning the reading.**

1

PASSION & PERFORMANCE
One Cannot Exist Without the Other!

"Heightened arousal enhances performance"
Sports Psychology (1993)

"The fiend (inner passion) is party to every work of art"
Fydodor Dostoevsky

"A writer must be in a lustful excitement when writing of love"
Ian Fleming, creator of James Bond

No great leader, athlete, artist, entertainer, scientist or entrepreneur is without abnormal passion. How do you know if you are abnormally passionate? You are driven beyond the norm, are easily aroused, and ooze enthusiasm for life, love and at times lust. Passion manifests itself in hyper-like kinetic energy, enormous zeal, and sometimes, physical ardor. Passionate people pursue dreams and fantasies with great intensity. They also tend to excess in most things. They are sometimes referred to as driven, wanton, licentious, depraved, or decadent. But such people also get a lot done in short periods of time. They act like maniacs on a mission that is often of their own creation.

IS TALENT IMPORTANT? Talent can enhance the trek, but it is hardly the most important factor in any great success. The best singer doesn't always get the role, just as the most qualified individual doesn't always get the job. But what makes some people more equal isn't just contacts and influence, which can happen, but it is a lust for life, a zest, that separates them from the pack. Amelia Earhart was never even in the top ten of female pilots during her era, just as Madonna was a very mediocre entertainer. And the famous diva, Maria Callas wasn't even close to having the best voice in a field where such things are considered sacrosanct. Do you think Stephen King is the best writer? Not a chance! But he sells more books because he has that something special called chutzpah.

Passion differentiates winners from losers more than any other single factor. Talent without passion goes unrewarded, but passionate people with some talent can go right to the top. Consider Joan of Arc, Mother Teresa and Edith Piaf, three women with little natural ability, zero training in their calling, but women with limitless passion. Each rose to the top due to an unrequited passion. Millions of talented people can be found as waitresses, salesman, and pumping gas. They are underutilized more for a lack of passion than any other reason. Such people are often waiting for someone to recognize their talent. They do not understand that waiting for someone else to place you in a position to succeed is virtually impossible. Success always emanates from within never without. When encountering a closed door it must be knocked down and such temerity requires passion, never talent.

Passion and drive are catalysts. They can propel the ordinary into the extraordinary, and the competent to omnipotence. Passion is the only difference between mediocrity and excellence. The new MBA graduate wearing a 1500 SAT score as a badge of wannabe success will perish without passion. The driven visionary with no pedigree, a 600 SAT score, and a dream can go wherever they desire. Passion has a way of improving upon talent, but talent cannot make up for a person devoid of passion.

Without passion the most talented entrepreneur, actor, politician, athlete, musician, painter, or philosopher is destined to live life in the middle lane. Eminence requires drive and talent. Many MENSA members believe a high IQ will open doors. It will not. Others believe a Harvard MBA will make them great. Not so! An example is the elevated IQ scores of the Asian community that research studies have shown are due to fervor. If zeal can improve IQ, just think what it can do for a person writing a play or novel, or someone selling a house, hitting a ball, starting a new business.

PASSION & UNCERTAINTY. The writer is like a tennis player desirous of becoming a winner. Both must work on the difficult tasks that separate the also-rans from the winners. Writing the next bestseller is akin to hitting a backhand down-the-line. This happens to be a very difficult shot for an amateur and even difficult for a pro. The first time it is tried will probably end in failure. For success to occur it will take many tries and failures in a heuristic (trial & error) of misses and hits that will ultimately imprint success on one's subconscious brain. The same will be true of writing and in some respects can be even more torturous a journey.

Hitting a backhand down the line with consummate success, according to sports psychologists, demands repeated tries until one suspends the negativity called failure. In other words, it must be practiced until a person believes they have at least a fifty percent chance of success. Why? Because the beginning player is never confident enough to master such a shot, and this destines them for mediocrity, because they will not try what they don't think they can achieve. Success has little to do with any physical ability, only with a spurious belief in their destiny. This is the reason children learn quicker than adults. They don't have a lot of preconceived beliefs that bias their ability to perform. They learn new concepts faster only because they don't know they can't. *If you don't know you can't, you can. If you don't know you can, you can't,* a fundamental premise in most things.

TABLE 3

Probability of Success Curve

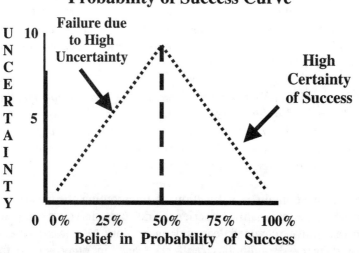

UNCERTAINTY & SUCCESS
Uncertainty increases until a person believes there is a 50% chance the outcome will be positive, only then does uncertainty decrease and belief increase. Success only comes after the failures that are part of the learning process.

PASSION & PEFORMANCE

Sports psychologist Rainer Martens in *Competitive Anxiety in Sport* (1990 p. 222) describes the above concept as the *Uncertainty & Probability of Success*. He illustrates this with an illustration with curves labeled Probability of Success (Table 3). This table illustrates the path of success. After passing the mid-point where a belief in the probability passes the 50 percent point doest the chances of success improve. Before that point there is a mental block that impedes success in any venture. The uncertainty actually increases with the negative belief and will suddenly increase when one believes in their ability. This is the story of self-esteem. Why? Success becomes a self-fulfilling prophecy. We often are unable to achieve because we are not sure we can and as soon as we get rid of those negative thoughts the chances improve dramatically. This is true in sports, but it is also true in business and the arts.

As indicated in Table 3 uncertainty rises precipitously until it hits a point where there is a 50/50 chance of the belief in a positive or negative outcome. The strange thing about this concept is that the highest uncertainty does not occur when a zero belief in success but when it approaches fifty-percent. In other words, the uncertainty is highest when one has thought about failing. In the above example of hitting a tennis backhand down the line, the player can only execute the shot after they have tried it many times and finally begin to believe in their ability. In a similar way business leaders must suspend their own insecurity in order to give themselves the greatest chance of success. More simply, success has more to do with the belief in succeeding than in any ability to perform. Martens (1990 p. 222) wrote:

> *Uncertainty about winning or losing in competition can be determined by the person's perceived probability of success or probability of failure...uncertainty increases to a point at which there is an equal chance of the outcome being positive or negative after which no uncertainty exists.*

Mastery in any domain is a function of overcoming the negative. Skiers exhilarated by the panoramic experience and majestic views are better skiers because they have relegated fear and uncertainty to a lesser role than any potential danger. Passion has replaced fear. In other terms, they have removed head from the equation. When a person is enjoying the experience, of say flying down a steep mountain, they function better than if they think about it. The body will respond to any problems but when the head intervene it tends to give the wrong messages to it. How many men and women have sat down on the snow and cried because they engaged their mind in the process. Children learn to ski easier than adults for this very reason. They envision falling as a positive. Adults view it as a negative. One could care less about falling they other allows it to debilitate them.

In this sense passion and expertise are inextricably tied together. Sales success and failure is another example of this principle at work. Sales people without passion seldom go the same distance as those driven. Consequently, data shows those with drive make 80 percent of all sales. Why? Because they tend to make five calls before giving up, whereas the less driven quit after two or three calls. This equates to the 80/20 rule where 20 percent of the sales people make 80 percent of the sales. Stated in terms of the Uncertainty Chart, the passionate achieve more because they continue to blast forward regardless of the rejections during that upward slope.

What if George Bernard Shaw had quit after writing those first six rejected novels? He would have failed and the world would never have had *Man & Superman* and *Pygmalion* (My Fair Lady). What if Einstein had quit physics after being denied a teaching assignment? Relativity would have had to wait. And what if Walt Disney would have scrapped *Disneyland* when the Board said it was a "stupid" not deserving to be funded? Walt sold his home and hocked his insurance policy to buy that land in Anaheim and that is how the Disney empire came about.

LUST – THE FUEL OF LIFE

It is difficult to name one eminent person without high drive. The world's greats were all driven, people on a mission that refused to be defeated. People like Napoleon, Darwin, Freud, Madam Curie, and Maria Montessori were so driven nothing could keep them from pursuing their dreams. In a similar way lust and love dominated the life of Isadora Duncan, Carl Jung, Picasso, Babe Ruth and Jack Kennedy. Had these individuals been less driven they would have never made their mark on history. And they would not have been so denigrated about their seductions. But the bad comes with the good in all things. Lust opened important doors but also led to many illicit romances. Had they been lest lustful they would have met a more ethical set of standards for society but they probably would not have been in this book. Lust pervaded both personal and professional and that is the way it has to be.

LUST – A DOUBLE-EDGED SWORD. The lustful are movers and shakers and such people sometimes shake the wrong trees. Lust can be used to motivate people to Herculean effort as has been found in Napoleon in battle and in Jim Jones in the cult debacle in Jonestown. It makes us better and makes us so rabid it can produce less than desirable behavior. It is the Dr.

Jekyll and Mr. Hyde syndrome revisited. Validation comes from many sources including Napoleon Hill, a man who spent his life looking into the qualities that led to greatness for America's early tycoons like Carnegie, Mellon, Edison, Ford, J.P. Morgan and FDR, tyrannical men who altered the face of America. Hill shared his findings in *Think & Grow Rich* (1960 p. 187). He wrote, "*Personal magnetism* is nothing more nor less than sexual energy. Highly sexed men are the most efficient salesmen." Freudian psychotherapist Wilhelm Reich spent a great deal of his life researching the subject and spoke of his findings in the *Function of Orgasm* (1973 p. 21) in which he said, "Sexuality is the function around which the life of society as a whole as well as the inner intellectual world of the individual revolves."

Success and seduction are strange bed partners, but they are inextricably tied together like beer and pizza. But seduction isn't always sexual. It can be sublimated into work as Freud so eloquently pointed out in his work on Leonardo da Vinci. Freud also wrote a paper on Dostoevsky's epilepsy and other dysfunctions that were precipitated by an inner rage spawned by his father's murder and castration. Michelangelo and Tesla both refused to marry because they felt that sex and creativity were a zero-sum game with a loss of one attributed to the gain in the other. Love reduces the ability to innovate and when someone is so driven as Leonardo and Tesla they died virgins according to biographers. Some have been so driven they were able to do both in excess as seen in Picasso, Duncan, Chaplin, and Wilde.

SEXCESS. James Michener saw himself as driven and wrote, "I was driven by the passion to produce good books." A student hearing Margaret Mead lecture said, "The sex appeal of her mind was absolutely captivating." Author Anne Rice was aware of a seething inner libidinal drive and wrote, "I'm overly obsessed with sex, it pervades my writing." Romance queen Danielle Steel says, "When I take on a new book, I become totally crazed, in a trance and will go a month without leaving the room." Such passion produced four failed marriages, seven children, and close to 500 million book sales.

Catherine the Great used lovers to help wrest control of Mother Russia. The Russian Empress spent the equivalent of $1.5 billion on her paramours. Howard Hughes set up young starlets in houses all over Southern California to be ready and waiting for his occasional visits. Such is the drive of excessive libidinal drive. Casanova only survived through seductions. He left us with a 4000-word memoir encompassing 12 volumes that credited chocolate as an aphrodisiac while documenting 18th century morality. Casanova purportedly fell madly in love with each of his conquests showering them with gifts and undivided attention. Attentiveness was key to his successful seductions. In a slightly different way John F. Kennedy and Bill Clinton used attractiveness and attentiveness to get elected to office. Virginia Woolf and Sylvia Plath wrote erotically as does Anne Rice. These women used passionate words to excite and to sell books.

What got Clinton elected, also almost got him impeached. That seems to have been lost on the political pundits in Washington. Those voters who put him in office had bought into that charismatic appeal that was little more than a strong libidinal drive that had been with him since college. He had not changed, but the Democratic voters thought that in the White House would change his spots, from a seductive governor of Arkansas to an ascetic President. Not a chance for such a transformation. It never happens and never will. Some said, "Yeh, but he didn't have to do it in the White House?" But he did have to since he was a high testosterone male with a need to prove he was better than most men and could get away with what most men wouldn't even dare. The titillation of such a challenge is more intense than the seduction. Hyper-intensity and satyriasis are innate in the Clinton's of the world. They are exciting and that gets them votes, but they are not about to become less than what they are once in charge.

Cleopatra was not much different from Clinton. Her only real edge over a brother competing with her for the throne of Egypt was her seductive power. She turned to her strength and used it with great effectiveness to gain the throne by seducing Caesar. Naming her child Caesarian was an act of genius. As the old adage says, `one must dance with who brung ya' and those qualities that lead to success must be tapped in continuing it.

Hyperactive libidos present in the likes of Cleopatra, Kennedy or Clinton become instruments of power and they are not about to wane once in power. Fanaticism is inter-woven in an individual's psychological makeup and thinking such people will change is gross naiveté. Such highly charged libidos are actually turned on by the risk of doing what lesser people only fantasize about. The idea of a liaison with the secretary just outside the door and the wife somewhere in the house is a turn-on for the hypersexual personality like Kennedy and Clinton. What is excess to most is part of the game to those with great vitality.

IS PASSION A CATALYST FOR PRODUCTIVITY?

Ardor is critical to super success in virtually any venue. Passionate people just plain get more done. They work longer hours, are intense to a fault, have an unquenchable ferocity, and refuse to quit long before their adversaries.

Normal people experience normal success and typically have a rather normal drive. The super-successful have abnormal drives, but are far more prone to abnormality on almost any scale. The more driven the person, the more productive they can be. The more abnormal the person, the greater the chance they will be abnormally successful. That is the essence of drive and productive output. Eminence doesn't exist without intensity. Is there a downside? Always! Many bodies are left in the wake of the truly driven personality. A quick look at the lives and lusts of the eminent producers in the world illustrates this point. Casanova, Napoleon, Hitler, Hemingway, Madam Curie, and Margaret Thatcher were obsessive personalities.

Passion pervaded the life of Casanova. It began with his preparation for the priesthood when he dared seduce two nuns during his training for the cloth. The *menage a trois* experience overwhelmed him and he was soon hooked. His penchant for such acts drew the attention of the Inquisition making him *persona non grata* as a priest. Later in life the philandering vagabond returned to Florence. He met and fell in love with a young girl and proposed marriage. But when she took him home to meet her mother he was shocked to find the mother had been one of his early conquests. His betrothed was his own daughter. Not discouraged, this lustful man began a long intrigue with both women, discussed at length in his later autobiographical writings. The name Casanova would be unknown today except for his perverse passions.

Carl Jung was a passionate psychotherapist who believed in allowing all feelings to seek fulfillment. He wrote, "Everything in the unconscious seeks outward manifestation, and the personality too desires to evolve out of its unconscious conditions and to experience itself as a whole." The Swiss master practiced what he preached and allowed free reign to most of his most perverse fantasies. He married the metaphysical with the scientific and attracted many disciples to an ideology that included free love and polygamy.

Albert Camus was a philosopher whose name was synonymous with female conquests. He decided early in life to give free reign to his innermost needs and passions. No woman was safe when he was near. He wrote, "When you have seen the glow of happiness on the face of a beloved person, you know that a man can have no vocation but to awaken that light on the faces surrounding him." Of course most of the faces he observed were female as he was an insatiable cad.

OPTIMAL AROUSAL & PERFORMANCE. See Table 4 for the inter-relationships between arousal and performance where relaxation and anxiety are two extremes interacting with boredom and hyper-activity. Optimum execution in any discipline – sports, writing or business - is a function of placing oneself in the middle where the zone or flow state exists. One must be relaxed but stimulated and calm but excited to get into a zone state. As in most things too much of anything is not good and moderation is best.

TABLE 4

OPTIMAL AROUSAL & PERFORMANCE

An optimum level of stress and arousal is required to excel, too little will make you boring or fall asleep, too much and you become hyper or anxious

HIGH STRESS

UNDERSTIMULATION
BOREDOM/FATIGUE

OVERSTIMULATION
ANXIETY

LOW
AROUSAL

OPTIMUM
PERFORMANCE
ZONE

HIGH
AROUSAL

SLEEP
RELAXATION

EXCITEMENT

LOW STRESS

PLEASURE PRINCIPLE. Freud defined high sex drive as psychic energy. His term for sex drive was the *pleasure principle* and also psychic energy. He believed "sublimation of unsatisfied libido was responsible for producing all art and literature" (Storr 1989 p. 74). Freud studied artists and writers to determine the role played by sex, or the lack of it, in their drive for success. He concluded that Leonardo had sublimated sex drive into work and wrote, "It is fairly clear that the impulse to every kind of aesthetic creation is psychologically connected with courtship... Societies that have been conventionally virtuous have not produced great art" (Russell 1987 p. 216).

Psychologist Frank Barron spent years studying successful architects at IPAR - Institute of Personality Assessment & Research (IPAR) at the University of California at Berkeley. He concluded, "Creative people are accurate, sharp, observing and have a high sex drive." Other findings from this study are: (Taylor 1975 p. 5)

> *The creative individual turns from reality to fantasy where he gives full play to his erotic wishes. Creative behavior is an overt manifestation of sublimation, an unconscious process through which libidinal or aggressive energies are converted into culturally sanctioned behaviors.*

EXCESSIVE LIBIDO. Few individuals in history have ever had the hyper-sexuality of American basketball icon Wilt the Stilt Chamberlain. Wilt wrote in his 1991 memoir *View From Above* that, "lust is far more motivational to man than love." He was incorrect. His lust was the result of testosterone run amuck. Chamberlain admitted to having sex with 20,000 different women. In his words that amounts to "1.2 women a day, every day since I was fifteen years old" (Chamberlain p. 251). Chamberlain never married so he had the opportunity for such conquests. And since he was a superstar hounded by young female fans known to rock stars as "groupies," he was able to have so many multiple trysts. Such liaisons are called "star fucking."

Passionate people are found in all disciplines. They tend to live and die by their ardor but often ascend to a higher state than their more mellow peers. Their *will* opens more doors, breaks down more barriers, and inspires more due to an enthusiastic charm. Such people are far more interesting and exciting but the downside is their ardor doesn't often recognize limits. One political associate of Kennedy said no woman was safe around him, not your sister, mother or daughter. Such zeal attracts disciples but also turns off many would be associates. Such people are seldom seen with indifference. They are loved or hated and are often their own worst enemy. Excess is their forte and they thrive or suffer by their intensity as was the case with Oscar Wilde.

An example of such a man was Honore Balzac, the father of the modern novel. Balzac wrote, "I only have two passions, love and glory. If I'm not a genius I'm done for." His intoxication for glory led him to lock himself in an attic for years clothed in nothing but a monk's robe to remind him to remain celibate. Everything Balzac did was extreme. He was energy incarnate and could no more function normally than give up food or coffee. He worked eighteen to twenty hours a day seven days a week to document French society of posterity. His work was a *tour de force* with few equals in history. Balzac was so driven he stopped bathing for fear it would relax him and keep him from his workaholic schedule that destroyed him by age fifty. His death was not in vain since he left us with a wonderful documentary of nearly 100 volumes. He would write, "The days melt in my hands like ice in the sun. I'm not living. I'm wearing myself out in a horrible fashion" (Robb p. 294).

PASSION & BLISS

At the other end of the intensity spectrum is Joseph Campbell, the father of modern mythology. He saw libidinal drive as instrumental to overachieving but couched the passion in terms of following your "bliss" or your labor of love. He wrote, "No misfortune can be worse than the misfortune of resting permanently static." For Campbell "bliss" was an internal source of hyper-energy born of some passion. His passion was the derivation of icons and hero worship that led him to pursue mythology. His believed:

> *If you follow your bliss you'll always have your bliss; but if you follow money, you may lose it. Work begins when you don't like what you're doing. Make your hobby your source of income, then there is no such thing as work, and there is no such thing as getting tired.* (Toms p. 107)

Carl Jung was one of Campbell's intellectual mentors, a man he visited in his pursuit of man's motivations. Jung had written, "It is not Goethe that creates Faust, but Faust who creates Goethe." That is a telling statement about man's inner motives. Another testament to following your heart, not your head, or the almighty buck, comes from Berry Gordy, the entrepreneurial founder of Motown. After selling out for hundreds of millions in the early 90's Gordy wrote his memoirs and admitted, "I was obsessed. I couldn't wait to get to work in the morning and hated to leave at night" (Gordy p. 202). Isadora wrote, "I was so interested in my work that I got into a state of static ecstasy."

PASSION & PEFORMANCE

LIFE FORCE

The essence of life was called *Life Force* by Irish dramatist George Bernard Shaw. A fan of Nietzsche, Shaw had concluded that it was his inner *will* that drove him to special heights and made him more than his peers. His internal Nietzschean Superman or *will-to-power* was used in much of his work but never more poignantly than in his classic play about Don Juan in hell – *Man & Superman* (1903). Passion for Shaw was the epicenter of man's worth and his ability to overachieve. With it no door would remain closed and without it he might as well get a job in the mines. The drive to alter another human to fit one's ideal was behind his classic play *Pygmalion* – My Fair Lady. He was Professor Higgins changing a lowly flower girl into a sophisticated lady. Shaw came about his *life force* beliefs through extensive study of Karl Marx whose work motivated him to co-found the British Labor Party despite being Irish. He saw Marx as the archetype of a man tapping into his *will* to alter the world with his classic *Das Kapital*.

PASSION & PEFORMANCE

Regardless of man's talents or ambitions, no true success will be found without trait or success anxiety that is labeled arousal by sports psychologists. A person must get excited or go nowhere. They must get *psyched up* or they will never be able to make into that place athletes call the *zone*. The so-called *zone* or *flow state* of emotional commitment can only be achieved between that point of getting *psyched up* and getting *psyched out*. No matter one's discipline the ability to perform at an optimum level depends on arousal up to a point but not beyond that point. The middle is magical and the objective of all people. A person knows when they are in that state. It is when you have the power of total focus, intensity, insight, and lucidity. Whatever you touch works, and you feel like you can conquer the world.

Anyone who plays a sport that is competitive and demands optimum eye-hand coordination like squash, basketball, tennis, golf, racquetball, knows how important it is to get in the zone. The state is often described as "relaxed concentration," a point when you are without anxiety but are highly focused. If too relaxed you become nonchalant, cavalier and lose focus. If too focused it is easy to become intense and so anxious it becomes counter-productive to optimal performance. That is when golfers through golf clubs, tennis players throw down their rackets, and executive throws a tantrum. Unrealistic expectations are rampant in the *psych-out* area. Lack of zeal keeps a person out of the zone and too much takes them too far.

TABLE 5
PASSION & PERFORMANCE
Arousal Theory of Performance & Creativity
Passion Improves Performance up to a point and then declines until it interferes with Performance

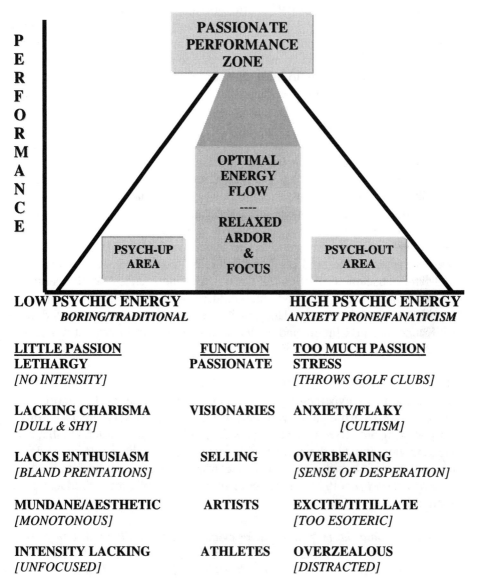

HIGH

P
E
R
F
O
R
M
A
N
C
E

PASSIONATE PERFORMANCE ZONE

OPTIMAL ENERGY FLOW

RELAXED ARDOR & FOCUS

PSYCH-UP AREA

PSYCH-OUT AREA

LOW PSYCHIC ENERGY
BORING/TRADITIONAL

HIGH PSYCHIC ENERGY
ANXIETY PRONE/FANATICISM

LITTLE PASSION	FUNCTION	TOO MUCH PASSION
LETHARGY	PASSIONATE	STRESS
[NO INTENSITY]		*[THROWS GOLF CLUBS]*
LACKING CHARISMA	VISIONARIES	ANXIETY/FLAKY
[DULL & SHY]		*[CULTISM]*
LACKS ENTHUSIASM	SELLING	OVERBEARING
[BLAND PRENTATIONS]		*[SENSE OF DESPERATION]*
MUNDANE/AESTHETIC	ARTISTS	EXCITE/TITILLATE
[MONOTONOUS]		*[TOO ESOTERIC]*
INTENSITY LACKING	ATHLETES	OVERZEALOUS
[UNFOCUSED]		*[DISTRACTED]*

PASSION & PEFORMANCE

Those lacking intensity are destined for mediocre performance whether it is in winning an election, pursuing a relationship, closing a sale, or operating a business. Research scientists use an inverted U model found in Table 5 to illustrate the inter-relationships between being "psyched-up" and "psyched-out." When learning to play the game of business or a sport it is critical to be charged up enough to overcome adversity but not too much to impair performance. Professional golf instructors have found that women are easier to teach than men. Why? Because women begin with fewer expectations and therefore do not get psyched out and consequently follow instructions better than most men. The average male engages ego and attempts to hit the ball a mile before knowing how to hit it ten feet. Optimal performance is a subtle area between two extremes (see Table 5).

HISTORY OF PASSION & SUCCESS

As discussed earlier, Cleopatra was a seductress. She seduced two of the more notable men in history – Julius Caesar and Marc Anthony, not for emotional gratification, but to secure power. Passionate persuasion was her forte and no duplicity was beyond her. It allowed her to become Queen of Egypt. A millennium and a half later the lovely would be Empress Sophie Vonhalt-Zerbst recruited two lovers to overthrow her idiot husband who was about to imprison her and put his mistress on the throne. Her ploy worked and Sophie became Catherine the Great. "Uterine frenzies" as she described them, dominated her rule, and she would come down as the most seductive monarch in modern history. Her long procession of paramours dwarfed those of Kennedy and Clinton and included the European court wit Casanova. Speculation has him gracing her royal bed.

MANIA & ARDOR. Scientists have tied manic-depression to high sex drive in addition to its hyperactivity dimension. Many of the world's most noted leaders were so afflicted as were half of these subjects. Hyperactivity drove Napoleon, Lord Byron, Nikola Tesla, Mark Twain, Hitler, Stalin, and Hemingway. It made them impossible mates but gave them a decided edge in competing with less driven peers. According to Kay Jamison who wrote in *Touched With Fire* (1993) such people are more capable, more productive and more driven:

> *Hypomania is prima facie evidence for intellectual and artistic achievement. Who would not want elevated and expansive mood, inflated self-esteem, abundance of energy, less need for sleep, intensified sexuality, and sharpened and unusually creative thinking.* (Jamison p. 103)

SYBARITIC GENIUS

Let's take a quick look at a few of the most successful leaders in history who were so inclined. A seductive style made them magnetic, but was also instrumental in their immense success.

NAPOLEON. Napoleon Bonaparte was passion incarnate. Hyper activity dominated everything in his life including playing cards, fighting battles, seducing women, and writing verse. His charismatic flare helped him seduce a nation despite not even being a citizen. He was born in Corsica and spoke broken French. And the paradox of his life was taking over France on a platform of nationalism when he wasn't even French. The Little Corsican out-worked, out-thought, out-witted, and out-romanced his adversaries. Strangely, he was first attracted to much older women, not uncommon in ambitious men. Why? Because they were well connected, had money to finance ambition, and were experienced paramours. Napoleon's first true love was a young damsel named Desiree. When that relationship faltered he took up with the 60 year-old Mademoiselle de Montasnier, a woman old enough to be his grandmother. He then took up with 40 year-old Madame Permon. When he finally decided to take a wife it was a court favorite, Josephine, a woman ten years his senior and a notorious nymphomaniac. She confirms the Napoleon mystique and hyperactivity. "I was alarmed at the boundless energy of the man, that energy which animates all his doings." Napoleon was infamous for wild soirees across Europe where horses could not keep up with his pace and would perish. He dictated to four secretaries simultaneously on different subjects without missing a beat.

ADOLPH HITLER. Hitler was also bipolar. His symptoms included wild reveries and emotional outbursts that alarmed his associates. Women would swoon at his words and the wives of the German industrialists were so taken they financed his Nazi Party. But they gave him the money personally that he sequestered away to insure control. The Fuhrer's nickname while in Munich was King of Munich, supposedly as testimony to his prolific sexual abilities. One biographer wrote, "Women's gushing adulation carried to the pitch of religious ecstasy" (Landrum 1996 p. 288). Biographer Stein wrote, "He had the magnetism of a hypnotist, the force of an African medicine man." These German women were Helen Hanfstaengl, Winifred Wagner, Elsa Bruckman, Helene Bechstein, and Gustav Krupp's wife - the richest industrialist in the land. Biographer Alan Bullock wrote, "Men groaned or hissed and women sobbed involuntarily caught up in the spell of powerful emotions" (Landrum 1996 p. 284) as he spoke.

Socialite Elsa Bruchman said, "I simply melted away in his presence. I would have done anything for him." A young German who was against his ideology once heard him speak and came away saying, "I forgot everything but the man. The intense will, the passion of his sincerity, seemed to flow from him into me. I experienced an exultation that could be likened to a religious experience" (Hershman and Lieb 1994 p. 149). Such inflamed rhetoric attracted legions of dedicated disciples that were willing to follow him anywhere and did. This loser took over a major nation through the power of passionate words that flowed like lava from a seething inner passion.

ERNEST HEMINGWAY. The master of the short story was also a master of seduction and fueled by a bipolar personality. F. Scott Fitzgerald said, "He had to have a new woman for every new book." A heroic pathos pervaded his life and work. He had to catch the biggest fish, bed the most beautiful woman, fight the toughest guy in the bar, and drink the most booze. Mania preoccupied his writing and life. It made him successful at his craft and unsuccessful as a husband and father. He was married four times but was never faithful. One mistress, the wife of the head of Pan American Airlines tried to kill herself because of him, while Pauline, his second wife succeeded.

Psychologists have found a relationship between high sex drive, suicide, mania and bipolar disease. Hemingway's life and lusts give credence to these afflictions. His father, brother, sister and granddaughter all took their lives. Irving Wallace wrote, "as a young man in Paris, Hemingway's sex drive was so strong he had to make love three times a day. He ostentatiously consumed sex-sedating drugs to quiet his raging libido" (Wallace p. 209). Hemingway boasted of bedding Mata Hari, an Italian countess, a Greek princess and numerous prostitutes all during his first marriage.

EDITH PIAF. The French chanteuse was notorious for an inability to sleep alone. Rather than spend one night without a man she would walk out of her hotel and down the street and pick up any stranger that was a willing partner. The Little Sparrow was in love with love. Every hit tune spoke of love and romance, something she never found in a tragic life that went unfulfilled. She admitted, "I cannot stand being alone," and "Love conquers all." She began one-night stands in her teens and never stopped until she died at 48. Piaf believed "you only really get to know a man when you've been to bed with him. You learn more about a man after one night in the sack than you do in months of conversation. When they talk they can fool you, but they can't kid you in bed" (Bertreaut 1973 p. 201). Bertreaut wrote, "She lived each day as if it were her last."

SYBARITIC GENIUS

Passion dominated every aspect of Piaf's frenetic life. It made her irresistible to a diverse group of fans including Jean Cocteau, Maurice Chevalier, Marcel Cerdan, and Yves Montand. She mentored Montand and then married him. He wrote, "Edith only sang best when she was madly in love. She was magnetic. No one could resist her." Her stepsister said, "Everyone was sucked dry by her single-minded passion" (Bereaut p. 69). An endless succession of love affairs and drugs took their toll, but when her true love Marcel Cerdan died unexpectedly in a plane crash her life ended. Love and passion dominated her life. Her music of love included hits, *La vie en rose, C'est magnifique, La vie, l'amour and Non, je ne regrette rien.*

THE DARK SIDE OF PASSION

Cultists and would-be messiahs have passion. Jesus, Mohammad, and Ghandi had it. Psychotherapist Carl Jung was so mesmerizing he had a sect of female fans who left their families to be near him in Switzerland. But the most despicable use of passion to seduce is found in the lives and lusts of Jim Jones, David Koresh, Georgie Ivanovitch Gurdjieff, and Bhagwan Shree Rajneesh. These gurus used their enormous powers of persuasion to serve personal ends. They spread a divisive gospel aimed at the seduction of unsuspecting and needy individuals - mostly women. They enthralled with grandiose ideas and the promise of salvation but only after threats of death, all aimed at gaining emotional and physical control over their flock. Jones was bisexual and insisted on *ménage a trios* trysts with his faithful. He led a band of disciples to Jonestown in South America and when he sensed his control waning he duped 900 disciples into committing mass suicide via cyanide laced Koolaid. Koresh dreamed up the immolation of 86 disciples in the Waco, Texas carnage. Strangely, both of these psychotic demagogues, ended their own lives with a self-inflicted bullet to the head.

David Koresh was a notorious pedophile. Jones justified his male seductions as a cleansing of the disciple's homosexual tendencies. There were a number of instances when Koresh seduced wife, husband and child of the same family. His perversity knew few limits. He married the fourteen year-old daughter of one of his followers and she bore him three children. Then he took up with her twelve-year old sister. All of this took place in the name of spiritual enlightenment.

Georgie Gurdjieff was a Russian born healer who established compounds in Paris, London and the United States. His penchant was for authoritarian power. He demanded total obedience from his needy subjects. Gurdjieff was

33

totally unscrupulous and would sleep with any member of his compound that he found attractive, and then cast them aside if they turned up pregnant.

Rajneesh was born in a remote state of India. He gained national attention with his 93 Rolls-Royces, all bought by devoted disciples. Sex for him was the true path to enlightenment. One of his many rituals included making young females wear transparent dresses with no undergarments. His reasoning? Because clothing interfered with the effective flow of energy required for their healing. He preached the complete surrender of one's mind and body to a Master – and that would be him, as the pathway to salvation. Male members were encouraged to eat ripe mangoes that had first been introduced into a woman's vagina. On arriving in America he proclaimed, "I am the messiah America has been waiting for," (Storr p. 57). He preached freedom and the sad commentary on the emotional state of America is that he was able to attract 2500 permanent, and an equal number of part-time members, to live and love on his 64-acre Oregon commune. He talked his disciples into funding the cost of his lifestyle to the tune of $5.75 million. Eighty-three percent of his flock were college educated, and amazingly 64 percent had bachelor's degrees, 36 percent had graduate degrees, with 12 percent holding doctorates.

LIBIDINAL LUNACY. Psychiatrist Anthony Storr draws the parallel between love and lunacy, saying love can be irrational to the point of inducing madness. In *Feet of Clay* (1996 p. 189) he wrote, "Like other irrational experiences, or periods of mental illness, love may open doors of perception which otherwise might have remained closed." Freud was the first to combine love and insanity. He said, "Love is the normal prototype of the psychoses." He believed sex drive could be used in physical releases or be sublimated into work energy and when not could cause dangerous side effects. He spoke of Leonardo's ascetic lifestyle and Dostoevsky many obsessions as examples. Most people have a sense of such dysfunctional behavior when totally immersed emotionally in a person or a project. Irrationality reigns supreme in such cases.

> The following chapters will be structured on a subject such as #1 Dysfunctional Passion or #2 Sex Appeal & Passion. Two subjects (Duncan & Hughes in Chapter #1) will be used to validate the points of passion to that nuance of success. The two featured subjects will be reviewed in the beginning to provide a substantive overview for the reader.

2

PASSION TO BE DIFFERENT

Isadora Duncan

Howard Hughes

"LOVE SHOULD BE A PASTTIME
AS WELL AS A TRAGEDY"

"SEDUCTION IS MY STYLE"

"No great genius is without some mixture of insanity" (Aristotle)

"Innovators are, at best, mildly sociopathic, and at worst completely insane" (Winslow 1989)

"Mad passion or passionate madness is the reason why psychopathic personalities are often creators and why their productions are perfectly sane"
Jacques Barzun, *The Paradoxes of Creativity*

ISADORA DUNCAN
FREE SPIRIT & CREATOR OF MODERN DANCE
b. San Francisco, California May 27, 1878
d. Nice, France Sept. 14, 1927

NOTABLE TRAIT: PRACTICED FREE LOVE

PHILOSOPHY: "ONLY UPON AWAKENING THE WILL FOR BEAUTY CAN ONE ATTAIN BEAUTY"

SELF-ANALYSIS: "I AM A PURITAN PAGAN"

MOTTO: "I'M A REVOLUTIONIST"

MARITAL STATUS: MARRIED RUSSIAN POET SEREI ESENIN AT 44 TWO CHILDREN DEIDRE AND PATRICK

RELIGION: VOCAL ATHEIST

INNOVATION: CREATOR OF MODERN DANCE

PASSIONS: "ISADORA COULD NO MORE LIVE WITHOUT LOVE THAN SHE COULD WITHOUT FOOD OR MUSIC" (FRIEND DESTI)

AGGRESSIVENSS: "I WAS SO INTO MY WORK I WOULD GET INTO A STATE OF STATIC ECSTACY"

THRILL-SEEKING: FEARLESS SPIRIT

CHARM: "NO RELIGIOUS EXPERIENCE EVER MOVED BELIEVERS TO HIGHER ECSTACY THAN ISADORA'S DANCE" (DESTI)

EGOISM: "TERPSICHORE TAUGHT ME TO DANCE"

ECCENTRICITIES: "I'M A REVOLUTIONIST" 3 CHILDREN FROM 3 LOVERS OF DIFFERENT NATIONALITIES

MANIAS: "SLEPT LITTLE. SHE ACTED LIKE A PERSON DEMENTED" (DESTI 133)

HOWARD ROBARD HUGHES
DASHING TYCOON & MOVIE MOGUL
b. Houston, Texas December 24, 1905
d. Princess Hotel, Acapulco, Mexico April 4, 1976

NOTABLE TRAIT: POWER OBSESSED MANIC-DEPRESSIVE

PHILOSOPHY: "I CAN BUY ANY MAN OR WOMAN"

SELF-ANALYSIS: LIFE OF DEBAUCHERY WITH BOTH SEXES

MOTTO: "SEDUCTION IS MY STYLE"

MARITAL STATUS: MARRIED ELLA RICE AT 19, JEAN PETERS AT 52, TERRY MOORE ON YACHT; NO CHILDREN

RELIGION: NON-PRACTICING FUNDAMENTALIST

INNOVATIONS: STARMAKER WHO BUILT LARGEST PLANE EVER BUILT – SPRUCE GOOSE

PASSIONS: BISEXUAL; SLEPT WITH JEAN HARLOW, SUSAN HAYWARD, GINGER ROGERS, BETTE DAVIS, KATHERINE HEPBURN, AVA GARDNER, LANA TURNER, CARY GRANT, & TYRONE POWER

AGGRESSIVENESS: "HE HAD TO WIN AT ALL COST"

THRILL-SEEKING: LIVED LIFE ON EDGE SEVEN PLANE CRASHES

CHARM: A DASHING POWER MONGER WHO PROPOSED TO WOMEN ON THE FIRST DATE BUT REFUSED TO FOLLOW THROUGH AS IT WAS ONLY A PLOY

EGOISM: MASTER OF HYPE AND LISTENED TO NO ONE; OWNED LOUELLA PARSONS & HEDDA HOPPER

ECCENTRICITIES: BIPOLAR, RECLUSIVE & WACKY HYPO-CHONDRIAC; HIRED PEOPLE TO CATCH FLIES

MANIAS: KINKY SEX, DRUG ADDICT, MANIC-DEPRESSIVE, OBSESSIVE COMPULSIVE WHO BOUGHT PEOPLE AND FINANCED THE BAY OF PIGS INVASION

SYBARITIC GENIUS

SEX, POWER & THE RENEGADE PERSONALITY

The above quotes by Aristotle, Winslow and Barzun offer evidence for the relationship existing between abnormality and creativity. Passion and drive fuel that relationship since it takes great fervor to oppose tradition or oppose the established order of things. Renegades like Isadora Duncan and Howard Hughes were passion incarnate, but they were equally off the wall. The combination made them enormously innovative and also radical members of society. Neither adhered to any convention - social, religious, moral, marital, or governmental.

It is no accident that normal success comes from normal people and abnormal success comes from the work of renegades. All innovation emanates from the fringe. Why? Because there are no wins where the pack lives. One must be prepared to violate what is to create the new. Creative people always come armed with great passion, temerity, and a renegade nature. They must be mavericks and be prepared to destroy what exists to create anything new or novel. Think about it? No new house can be built where an existing one sits. Building a new one demands destruction of the old. That is the nature of all innovation.

Had Isadora Duncan accepted ballet modern dance would never have been born. Had Howard Hughes killed off the Spruce Goose when he knew it would never fly, which happened shortly after he began the design, he would not have blown $75 million on a stupid project. But he would not have become the dominant satellite supplier through his Hughes Aircraft venture. He always looked beyond immediate wins to see the larger picture often lost on the short-sighted. He paid a horrific price in the short run but owned the business in the long.

MEDIOCRITY LIVES IN THE BOX. The world's educators train children to conform and adapt, and to not rock the boat. Such training insures they never disrupt a classroom but also conditions them to be less creative. Such methods led Edison, Einstein, and Bucky Fuller to drop out of school. It is why Einstein said, "I was an upstart heretic. But few people are capable of expressing with equanimity opinions which differ from the prejudices of their social environment." Ironically, the Father of Relativity became an educator but he detested it. He wrote on his blackboard at Princeton, "Not everything that can be counted counts, and not everything that counts can be counted." That is the essence of creativity outside the box.

The creative genius must deviate from the norm. If they were normal their creations would be normal. It is only by living outside the box of conformity that they are able to be abnormally creative. A vast amount of data validates this argument. Einstein didn't wear socks, Nikola Tesla wore white gloves each day and threw them away and never had a date his entire life. Bucky Fuller went two years without speaking to anyone including his wife. Howard Hughes ate just 12 peas each meal. Oscar Wilde, Colette and Madonna were bisexual. Bertrand Russell, Isadora Duncan and Carl Jung to practiced free love. Charlie Chaplin had stage freight to such a degree he once stood frozen while a man drowned. Such people see life through a unique filter. They are not only different, but different in a way more normal people do not understand and consequently they have difficulty working in a conventional organization.

Some people cannot tolerate different. Traditionalists want to place everyone in a box. The visionary does not tolerate such constraints and in fact, will rebel in such an environment. That is why Einstein invented relativity working in a post office. No university would hire him despite his genius. It is why Frank Lloyd Wright was called the "Anarchist of Architecture" by the *New York Times* and was called Frank Lloyd Wrong for daring to "destroy box houses." It is why Ayn Rand was called the "Radical Revolutionary," and why Picasso said, "Art exists to be used against the established order. The painter must destroy to create."

PROMETHEAN PASSION. In the Greek Classics, Prometheus was a mythical god who defied Zeus by stealing fire from the heavens in order to bring science in the form of light to mankind. Consequently, Prometheus has come down to us as the symbol of creative genius and as a defiant spirit. The subjects in this work were all Prometheans who defied convention and therefore altered their discipline like few others. Larry Ellison stole the idea for an integrated database software system that has catapulted Oracle into the second largest software firm in the world behind Microsoft. Ellison was not the first to do such a thing. Bill Gates didn't have a clue how to develop the software system he agreed to design for IBM. But he took the contract, went out and found one to modify to fit his needs, and so was borne Microsoft. That is the nature of the entrepreneurial genius. They dare what others see as ludicrous, and see opportunities that others see as danger. Carl Jung defied Freud as only a Promethean could do and in so doing created his own psychological terminology that has bequeathed us with concepts like introversion, extroversion, Archetypes, Collective Unconscious, Synchronicities, Anima & Animus, and the Syzygy.

SEX & POWER. In the book *The Anatomy of Sex & Power* (1990 p. 31) author Michael Hutchison wrote, Sex and Power are inextricably intertwined." But seduction is always a two-way street. For every seductor there is a seductee. Did Clinton seduce Lewinsky? Or did Lewinsky seduce Clinton? No one will ever know. But we do know it was a mutually agreeable relationship pursued by two consenting adults. To make American taxpayers pay millions for such a dalliance is not only illogical it has been viewed in Europe and Asia as just plain stupid. Was President Clinton guilty? Yes, for poor judgment that would become a political football paid for by the public.

DYSFUNCTION & SUCCESS. The two individuals personifying super success and abnormality in this chapter are Isadora Duncan and Howard Hughes. Both were iconoclasts who pursued passion as if it were about to become extinct. Duncan was about as radical as any female who ever lived. She said, "I have constantly danced the Revolution and the call to arms of the oppressed. On the night of the Russian Revolution I danced with a terrible fierce joy" (Duncan p. 334). This free soul advocated doing what one wants as long as it was not destructive. She believed in free love, children without marriage, paganism, and dancing without shoes. She said, "I'm a revolutionist. All geniuses worthy of the name are. Every artist has to be one to make a mark in the world" (Desti p. 118).

Hughes was equally radical, but power and financial influence were his weapons of seduction not the seductive grace and elegance of Duncan, although Hughes quite dashing in his youth. Hughes had a fetish for beautiful people, men or women. He became obsessed with the Miss Universe contest and made extensive lists of the contestants and tried to tie them all up to contracts. Hollywood, considered Hughes perverted, and that takes some doing. His penchant for voyeurism and other abnormal seductions was legend. He had bizarre eating and living habits and once went many years without wearing any clothing. He held meetings on the toilet and refused to shake hands with his top aids for fear they would infect him. The manic-depressive Hughes disappeared many times and experienced many emotional breakdowns. He was obsessive-compulsive, Machiavellian and lived life far beyond most men. Hughes would jump into a plane without having the slightest idea how to use the controls and then crash it. His last crash resulted in internal injuries that left him a drug addict.

ISADORA DUNCAN – PERFORMING ARTS

At age five this precocious child told her teacher "There is no Santa Claus." Freedom of the soul and mind were highly important for this child of two itinerant artists. Isadora lived what would have been considered a lonely early life on the streets of San Francisco. She was a "latchkey" kid since her mother Dora Gray worked two jobs to support her and her older brothers and sister. This was in the latter part of the 19th century when such freedom for a young girl was quite unusual. W now know that such freedom builds self-sufficiency but with all such freedom comes danger. Isadora wrote in her memoirs that her early freedom was instrumental in her later success.

Duncan was the 4th born of five children of an itinerant poet Charles Gray and a musician mother. Isadora wandered the streets of San Francisco and Oakland while her mother worked. She wrote, "As a child I wondered alone by the sea and followed my own fantasies. I was already a revolutionist. The finest inheritance you can give a child is to allow it to make its own way" (Duncan p. 21). From that point she refused to be controlled. Freedom set her free and imprinted an independence that knew few bounds. She saw freedom as the catalyst for the good life and used it to create a whole new dance based on the freedom of movement and free-flowing gowns. It also became the basis of her personal life and loves. She defied all tradition and convention including ballet, which she loathed. As a dance innovator she opened avant-garde dance salons in Berlin, Paris, Athens, London, and St. Petersburg.

Isadora was a rebel from early childhood. Her mother enrolled her in dance class and she lasted all of one hour, and proclaimed that ballet was, "ugly and against nature" (Duncan p. 21). She later described it as "deforming the feet until nothing is left but to deform the brain. The solar plexus is the central spring of all movement." That philosophy grew into a dance concept she described as a "central inner force." Her success emanated from a kind of spiritual inner passion. She was committed to marrying Greek classics, music, art, sculpture, and poetry into one divine set of movements.

But it would be freedom of movement that became central to her being and her style of dance. It was pervasive in her life, work, thoughts, and romances. Love was freedom to her and was manifest in the dance of Aphrodite - the soul. She refused to capitulate to anyone or anything, and was passionately dedicated to "following my fantasy and improvisation. I was possessed of the dream of Promethean creation" (Duncan p. 213).

Isadora was in "revolt against puritanical tyranny," and in her memoirs described herself as a "Puritanical Pagan." This iconoclast believed she was special and not subject to the rules of ordinary mortals, quite the stance for a girl who only made it through the 4th grade and one hour of dance lessons. She had made up her mind to rebel quite early in life and later described herself as a "Revolutionist. All geniuses worthy of the name are. Every artist has to be one to make a mark in the world today." Historian Daniel Boorstin said her entrance into European society was "scandalous." He wrote, "Isadora shocked society audiences in London and Paris by her bare feet and legs, her clinging and revealing costume, and her free movements, and then gave an irreparable jolt to the classic ballet of Imperial Russia."

The mother of modern dance lived in accordance to her radical philosophy of life. She was a wild child without morals according to American journalists of the era. She dared to have children by married men who she wouldn't have married had they been single. Her lovers were titans. Gordon Craig was the son of British actress Ellen Terry. He fathered her daughter Deidre. When that relationship ended she took up with the scion of the Singer sewing machine empire Paris Singer. He fathered her son Patrick.

An example of Duncan's rebellion came when Singer put $250,000 down on a piece of property to house her dance academy in New York City. When she went to review the property that cost $5 million, she told him, "I can't work here. It smells of horses." In this respect the renegade Aphrodite was her own worst enemy. Once she had danced to honor the Russian Revolutionists, who she identified with passionately and her boyfriend abandoned her.

PSYCHOSEXUAL ENERGY

Isadora was in love with love. She desperately wanted to marry the dance with the arts, philosophy and the Greek Classics. She wrote, "Each love affair in my life would have made a novel, and they all ended badly" (Duncan p. 348). But she never stopped trying. When she made her first major commission she took all the money, moved to Athens and bought a mountain where she intended to found her dance academy in the likeness of Plato's Academy. Romantic passion led her to such decisions that proved folly, since the mountain had no water and she lost all her money.

Duncan met and fell in love the first time in Berlin. Gordon Craig was a stage designer on tour with a wife in England. Deidre and Patrick were killed in a tragic auto accident in the Seine. After their deaths she went into a deep depression and then as only Duncan would, she took off for Rome to find a man to father another love child. She lived with friend Eleanora Duse and became pregnant by an Italian sculptor. Soon after the child was born it too died, leaving Isadora despondent and with nothing but her dance.

RENEGADE SPIRIT. Agnes de Mille wrote of the nonconformist, "Isadora cleaned away the rubbish. She was a gigantic broom. There never has been such a theater cleaning. She was totally unpredictable. She would make a date with a new gentleman that appealed to her and would arrange to meet him at a Parisian restaurant. In the interim she and would invite a wide assortment of nefarious characters from her Parisian nightlife. When her new friend arrived he was aghast at the sight. He had imagined a quiet night alone with the Barefoot Contessa only to find himself surrounded by a motley group that looked like something out of a Star Wars bar scene. Biographers describe her holding court with a diverse entourage including beggars, poets, artists, actresses and an occasional bum. Pedigrees were of no interest to this free spirit, only a lively spirit and desire to enjoy life. She liked to say, "life is a dream, a spiritual vision," and that true beauty was only possible if one "awakened the will for beauty."

CAPITULATION TO MARRIAGE. Isadora finally broke her lifetime vow not to marry at 44. But the motivation wasn't romantic or fleeting beauty. It was something else. She had met a young Russian poet while performing in St. Petersburg Russia. Always impulsive and impatient she was in a mad love affair with Servie Esenin, a 26 year old who was mad. In Stalinist Russia, a citizen was not allowed to leave the country unless married. When she received an invitation to tour America, she agreed to marry him, for the sole purpose of his company on tour. Esenin was a blond god who reminded her of her dead son Patrick. In fact Esenin was not much older than her son would have been. When she was offered a tour of America she asked him to accompany her and it ended in a marriage that was the worst decision in a turbulent life. Esinen turned out to be an epileptic and prone to violent rages. He appears to have been a substitute for a lost father and dead son. But she was "in love" and that led her to make the worst decision of her turbulent life.

While touring America and France, Esenin destroyed hotel rooms. He was deported from both countries for disruptive behavior. Everywhere he went he went on a tirade from alcohol and spent every cent she earned. She agreed to pay the damages to their hotel rooms but she didn't have enough money. He also beat her unmercilessly. He threatened to kill her daily. And when she ran out of money he left her destitute in Paris and returned to Moscow. They never divorced, but she stood by him when the officials were prosecuting him for his illegal marriage to the granddaughter of Tolstoy. The madman finally hung himself while in the throws of a fit in 1925.

CHARISMA.. Isadora had charismatic power. People found it difficult to refuse her. Even her mother was talked into accompanying her on a wild trip to Chicago when Isadora was only sixteen. They came close to starving to death in the Windy City. Then she came across an ad in the *Chicago Tribune* announcing the arrival in town of the great Augustin Daly. Isadora decided the famous impresario should be aware of her great talent. She brazenly walked into the theater and began telling him of her unparalleled talents. She said in non-stop staccato:

> *I have discovered the dance. I have discovered the art which has been lost for two thousand years ... I bring you the idea that is going to revolutionize our entire epoch ... I am indeed the spiritual daughter of Walt Whitman ... I will create a new dance that will express America. I bring to your theater the vital soul that it lacks, the soul of the dancer* (Duncan p. 31).

Daly was aghast at this impetuous teen and not sure she may not just have something special offered her a part in a New York City pantomime. Isadora and her mother Dora left for New York, and in classic Duncan style, she wired siblings in San Francisco, and told them she was on her way to fame and fortune and to catch a train for New York. Optimism soon turned to bitter reality as she walked from 180th street in Manhattan to 29th for a job in the chorus. She wrote, "I didn't' eat lunch because I had no money so I used to hide in the stage box." Then the hotel in which they were living, the Windsor burned to the ground with all her clothes. She used her wits to seek her fortune in London riding steerage in a cattle boat but was so mortified by the experience used an alias Maggie O'Gorman.

With her mother and brother they slept on park benches in Hyde Park and confessed, "We denied ourselves food to appear well-dressed and prosperous" (Duncan p. 54). When the elements came close to destroying them in a harsh London winter she walked into the elegant Dorchester Hotel and told the bellmen, "Our trunks have been delayed but should be here by taxi shortly.

Please show us your finest quarters." She wrote, "I informed the night porter that we had just come on the night train, that our baggage would come from Liverpool, and to order breakfast to be sent up to us" (Duncan p. 52). They were given a room and ordered palatial meals by room service until found out the next day and evicted. But charisma came to her rescue as she was hired to dance in salons in London and then in Paris. While performing in Paris a German producer became enamored of her free form style and invited her to dance in his Berlin music hall. Isadora was destitute and hungry. Bur for her art was more important than food, and she had always considered herself an artist even when dancing on the streets of San Francisco. She scoffed at his offer, first turning down 500 francs, then 1000 francs, and finally telling him, "No! My art is not for a music hall. I am here to bring about a great renaissance of religion through the dance. I would refuse ten thousand, one hundred thousand. I am seeking something you don't understand."

INTELLECTUAL INTEGRITY AT ANY COST. When she finally made it to the Berlin stage she caused a riot. After her performance she was interviewed by the German press and spoke of her dance as a "The art of liberation for women". She ended her sermon with a speech on the right of women to love and bear children without marriage or permanent relationships. Her speech was received with gasps of shock from the wives of German industrialists who were quite happy in their roles. The press called her words, "SCANDALOUS!" Her response? "Any intelligent woman who reads the marriage contract and then goes into it, deserves all the consequences" (Duncan P. 181).

Isadora's principles cost her dearly. The renegade lost millions in fees and countless valued relationships due to libertarian diatribes and rebellious comments on the landed gentry, the very people who paid to see her perform. One example took place at the New York City Metropolitan Opera on March 1917. This was the day of the Russian Revolution and the iconoclast saw fit to dance in tribute with the music of Wagner's *Marseillaise* performed in a "terribly fierce joy." At the time Wagner's work was the symbol of Germanic tyranny. Such things were of little consequence to the self-proclaimed revolutionary. She followed with the "Marche Slav" in complete contempt for everyone in the audience since the Russians and Germans were allies. Paris Singer was her lover at the time and the benefactor of capitalism walked out and left her. With that brazen act she lost his support for building a New York Dance School, and in fact didn't have the funds to return to Paris. She was forced to hock a diamond necklace he had given her to finance the trip back to France. The introspective but self-destructive Isadora reflected later, "My art impulse was too strong for

45

me and I could not arrest it even to please one I loved" (Duncan p. 225).

REVOLUTIONIST. Isadora was a revolutionary, but never a Communist as reported by the media. Her sympathy for the Russian Revolution was based on many appearances in St. Petersburg and Moscow and her own identification with the working classes. But the media continually cast her as a card-carrying Communist. The truth was that Isadora was apolitical, with only one allegiance – art. For her creativity was born of rebellion. She needed to destroy existing dogma, and was forthright with the media, "I am not an anarchist or a Bolshevist. I'm a revolutionist." (Duncan p. 118).

HEDONIST. Isadora was most recalcitrant in her love life. She had met and fallen madly in love with designer Gordon Craig. Their tempestuous love affair was ill-fated from the beginning. It also became headline news around the world and her reputation suffered. In America the puritans felt she had made a mockery of marriage by carrying on with a married man and then daring to openly revel in having his child. From that point she was *persona non grata* in America. They ignored her convinced she was depraved. While her native country defiled her, Europe deified her. The continent found her *avant garde* behavior refreshing.

Isadaroa was fearless. Her daring and panache were without peer. When she met Paris Singer and ran off with him on his yacht he already had a wife and five children. That relationship only contributed to her renegade image. She was a darling of the press due to her provocative dance, sheer costumes, barefoot dancing, yacht parties, elegant soirees that all kept her in the limelight. She and Paris raced uninhibitedly across Europe defying all established tradition.

MANICNESS. Isadora's psychic energy led to fits of mania in her work and personal life. She was a perfectionist who often danced through the night oblivious of time, food, or fatigue. She wrote of her obsessive passion saying, "I got into a state of static ecstasy." Friend and biographer, Mary Desti told of her manias, "She acted like a person demented. Nothing could stop her. Isadora would not sleep a wink and was in a state of the wildest excitement. She decided not to go to bed but to go from restaurant to restaurant, night club to night club, anywhere and everywhere for excitement" (Desti p. 133).

Isadora wrote, "Nothing seems to exist save in the imagination". It was her inner source of power that was used to revolutionize the dance. She documented her "inner-self" and "spiritual vision" with an eerie surrealism:

I feel the presence of a mighty `power' within me, which listens to the music ad then reaches out through all my body, trying to find an outlet for this listening. Sometimes this power grew furious, sometimes it raged and shook me until my heart nearly burst from it's passion (Duncan p. 224).

FREEDOM TO THE END. Isadora's free-spirit pervaded her life and her death. She was in Nice on holiday, although life was holiday for Isadora, when she decided to have a handsome driver selling Bughatti sports cars to take her for a spin. She waved to her friend Desti saying, "I'm off to the moon, so don't be surprised if you don't see me again." Decked out in traditional free-flowing dress replete with a six foot long scarf, she jumped into the exotic sports car and screamed to the waving crowd, "Adieu, mes amis. Je vais a gloire" [Farewell my friends. I go to glory]." The driver hit the accelerator and the high-powered sports car leapt into the balmy Nice evening. Isadora's long free-flowing scarf caught in the rear axle and in one terrible bone-crunching instant snapped Isadora's neck severing her jugular. She died as she had lived as if in a Greek tragedy. She was forty-nine.

SYBARITIC GENIUS

HOWARD HUGHES – POWER HUNGRY INDUSTRIALIST

Few men were as dashing, volatile, or as perverse as the billionaire Howard Hughes. He was a product of an entrepreneurial father and a hypochondriac mother and the combination clearly conditioned him for a wacky and bizarre life lived on the edge. He was a paradox, an egomaniac who listened to no one, and an inveterate explorer and innovator. He was a control freak who was unafraid of test piloting the fastest and sleekest aircraft, yet was afraid of a common housefly. Everything in his life had to be on his terms, including women, employees, movie production, and real estate ventures. He was the master and controlled his destiny but never his life.

Hughes refused to touch a doorknob without tissues or shake hands with his most intimate executives. He wouldn't allow his wife Jean Peters sleep with him for fear of contamination. Yet he didn't bathe for years and was a dirty and disheveled human. He had to control every nuance of his life but in the end couldn't even control his bodily functions. Hughes was power hungry and bought those he couldn't control. Women were attracted to him for his flamboyant style, money, and star-making power. The life and loves of Howard Hughes were more bizarre than provocative.

During the Las Vegas years Hughes was a recluse. But in heyday as a movie tycoon he was a *bon voyant* playboy with dashing good looks, fast cars, and a sleek body. By the time he ended up as Mr. Las Vegas he had survived seven major plane crashes and was anything but a playboy. Even the addiction to Las Vegas was a mystery since he didn't party, gamble, drink or need to hire prostitutes. By this time he was a drug addict due to the extreme pain ravaging a body virtually destroyed by his many scrapes with death in airplanes. During his stay at the Desert Inn he had only one of his previous obsessions, voyeurism. He watched erotic movies day and night as a fantasy escape into a glorious past.

Power made him and ultimately destroyed him. During his heyday, he slept with virtually any woman he wanted. Many saw him as a ticket to the top, others were intrigued by the richest man in the world. But Howard wasn't just content with sleeping with them. He had to control them and own their bodies, minds, and spirits. A few bought into his game and paid the price. Others just signed contracts with his movie company RKO and stayed in his houses located in and around Southern California. Few saw him as such a control freak since he was pathologically shy, suave, and charming. To many he was irresistible. To others he was demented. To posterity he was a satyr.

SYBARITIC GENIUS

PROFESSIONAL HISTORY. The Hughes reputation is legend. During his early career he was a press darling in the likes of today's Tiger Woods, Michael Jordan, and Donald Trump. He was a master of hype who owned the likes of Walter Winchell, Louella Parsons, and Hedda Hopper. All were flown anywhere in the world on TWA airlines for free. Consequently, no negative stories about Hughes surfaced in the scandal papers. Few biography buffs are aware that Howard Hughes pioneered commercial aviation. He was also a star-maker during the epic era of Hollywood. What is remarkable is that Hughes taught himself the craft of moviemaking, how to direct, and produce. He never finished high school but was obsessive about what he wanted to know and had a photographic memory.

Excess ruled the flamboyant life of Hughes. Everything he did he had to do to an extreme and that included buying companies to seducing women. He loved the beautiful people and was bisexual so Cary Grant and Tyrone Power were prime targets and ultimately conquests. Grant flew anywhere in the world free of charge and once was the only person on a transcontinental flight. Anything that appealed to Hughes was fair game. He either bought it or seduced it and sometimes did both. One example was the making of the WW-I movie Hells Angels. Hughes didn't rent the planes as a prudent producer, he bought enough planes to make him the proud owner making him the third largest Air Force in the world. *Hells Angels* (1930) took eighteen months to film at a cost of $2 million. That was an incredible investment at the time and when finished was worthless since the first talkie, Al Jolson's *The Jazz Singer* was released with sound. The inveterate Hughes scrapped the footage and began over. Associates assumed he had gone mad.

His movie had to be the greatest ever made and employ the wildest air fights, the sexiest women, and the most furious action and sound affects. Hughes fired the director and assumed the role himself and then went out and interviewed the worlds' most beautify women. He selected an unknown teenager Jean Harlow. He was the owner, Director, Producer and sometimes stunt pilot. He almost died once by jumping into a vintage Thomas Morse fighter and took off without the faintest idea of how to manage the controls. At four hundred feet the plane went into a spin and crashed at Mines Field in Inglewood, California. Hughes was pulled unconscious from the crumpled plane with a crushed cheekbone and abrasions. In a German bomber scene two pilots parachuted out after placing the plane in a suicidal dive but one never made it and the movie scene at the theaters included the body of Phil Jones who was unable to get out of the plane. Hughes was thrilled with the realism. Conventional strategy or tactics were never

SYBARITIC GENIUS

important in the volatile life of Hughes. The sultry teenage sensation Jean Harlow became a star and became a lover. When finished the movie cost a mind-boggling $4 million dollars. Hughes never recouped his investment, but the movie had marvelous reviews and he was on his way as a boy wonder producer.

During this period Hughes became enamored of the burgeoning airlines industry. He set the record for a round-the-world trip in his Lockheed 14, breaking Wiley Post's world record by a remarkable 50 percent when he landed in New York in 1938. He financed the trip himself to the tune of $300,000 but once again it made him an icon in that world that would ultimately make him the world's richest man. Methodical planning and stringent goals were critical to his mission and would forever link him with commercial aviation. After that the acquisition of TWA, and later Air West, were just other toys for his pleasure. He often worked 24-36 straight hours without rest. He was a Type A and control freak beyond compare. When his first wife Ella Rice caught him in bed with Carol Lombard, she divorced him and moved back to Houston. They were childless.

MONEY POWER. This "eccentric madman" led a thrill-seeking, provocative life that included multiple seductions of both sexes on a daily basis. He was an insatiable lover. A movie of his life could never do justice to his flamboyant lifestyle. The most glamorous women and men in Hollywood lined up to sleep with him. He bought governors, congressman, the media, and financed the Bay of Pigs invasion. According to biographer Higham (1993) he was "almost comically corrupt." No one was beyond his influence. He bought the allegiance of President Franklin D. Roosevelt's son Elliot by setting him up with one of the actresses he had under contract – Faye Emerson. He gave Elliot $75,000 in cash to carry on the affair, but it backfired when the fell in love and married. He also financed a business venture of Richard Nixon's brother Donald.

The reckless abandon with which Hughes operated appealed to the media, and his dashing good looks and power mesmerized women. In his case, success did breed success. His father had taught him that he could buy his way out of most jams or into most institutions. Hughes first successful conquest took place in Hollywood when he bought the contract for Billy Dove in 1929. At the time she was considered the most beautiful woman in the world and Hughes had to have her for his studio and his bed. He offered her gigolo husband $325,000 [$10 million in today's money] for her body. Her husband accepted. Then he paid Warner Brothers another $335,000 for her contract calling for five movies. Her sexual duties were fleeting since he caught her in bed with co-star George Raft. Then her movie bombed leaving Hughes with a horrible return on his investment.

OBSESSIVE-COMPULSIVE. Hughes was an obsessive womanizer with a fetish for breasts and fellatio. His sexual antics included proposing marriage to starlets he didn't even know including the young Elizabeth Taylor. He offered Liz $1 million dollars to marry him. His paranoia ran amuck in his contracts. He insisted his starlets could not ride horses, motorcycles or bicycles. When he began the movie *The Outlaw* starring Jane Russell he became so obsessed with showing her ample mammaries to the world he spent many sleepless nights designing brassieres that could pass the stringent Hollywood censors. To his credit Hughes ended up with some innovative bra designs that are now commonplace.

Biographer Higham (1998) described Howard's film making obsessions as a "Masturbatory frenzy." Higham wrote, "No other individual in Hollywood had so completely released his sexual urges on the screen, and nobody would for decades." *The Outlaw* was banned. But Hughes refused to shelve it and filed a $5 million dollar lawsuit filed against the Motion Picture Producers for interference with free trade. He prevailed when a liberal San Francisco judge found "nothing disgusting in the female breast."

PSYCHO-SEXUAL DRIVE. The depravity of Howard Hughes knew few bounds. If he couldn't own a woman he wasn't interested in her. While in his 20's and 30's he regularly slept with two, three, and four women in one day. Often he mixed in a male star like Cary Grant or Randolph Scott. Biographers describe him sleeping with Ginger Rogers in the morning, Bette Davis at noon (she was married), Rita Hayworth in the afternoon, and another that night on his yacht. He was infamous for sailing beyond the legal limit and arranging a mock marriage ceremony with voluminous amounts of alcohol and music to set a romantic scene. He would spend the night with the starlet only to inform her in the morning that it was great fun but a lark. Terry Moore tried to hold him to it but he prevailed.

Many of the most famous names of Hollywood graced his bed including Jean Harlow, Billy Dove, Ginger Rogers, Susan Hayward, who had an abortion with his child; Lana Turner, Ava Gardner, Linda Darnell, Ida Lupino, Debra Paget, Jean Tierney, Mitzi Gaynor, Barbara Hutton, Barbara Payton, Yvonne de Carlo, Joan Fontaine and a woman who he really cared for Katherine Hepburn. Terry Moore became pregnant by him. He married Jean Peters in 1957 when he was

SYBARITIC GENIUS

52 and in declining health and two years after a vasectomy. They married under assumed names – G. A. Johnson & Marian Evans - in Tonapah, Nevada on Jan. 12, 1957. During this period he maintained a bungalow at the Beverly Hills Hilton but Peters was only allowed brief visits. Among his eccentricities was insisting that nudie magazines like Playboy be only delivered by a bachelor.

CONTROL FREAK. Hughes was a control freak. What he couldn't buy he tried to control. An example was his strange purchase of the Desert Inn Hotel in Las Vegas. He always booked the suite, but on once occasion he was told it was already reserved for Jack Nicklaus and Arnold Palmers since the Tournament of Champions Golf Tourney was being held. The distraught Hughes was furious and made an offer that was ridiculous - $13 million that did not even included the property. In that era the prestigious event was held each year in Las Vegas and golf's golden boys Palmer and Nicklaus stayed in the penthouse. Hughes bought the hotel and cancelled the tournament on April Fools Day 1967. The irony is that Hughes did not gamble, drink or attend shows. It was his suite and if he couldn't have it, he would buy it. This began a long list of acquisitions in Las Vegas that ended with his ownership of one-third of the states casinos. He became a nocturnal animal watching movies all night with the hotel's windows painted black. When the all-night TV station KLAS changed its venue he was incensed, bought the station, and installed programming that he liked.

EARLY LIFE INFLUENCES

Howard Hughes was born on Christmas Eve, 1905, to Dallas socialite Allene Gano and a wild philandering oil wildcatter Howard Hughes, Sr. Howard Sr. was a live- on-the-edge entrepreneur and womanizer. He was a high roller and Type A workaholic who was never home, leaving his hypochondriac wife to care for Sonny. Allene was told she was unable to have any more children and dedicated her life to her only son. Allene feared germs and infections. Her preoccupation was transferred to Sonny. Sonny learned early to feign illness to get out of work or to cover other problems. It would carry into his adulthood. Biographers suggest that his mother "was obsessed with her son's physical and emotional condition, and helped instill in him lifelong phobias about his physical and mental state" (Bartlett & Steele p. 45). As a teenager Howard supposedly contracted polio and spent months in a wheelchair. He miraculously recovered when the doctors could find nothing wrong with him. Later when Hughes couldn't cope with a problem like the TWA debacle he would mysteriously disappear. It was his mental health therapy. His most notorious disappearances coincided with his three nervous breakdowns in his mid-thirties, early forties and early fifties.

SYBARITIC GENIUS

Hughes learned from his father to art of bribery. His father was working in Southern California after his wife died suddenly when Sonny was 17. He wanted the boy near him and when there was no room at the prestigious Thacher School in Santa Barbara, California, he bribed them and Sonny would spend a year there. During his stay Southern California Howard got to know his uncle Rupert who was a successful screenwriter but also a raging homosexual. Uncle Rupert seduced his teenage nephew and also introduced him to the exotic world of Hollywood. Sonny found the glitter of Hollywood intriguing and beguiling. The unconventional sex piqued his interest. When his father returned to Houston he removed Howard from school and then used his influence to have him accepted Rice University despite not having a high school degree. Then tragedy struck when his father had a massive heart attack and died suddenly on January 14, 1924. Howard was now eighteen.

At eighteen Sonny found himself alone in the world. One month later he dropped out of Rice University and began planning his future. He was already obsessed with death. He was understandably in a state of shock over losing both parents in quick succession despite having inherited $450,000, all in the form of Hughes Tool stock, of which he owned 75%. But the precocious teenager was to share the firm with his distant relatives. He immediately worked out a methodical plan to buy them out with the firm's own money, a concept later known as a leveraged buyout. Hughes was a master of such leverage from an early age. To further insure his status as an adult, he proposed to childhood friend Ella Rice and took over his father's business. Hughes spent his entire engagement period preparing a ten-page will in which he created the Howard R. Hughes Medical Research Laboratory. Such preoccupation with death and a will is not normal behavior for a nineteen year old about to be married. But he was already an indomitable spirit and now an executive. But he didn't want to run the place. His passion was in Hollywood. He hired a top executive, paid him well, bought a Rolls Royce, and headed west where he took up residence in the Ambassador Hotel on Wilshire,Boulevard. He made his first movie *Everybody's Acting* at twenty-one but no one took him serious.

A DEATH-WISH. Hughes operated in life as if he had a death wish. He took one risk after another in concert with his manic-depression. In September 1935, Hughes had just set a speed record at 352 mph with his personally designed [H-1] air racer. Amelia Earhart was one of the judges when Hughes ran out of gas because of limited fuel in an attempt to save weight. Rather than jeopardize his prize plane he didn't bail out and crash-landed. He survived but it only led him to make even more brash decisions that resulted in five more crashes. He was always the victim and the villain due to pushing the limits in all things. In May

1943, Hughes was the test pilot for a Sikorsky seaplane that he intended to build for the Air Force. When asked by an FAA official why a business tycoon was functioning as a test-pilot, Hughes responded, "Why should I pay somebody else to have all the fun." This would be his fourth crash, and the one with the most fatalities. Hughes crashed the Sikorsky and it sank immediately in 165 feet of water in Lake Mead near Las Vegas. Hughes was seriously injured with multiple lacerations of the face and was dragged from the wreckage in severe shock. He had miraculously escaped with his life. Passengers Richard Felt and William Cline died and aeronautics inspector Charles Rosenberg shattered his spine and never walked again. The crash was attributed to bad communications between Hughes and the ground.

In his last crash Hughes was also functioning as a test pilot. This time the Air Force found him guilty of pilot error but never pressed charges since he almost died and would never again be normal. Flying an XF-11 in Culver City on July 8, 1946 Hughes violated numerous FAA regulations. According to Air Force officials the crash could have been avoided if he had "attempted an emergency landing" instead of pushing the new plane beyond reasonable limits. They claimed "this accident was avoidable after propeller trouble was experienced" (Senate War Hearings p. 20) had Hughes exercised reasonable caution. Hughes had loaded the plane with twice the allotted fuel, retracted the landing gear against the rules, and violated the forty-five minute flight test limit.

One hour and fifteen minutes into the flight, Hughes crashed. He could have avoided disaster had he landed the plane in a field or on a road. The obstreperous Hughes refused and his decision proved disastrous. The plane hit a house in West Los Angeles, caught fire with Hughes trapped inside. Hughes had a collapsed lung and displaced heart and was unconscious when dragged screaming from the plane. He was in sever pain and not expected to live. He hovered near death for days and pure resolve saved him according to attending physicians who marveled at his recovery. Hughes aged ten years and would never be the same. Within five years he was functionally incapacitated - both mentally and emotionally. Drugs masked the pain but they destroyed him emotionally and mentally. A live-on-the-edge lifestyle had made him, and it had destroyed him.

DYSFUNCTIONAL ECCENTRIC

Howard Hughes refused to do anything in moderation. For him it was all or nothing. He was a driven man with a penchant for danger. When manic he was unstoppable. When depressed he went into seclusion or disappeared. He made his own rules and lived by his wits. He interviewed beautiful young women for a movie role and demanded they appear without makeup. His logic? So they could not cover blemishes. This eccentric once sold his Rolls Royce because it polluted the Los Angeles air, a move thirty years ahead of its time. Idiosyncrasies defined him. He was a lifelong insomniac who slept sparingly and often not at all. For years he ate the exact same meal. If it varied by one pea or the make of ice cream, the chef was terminated. His standard menu included a medium rare steak, 12 peas (no more no less) and vanilla ice cream. During the day he ate Hershey Bars, pecans, and whole milk all contributing to his constipation. The oddball once spent 48 straight hours sitting on a toilet holding business meetings during his vigil.

When Hughes was unable to control something he either destroyed it or retreated from it. When unable to meet the $400 million indebtedness at TWA he suffered a nervous breakdown and disappeared. He had created the dilemma by buying 63 jetliners from Convair and Boeing. His chief engineer at TWA, Bob Hummell, said he became disoriented during this period and would talk non-stop for ten hours. At the time Howard and some associates were on a flight that landed in Shreveport. Howard mysteriously disappeared, and was later found in jail having been arrested as a vagrant. A week later he disappeared in Florida and was not found for three months. When he reappeared at the New York Plaza Hotel he was dressed in a tuxedo and sneakers carrying two douche bags and a dental drill in a black bag.

A LONELY HERMIT. Hughes' mania and obsessive need for control became his Achilles Heal. He used and abused women, but if he had allowed one to get close, she may have been able to save him when he became dysfunctional. But he never trusted women. He used them and discarded them. He was suddenly a prisoner in his own asylum. While incarcerated at the Desert Inn he had no one to turn to for help. He desperately needed someone he could trust to get him medical help. Unfortunately he had no friends, only employees. Those within his inner circle were people who would benefit from his incapacity. His guards and administrators didn't want him normal. Their very jobs depended on him being a non-functioning human being. They were the keepers of his private refuge, and they adroitly kept him secluded and adjudged sane in an act of self-preservation. Hughes had created a self-imposed sanctuary where he was the prisoner.

SYBARITIC GENIUS

A LASCIVIOUS BIG T PERSONALITY

Howard Hughes was blessed with good looks, money and a resilient spirit. He gambled away most of these gifts for power and influence. Business acumen and a maniacal work ethic fueled by unabashed passion made him into one of the world's richest and most powerful men. The irony is that when he reached the top he was no longer able to enjoy the fruits of his work. By his early fifties he was impotent from the drugs and so many bodily injuries. He had long since lost all friends - including lover Cary Grant. Hughes became an emotional cripple incapable of the most basic acts. He had gambled and won the battle of business and lost the war of life. His spoils should have been more in tune with the price he had to pay. Virtually every other subject in this book started in life with less of everything than Howard Hughes but few ended up so barren. The sad thing about Hughes is that he worshipped at the altar of power, and when he finally had more than most kings he was functionally incompetent. Howard could buy men and women and spent much of his life doing so but in the end he was unable to buy contentment or happiness.

Rolling the dice for Howard Hughes had turned up snake eyes. A resilient will contributed to fame and fortune and a destitute personal life. There has been recent speculation that his bisexuality and drug habit led to his death by AIDS. There is now evidence that AIDS was in fact around at the time. It appears doubtful in Hughes case that he died of AIDS since he was sexually inactive after the mid-fifties. Drug addiction could have been a possible source of contracting the disease however his meticulous need for cleanliness also makes this possibility unlikely.

3

INSECURITY & PASSION

| Albert Camus | Larry Ellison |

"I don't believe in anything"   "I don't understand love"

"The more intense the inferiority the more violent the superiority"
Psychotherapist Alfred Adler

"For forty years I've awoke at 4 a.m. in a state of dread. Nobody will
want to read this, it won't work, I'll never fool em"
James Michener memoirs (1991)

Where gifted children are unhappy with themselves or with their
situations, they often turn eagerly – even desperately – to achievement to
fill the void" Webb, Meckstroth, Tolan (1982)

ALBERT CAMUS
PHILANDERING EXISTENTIALIST PHILOSOPHER
b. Mondovia, Algeria November 7, 1913
d. Paris, France January 4, 1960

NOTABLE TRAIT:	INSATIABLE LIBIDINAL ENERGY
PHILOSOPHY:	"TO KNOW IF ONE CAN LIVE WITH ONE'S PASSIONS – THAT IS THE WHOLE QUESTION"
SELF-ANALYSIS:	"SENSUALITY ALONE RULED MY LIFE. FOR A 10 MINUTE LOVE AFFAIR I WOULD HAVE RENOUNCED MY PARENTS"
MOTTO:	"ONE MUST LIVE WITH HER, SHUT UP, OR SLEEP WITH THEM ALL" – HE SLEPT WITH THEM ALL
MARITAL STATUS:	SIMONE HIE WHEN 19 FRANCINE FAURE WHEN 27; TWO CHILDREN
RELIGION:	ROMAN CATHOLIC WHO BECAME AVID ATHEIST
INNOVATIONS:	*Le' Etranger–[The Stranger]* (1942) ABSURDITY *La Chute -[The Fall]* (1956) NIHILISM
PASSIONS:	NEVER FEWER THAN TWO MISTRESSES
AGGRESSIVENESS:	"MAN'S MOST DANGEROUS TEMPTATION IS INERTIA"
THRILL-SEEKING:	"REVOLT IS HAPPINESS"
CHARM:	"IRRESISTABLE CHARM"
EGOISM:	"I DON'T BELIEVE IN ANYTHING"
ECCENTRICITIES:	"SLEEPING IS A WASTE"
MANIAS:	CIGARETTES, WOMEN & WORK

LARRY ELLISON
PLAYBOY ENTREPRENEUR & BILLIONAIRE
b. New York City, August 17, 1944

NOTABLE TRAIT: EGOMANIA, REBELLION & INSECURITY

PHILOSOPHY: "LIFE IS THE ENLIGHTENED PURSUIT OF HAPPINESS"

SELF-ANALYSIS: "WE WORK BECAUSE WORK IS AN ACT OF CREATION"

MOTTO: "PEOPLE I LOVE ARE ESSENTIAL FOR MY SANITY"

MARITAL STATUS: ADDA QUINN, NANCY WHEELER BARBARA BOOTHE; SON & DAUGHTER

RELIGION: RADICAL BUDDHISM

INNOVATIONS: RELATIONAL DATABASES

PASSIONS: "HE FELL COMPLETELY IN LOVE WITH ANYTHING"

AGGRESSIVENESS: SWAGGERING COMBATIVE STYLE IN ALL

THRILL-SEEKING: "IT'S EXCITING, IT'S A RUSH MAN" (ON NEAR BANKRUPTCY IN 1990); FLIES JETS AND RACES YACHTS FOR AMUSEMENT

CHARM: "HE'S WILDLY ENTHUSIASTIC, IT'S INFECTIOUS"

EGOISM: "HE THINKS HE'S GOD"

ECCENTRICITIES: "I NEVER ACCEPTED CONVENTIONAL WISDOM, IT SERVED ME WELL LATER IN LIFE"

MANIAS: "HE IS EXTREMELY INTENSE, HE WORE ME OUT"

INSECURITY BREEDS GREATNESS

Successful people often become great because of a mortal fear of failing. It is because they fear to fail that they don't. When such people come to a door that is closed, they knock it down. Most people are too afraid to violate existing dogmas and policies and consequently live within those bounds. Those who are insecure and allow it to dominate their actions are destined to a life of mediocrity, but men like Camus and Ellison, who were more insecure than 99 percent of the world's population, used their fears as motivators. How are they different? In a number of ways, but both had enormous ego drive and passion that overcame their basic insecurities.

Insecurity was the driving force of these subjects, but none so great as existentialist philosopher Albert Camus and Silicon Valley entrepreneur Larry Ellison. Both were passionate beyond compare and equally insecure. Neither felt loved as children and both confused lust with love as adults. Seduction became a means of feeling wanted as both grew up in foster homes and lacked in parental affection. Camus wrote eloquently, "There is no love of life without despair of life." His father had died when he was a baby and his illiterate mother was unable to cope. She sent him to be raised by those more capable but the price was the loss of motherly love. Ellison was the son of an unwed mother. When he came close to dying in early childhood she sent him to be raised by a distant aunt and uncle in Chicago. He hated them.

OVERCOMPENSATING FOR FEAR

Alfred Adler said, "We are all striving for superiority to overcome inner fears of insecurity" (Hoffman 148). He found that inferiority is central to overachieving and forms the basis of all ambition. Such overcompensation helped Ellison build Oracle into a mammoth giant. He had been let go or passed over in a couple high tech ventures in Silicon Valley and then fired from Amdahl at age 29. He was always ill-prepared to work for anyone and finally forced to start his own firm. And on April 26, 2000 he passed Bill Gates as the richest man in America with a net worth of over $50 billion.

In a similar manner fear of an early death drove Camus to become the world's most noted existentialist. When told he may not live past twenty-one he became a driven man, albeit in a torrent of invective of nihilism that would win him a Nobel Prize. Both men struggled with a raging inner turmoil. They desperately needed to prove they were worthy, not only of acceptance, but of excellence. Fear and insecurity permeated their lives. And one of their means of overcoming the raging insecurity was seduction. Ellison's first wife told a biographer, "He wants desperately to be loved." She quoted him having said, "I don't understand love. I don't understand people bonding together" (Wilson p. 38). Camus said, "To know if one can live with one's passions – that is the whole question." He was admitting that his inner drives and anxieties were pushing him beyond all normal limits and it scared him. Both men needed a constant flow of women into their lives to prove they were wanted. Physical love pervaded their very being. Conquest appears to have made them feel whole. Rejection devastated them.

Passion permeated life at Oracle as it did the words of Camus. Both men loved to defy and debate, and their arguments were always divisive. Ellison loved to argue and would do so with anyone on any subject. After a fiery argument on one side of an issue he would reverse his stance and argue just as vehemently on the other side. Why such a turnaround? To prove his superiority. He had to initiate a fight so that he could win it. The issues were immaterial. It was the need to win that turned him on. A similar need led Camus to write of rebellion and the absurdity of life that he likened to the *Myth of Sisyphus* (1942). Camus's whole philosophical system was based on revolt, nihilism and self-doubt. He wrote, "Suffering is nothing. What counts is knowing how to suffer."

INSECURITY AS MOTIVATOR. Insecure people are often their own worst enemy. They are often highly successful, but can be self-effacing and self-destructive. French chanteuse Edith Piaf was so needy, she went to extremes to find love. Unfortunately, she often found it in booze, drugs, or in the gutter. She walked the streets to find a man to share her bed for fear of being alone. The *Little Sparrow* Piaf had been abandoned as a child similar to Camus and Ellison. The loss of love left its mark. The basic insecurity led to a tormented life in which her motto was, "Love conquers all," but it also drove her to unprecedented heights in the world of entertainment.

French writer Colette had a similar propensity. She went to great ends to prove she was both wanted and seductive including scandalizing the *Moulin Rouge*. No price was too great for her success including appearing on stage with one breast exposed. That may not seem a big thing at the millennium but it was in 1910. She said, "When it comes to literature, I have an insecurity complex." This was after having sold 300,000 books before age thirty.

PSYCHOLOGY OF INSECURITY. Austrian psychotherapist Alfred Adler built his psychological system around insecurity. He used Mussolini to validate his hypotheses that "inferiority is central to the understanding of human nature." He believed "all goals and striving" resulted from internal feelings of inadequacy. Much of his work grew out of a sickly childhood when doctors predicted he would die. When the attending physician saved him he wrote, "At that moment I decided to become a physician," and he went on to dedicate his life to showing how insecurity could lead to superior effort. Overcoming adversity led him to say, "We cannot develop unless we struggle," a thesis found in every one of these subjects.

Fear is an awesome motivator as demonstrated by the life and loves of the *Little Tramp* - Charlie Chaplin. Chaplin's whole characterization was predicated on an insecure man trying to be more than he was. That was the psyche imprint of the *Little Tramp*. Growing up in a London slum and finding no respect was the genesis of Chaplin and his success. He was never so funny than when he was fighting futility, running for his life, getting run over, or being taken advantage of by the landed gentry. The Little Tramp was the classic underling who emerged from the tortured psyche of his creator Chaplin. This was never so pronounced as when he said in his autobiography that he sat in the window of his room in Coney Island and watched a man drown rather than risk saving him.

Adler described such behavior as "an over-compensation for some inner frailty or insecurity," adding, "The more intense the inferiority, the more violent the superiority" (Hoffman p. 176). He strongly believed that our early fears and anxieties lead inextricably to overachieving. These motivating drives emanate from the unconscious in a steady stream of energy leading to his maxim "We are all steered unconsciously by our guiding goals."

INSECURITY & ARROGANCE

Often insecurity begets arrogance. The insecure often disguise fear by overcompensating through arrogance. Appearing confident masks an inner fear of failure. Ellison is the poster boy for such behavior. Consider his audacious prediction to the media in the 90's that Oracle would replace both IBM and Microsoft as the preeminent software provider of PC and database software systems. At the time of his prediction Bill Gates at Microsoft controlled about 90 percent of all PC operating software in the world. In 1997 Ellison had the temerity to tell the media, "IBM is the past, Microsoft is the present, Oracle is the future." Such brashness was suddenly looked on in a new light in early 2000 when Oracle became #3 and he passed Gates as the world's richest man. The legendary playboy is the bad boy of Silicon Valley. One San Francisco venture capitalist said, "It would take a "forklift to carry his ego around" (Consol p. 1997).

SYBARITIC GENIUS

Ellison is arrogance carried to a different level. He has never quite forgotten his humble beginnings and feelings of inadequacy over being adopted. His approach was arrogance with a supercilious persona that is irritating and often obnoxious to his associates and potential mates. In order to offset his inner insecurities he dresses in sartorial splendor, flies his own jet fighters, lives in three palatial mansions, drives only the most fashionable sports cars, and is never without some dazzling female on his arm. He hates Gates, but it is deeper than a business thing. His adversary has what Ellison lacks. Bill was raised in a stable environment by highly respected parents and matriculated to Harvard even though he never finished. They have perversely similar personalities in that they are driven, Type A's, renegades, fearless, and are insufferably arrogant. But Gates could care less about his attire since he doesn't need outside acceptance from any peer group. Gates can be the nerd and not suffer the consequences. Not so with Ellison. He is driven to overcompensate for his lack of social or parental upbringing. He hated his Jewish stepparents, especially his father who called him a "loser" when growing up. Ellison's ex-wives speak at length about his need for love.

Bucky Fuller is another example of overcompensation leading to overachieving. Fuller was a "raging optimist," and wrote off all outside rejection as the rantings of the ill-informed or ignorant. Often he was correct but his going mute for two whole years was based on his need to go within to find the power to live outside societal acceptance. In a similar manner most writers refuse to read critical reviews of their work. However, the brilliant Fuller lived beyond the purview of most technologists. He predicted the Internet in the 60's in his monumental work *Critical Path*. He wrote, "Integrated electronic media broadcasting and computerized switchover." Will alter our world. Fuller lived in contempt of the establishment and liked to describe himself as the "world's most successful failure."

Dostoevsky was another such individual. The father of the psychological novel once said of his work, "My dissatisfaction amounts to disgust." Oscar Wilde wrote, "Behind every exquisite thing is something tragic" (Schmidgall p. 39). It is hard to believe, but the man voted as the greatest entertainer of the 20th century, Charlie Chaplin, had stage fright. Chaplin, Madam Curie, Howard Hughes, Walt Disney, and Tesla all attempted suicide as did Napoleon. It is all part of the complex puzzle of fear of ferocity. Camus was another raving egomaniac who was only masking inner fears. In one moment of introspection he said:

> *There is no love of life without despair of life. But people confuse love and marriage. True debauchery is liberating*

because it creates no obligations. In it you possess only yourself; hence it remains the favorite pastime of the great lovers of their own person.

In other words, insecurity and pomposity live within the same individual. It is often tied with passion and seduction.. It surely was the basis of Camus' debauching lifestyle since he needed to feel wanted and seduction gave him those feelings. The same was true of President John F. Kennedy. Kennedy never believed he was cut out to be a politician, let alone the President of the United States. His father Joe pushed him into a political career. Jack went along for the ride, but never really took himself too seriously. Senators and other politicians found him arrogant and brash and the reason was his overcompensation for a role he didn't see himself playing. Biographer Reeves spoke of his seductions as a function of his inferiority. Prep school roommate Lem Bilings said, "He knew he was using women to prove his masculinity, and sometimes it depressed him." (Reeves p. 95).

Bertrand Russell is another example of pomposity resulting from a need to satisfy some inner torment. Russell had an opinion on almost everything, yet he was quite insecure, and it drove him to search for the truth in all things. He wrote, "In adolescence I hated life and was continually on the verge of suicide" (Russell 1987 p. 317). He would later write, "The whole problem with the world is that fools and fanatics are always so certain of themselves, but wiser people so full of doubts.

CREATIVE GENIUS & DISCONTENT. British psychiatrist Anthony Storr (*The Dynamics of Creation* 1993) labeled "divine discontent" as the defining element of creative genius. He wrote, "man's discontent is his most precious attribute which spurs him on to creative achievement" (p. 244). Validation can be found in the lives and work of many creative geniuses like Charles Darwin, Karl Marx, Madam Curie, and Walt Disney. All experienced emotional breakdowns just prior to their innovative successes and most attempted suicide at some point in their volatile careers. Many like Walt Disney couldn't stand the humility of defeat and attempted suicide when faced with failure. Ironically, each of Uncle Walt's eight breakdowns coincided with the creation of a masterpiece like Mickey Mouse, Snow White, Fantasia, and Disneyland. Both Freud and Jung were in the throws of a nervous breakdown when they produced their most remarkable breakthroughs – *Interpretation of Dreams* and *Symbols of Transformation*. Storr called this period of Jung's life his "psychotic period." Jung sensed dementia overwhelming him and it frightened him. But his psychotic time proved to be his most creative due to a prescient insight and lucidity. He wrote, "When you reach rock bottom and nothing can be worse is when you discover inner peace." At this time the BBC asked him about religion, and he said, "I don't believe. I know" (Hannah p. 124).

Ted Turner told David Frost in October 1991, "You won't hardly ever find a super-achiever anywhere who isn't motivated by a sense of insecurity." Ted admitted to being bred to be insecure by an alcoholic father who felt that "insecurity bred greatness" (Whittemore 1990). Whittemore said, "Turner's came from an extreme form of insecurity and vulnerability... the driving force behind his inexhaustible need to achieve" (Landrum 1993 p. 222). Buckminster Fuller had so much discontent he walked to Lake Michigan intending to end it all, but experienced an epiphany. He went on to produce 2000 patents and write 25 books. Martin Luther King said, "The children of darkness are frequently more delusional and zealous than the children of light." Larry Ellison told CNN in May, 2000, "You can't conform in business. If you do you will lose, unless you are prepared to be different."

ANXIETY, FEAR & SUCCESS. Anxiety and fear can spur one on to great achievement. Hegel described it in *Phenomenology of Mind* as "growth through struggle." Anxiety and stress studies show how the onset of anxiety releases adrenaline to enable a person to fight harder. We know that when fighting harder more battles are won. In *Anxiety, Phobias, & Panic* scientist Peurifoy wrote, "High levels of creativity, extreme competence, and manic work ethic are by-products of anxiety" (*USA Today* Aug. 18, 1997).

By age thirty-five JFK had received the last rites from the Roman Catholic Church three times. By his late twenties he feared he would die of Addison's Disease, a diagnose by a London physician in 1947. The physician told female friend Pamela Churchill, "he doesn't have a year to live." When George Smathers told him to slow down he responded, "The drugs will finish me off by the time I'm 45. The point is that you've got to live every day like it's your last day on earth. That's what I'm doing" (Russell p. 95).

FEAR - CATALYST OR CRUTCH. A fine line separates those who use insecurity to motivate and those who allow it to destroy. The demarcation lies in the *will* or internal self-image. Those with an indomitable will seem to overcome and use the negatives of life to push them to greater achievement. Others allow adversity to win as they just give in. Such people usually are lacking in a strong enough self-image to fight off the negative. Ego can offset any rejection, but it requires externalizing the negatives. Notice the egoists who overcome insecurity. They tend to blame ineptitude on something outside themselves. Fuller blamed ignorance. Others like Babe Ruth chalked up his strikeouts to the cost of going for broke. Buying into rejection personally only reinforces a fear and insures failure. Such people become victims to justify their rejection. They blame failure on bad luck, the system, or being dealt a bad hand. They are often right in their assessment but the great use the adversities as motivation and refuse to allow failure to result.

Examples of fear leading to greater success are pervasive in history. Stephen J. Cannell, writer-producer of such winning shows as Adam-12, The Rockford Files, Baretta, Hunter, Wiseguy and The Commish was a total loser until mid-life. He flunked the first, fourth, fifth, and tenth grades and was asked to leave school due to ineptitude. It wasn't until age 35 that he discovered he was dyslexic. "Deep down I figured I wasn't the brightest guy around. My attitude was always, who cares? But writing became my passion" (*Investors Business Daily* p. A8 6/14/99). Anton Wilson wrote in *Quantum Psychology* (1990) of a Chicago girl who began school and was tested as slow. She proved the test was correct and became a slow learner and even worse student. On entering high school the girl was tested once more. This time she scored in the top 1 percent of her class, placed in an accelerated class, and graduated with honors. Her tests were a self-fulfilling prophecy.

CLINTON & ELLISON. An eerie similarity exists between President Bill Clinton and Larry Ellison. It has made them close friends. Both were born at the end of WW-II, grew up without a father, are bright, have huge egos, are charismatic beyond belief, play a musical instrument, are somewhat unscrupulous, Machiavellian, and worked their way to the top using wit and charm. People love them or hate them. Both can talk their way out of jams of their own making. Clinton barely escaped impeachment with the Lewinsky affair. Ellison contributed to his presidential campaign in 1996, not because of any interest in the Democratic platform, but because he identified with Clinton as a soul mate. Both were raised by surrogates, never knew their birth father, are renegades, charming, and are philandering users of women.

In his youth Ellison spent much time talking his way out of parking tickets. Later he would use his talents to escape clandestine sexual debacles in much the same way as Clinton did with the Lewinsky and other scandals. Both men believed they were special and governed by the standards of lesser beings. They live life on the edge more than most and that is what sets them apart and makes them more successful than others. Both are cavalier about their right to seduce. They assume seduction is some fundamental right of passage. Both have gone through life with a little boy attitude that appeals to nurturing women, but often infuriates male adversaries. Neither show up on time exasperating dedicated employees steeped in structure.

ALBERT CAMUS - EXISTENTIALIST

Insecurity was the driving force behind the life and lusts of French philosopher Albert Camus. Self-doubt dominated his life, his work, and his success. It even pervaded his philosophy in term of nihilism and an ideology of the "absurd." Intrinsic insecurity led him to seduction of fans and females. Every woman who crossed his path was fair game.

Camus began life in abject poverty in Algeria. His early life was beset by poverty and strife. His father Lucien was an agrarian peasant killed in WW-I shortly after his birth. His mother Catherine was of Spanish heritage. She was an illiterate cleaning woman who moved to Algiers when Albert was one but soon gave up on raising him and turned him over to relatives to rear. Life in Algiers was cheap during the years of his youth beset by World War I soon followed by the Great Depression. In 1928 when Albert was diagnosed with TB, a death sentence in that era. It wasn't long before the Nazi juggernaut took over his homeland and World War II began to be followed by the Cold War. All this set the stage for his role as a positive extistentialist, a nihilist on a mission to look into the foibles of mankind and the paradox of living during such a tormented and ruthless age. His philosophy of absurdity emanated from an internal fixation on despair and futility.

Self-doubt led Camus to excess in his work and play. He was consumed with a need to live life on the edge since he was in constant fear of an apocalypse personally and professionally. Life was cheap and such a sense of the tragic leads one to live for the moment and live it he did. And his work leaves posterity with a roadmap of that era, and by the millennium he had been acclaimed the most successful French writer of the 20th century. How could fear lead to such glory? Conditioning! The futility of life pervaded his work and spawned a "philosophy of doubt." During his teens he wrote, "I have a mad and avid thirst for everything, even sleeping is a waste" (Todd p. 49). Such a fatalistic view of life molded him into a nihilistic workaholic who lived life in double-time. It created a megalomaniac on a mission and nothing was sacred. As a teenager writing for an Algerian paper he wrote, "I am in a hurry to live a lot, with lots of experiences" (Todd pg. 49).

WRITING AS CATHARSIS

Camus wrote, "A novel is never anything but a philosophy put into images." And existentialism fit his philosophical imagery. His words tended to be therapeutic, but their message was aimed at hope. He was soon saying things like, "I don't believe in anything and it's impossible to live like this having killed morality inside me. I have no more purpose, no more reason to live, and I will die" (Todd p. 21). No greater sense of cathartic release can be found in literature. The inner despair is pervasive in his fatalistic rhetoric and philosophic invective. He wrote to exorcise those inner demons tearing at his soul. He knew he had been dealt a poor hand, but decided to play it the best way he knew how. And one of those ways was through passionate rhetoric.

His zealous words would earn him a Nobel Prize for Literature, but it was his positive existentialism that made him successful. Camus believed that it was okay to have a bad hand, but far more important to recognize the absurdity of allowing the hand to keep one from living a good life. In other words, it was okay that the world was nuts, but not okay to buy into the schizoid existence. This resulted in words that attracted a large audience who could identify with such a philosophy. It made him the spokesman for the "beat generation."

Self-doubt pervaded the very essence of Camus. He became a seething bastion of nihilism and uncertainty that would have destroyed a lesser man. He used his worst fears to build a system to overcome uncertainty, and to outwit a paranoid world. It became for him a philosophy of life of the negative. An indication of the basic insecurity of the man can be seen by his words after having won the grandest prize in his field, Nobel Prize for Literature. He returned to his home in Paris and wrote a letter to a female friend saying, "I can't write. I don't believe in anything including me." A friend who was present at his acceptance speech at the Nobel award ceremony was shocked at his stoop-shouldered persona. His words were not those of a literary genius, but of a defeated man. Camus rationalized his life as a positive motivator. He wrote, "My only riches are my self-doubts. It gives me more doubts than certainties. Success is a balm, but a temporary one, and an artists discontents remain incurable" (Todd p. 373). The work that earned him the Nobel Prize was *The Fall* (1957). He called the work "ugly."

PASSION INCARNATE. Camus married twice; the first time at age 19 to a drug addict Simone Hie. The marriage was short-lived. His second wife was a beautiful brunette from Algiers, Francoise Faure. The philandering philosopher was never faithful to any of his mistresses. He often carried on active affairs with three or four women during any given period. In a moment of introspection he wrote of his lecherous behavior and lusts:

> *Sensuality alone ruled my life. For a ten-minute love affair I would have renounced both my parents. It is painful for me to admit that I would have exchanged ten conversations with Einstein for a date with a pretty walk-on extra. But*

INSECURITY & PASSION

after ten dates with her I would usually be longing for Einstein, or serious books (Todd pg. 344).

He introspectively asked, "Can a man really live with his passions?" This was just one more example of his self-doubts over his lascivious behavior. He knew he was incorrigible but was unable to control his need for women. But he knew he was using them since he didn't believe they contributed to his work and in fact thought them to be a deterrent. He wrote, "Artistic creation means work minus sexuality" (Todd p. 157). But even as he said it he would be in bed with another woman. As only a philosopher can do he was objective about his raging libido and wrote, "To love someone is to grow old with them. I'm incapable of that kind of love. One must live with her and shut up or sleep with them all." He slept with them all but proclaimed, "Women inspire in us the desire to create masterpieces, and prevent us from finishing them" (Todd p. 185).

Womanizing is too soft a word to describe the lustful life of Camus. Despite being married to two gorgeous women, he carried on multiple trysts with two or three women for the greater part of his adult life. One of his mistresses was actress Maria Cesares. He wrote plays for her as he did for another British actress. An American journalist, Patricia Blake shared his attentions with Parisian Catherine Sellers. He had an insatiable sexual appetite. His marriage to Algerian Francine Faure was a total subterfuge. She tried to tolerate his philandering, as French woman are want to do, but it caught up with her in 1954. A few liaisons could be tolerated, but Camus abused the privilege. Francine went into serious depression and had crying fits that could not be stopped. Camus had her moved to a clinic for her own safety but she jumped out of a second story window and broke her pelvis. She underwent 23 electric shock treatments to no avail. Camus moved out of their house, torn by the guilt of an unfaithful husband and his need for freedom.

OVERCOMPENSATION. Insecurity permeated Camus' work. He wrote, "I am not a philosopher, because I don't believe in reason enough to believe in a system" (Todd p. 408). In his adamant denials he was confirming his philosophical bent. Could a non-philosopher write something like "The spirit of rebellion can exist only in a society where a theoretical equality conceals great factual inequalities" (*The Rebel* 1951 p. 20) or "Suffering is nothing. What counts is knowing how to suffer" (Todd p. 26). These are the ramblings of a man predisposed to question the plight of man on a perilous journey in a distraught world.

Success came early for Camus. He wrote his two landmark works - *The Stranger* (1942) and his essay *The Myth of Sisyphus* while still in his twenties.

Both became textbooks for the budding existential movement just after World War II. They peaked in popularity during the Cold War years of the late 40's and early 50's. It was in these works that Camus communicated his philosophy of freedom, a kind of optimistic nihilism, that was espoused first in *The Stranger* and then in the *Myth of Sisyphus*. His metaphorical use of the myth of pushing a rock up a hill was aimed at showing man's futile existence in a world gone mad.

It must be remembered that Camus grew up without electricity or running water. And by his mid-teens was told he was going to die before age 21. And that occurred at the start of the Great Depression. He outwitted death and was still alive and in Paris when the Germans occupied that city. He was unable to return to Algiers for six years. During the war he wrote for the underground newspaper *Combat*. Life was cheap. He could have been killed at any moment. When the allies liberated Paris he was fired from his job as he was seen as an ex-patriot on borrowed time. That forced him to live by his wits. His mother and brother were living in Algiers in daily fear of their lives. It is any wonder that Camus came to see the world as "absurd" and with few redeeming qualities. He began writing of "rebellion" and "revolt." His was an attempt at a kind of "humane stoicism." His legacy is well document in his works of the time, *The Plague* (1947), *The Rebel* (1951), *The Fall* (1956), and *Exile* (1957). He became a cult-hero for the beat generation of the late fifties.

RENEGADE. Camus was an iconoclast. He wrote, "I feel one must revolt to arrive at happiness – I revolt therefore we are" (Todd p. 296). He refused to conform. His works are but cathartic mind-dumps of his inner turmoil. In his best selling book *The Rebel* (1951) he wrote, "The only coherent philosophical position is revolt" (p.145). It is interesting that often spoke of just wanting to live a normal life, yet he was incapable of such a life. He had been conditioned to live the life he did and it made him and destroyed him. He adamantly refused to conform to any moral codes of behavior or to live within conventional guidelines. He did all things in excess including work, smoking, driving (he died in a car wreck), seductions, and philosophy.

Camus was a renegade on a mission of self-destruction. His early life in Algeria was a struggle for survival. He had no father or mother, therefore had no role models for when he grew up. Later, he admitted to being a horrible husband and father. Camus was eccentric in many ways, and interesting, if not terribly dependable. Much of his writings were rational excuses for his lascivious behavior. He personifies Anthony Storr's concept of the creative genius achieving due to a "divine discontent." Discontent dominated his existence. When his TB diagnosis ended any chance to be a college professor, anyone with an infectious disease wasn't allowed to attend a university in Algeria, and if they could do so, was not allowed to teach. That led him to a life of writing as a free-lance journalist.

Camus' most appropriate metaphor for absurdity in life was the mythical Greek story of Sisyphus pushing a rock up a hill and having it continually roll back down. He wrote, "Only an absurd man would spend his life pushing rocks up a hill with a preordained outcome." He viewed such men as failures, not due to their impossible task, but due to their refusal to see their plight. Man was supposed to look beyond the menial and get to the bigger picture and stop being used in such a paradoxical or dysfunctional situation. Those who could see the *absurdity* of life would prevail according to the Camus philosophy. Those unable to get beyond the paradox were destined to spend their lives pushing rocks up hills with no chance of success.

The existentialist is easily led to a life of debauchery as they hit a wall they say "to hell with it," and go get high. Such people in the period bought into the Fritz Perls ideology of the Gestalt Prayer, "I will do my thing, you do your thing, and if by chance we should meet so be it." It is only a short route to hedonism, free love, and sex, drugs and rock and roll. Pleasure becomes a ay of life and philandering justified on the merit of deserving a release from an unfair world, or an insoluble paradox. For Camus passion prevailed. He lived life on the very edge in all things. Unfortunately, his reckless lifestyle led to his premature death in an auto accident on his way to Paris in 1960. He was only forty-seven years old.

LARRY ELLISON, CEO ORACLE

Larry Ellison almost died at nine months in New York City where he was living with his unwed mother. His mother gave up trying to cope and sent him to live with a childless aunt Lillian in Chicago. Her husband Louis had grown children and as a much older man was ill-prepared to deal with the precocious and rambunctious boy. They attempted to raise him in the Jewish faith, but the boy was already rebellious by the time of his Bar Mitzvah, which he refused as silly. He told biographer Wilson (1997), "I saw no evidence for this dogma stuff."

Louis was an authoritarian and unprepared for such a recalcitrant child. By his teens Larry's step-father was calling him a "loser" and "incompetent." Larry grew up resenting authority figures and doubting all forms of dogma or rules. He admitted he began life with a vengeance aimed at proving his father wrong in his assessment that he would never amount to anything. Insecurity became a driving force and a reason to succeed. Ellison's combative and swaggering style gives testimony to a man on a mission.

Looking back on his early life, Ellison described it as horrid, but he often embellishes it to make his life more press worthy. He told biographer Wilson (1998 p. 23), "If fire doesn't destroy you, it tempers you," adding "Oh, it was a powerful motivation." Lack of inner confidence drove him to challenge the system. He masked his insecurity with an arrogance that has few equals. He has prided himself on being different and living life on his terms. That caused him to become quickly *persona non grata* in any organization requiring teamwork. After high school he split for California and worked for a series of high tech firms in Silicon Valley. At first he attended Berkeley while working part time but he was even unable to adapt to the rigors of classwork. He worked for Wellsco Data Systems, Fireman's Fund Insurance, and Amdahl Corporation. When Amdahl ran out of money Ellison was let go since he always showed up on "Larry time," regardless of the situation or importance of the meeting. Nothing was sacred to Larry Ellison. When he decided to start his own firm, Oracle, he asked an associate Stuart Feigin to join him. Fiegin told the media later, "The guy couldn't manage a lunch date." He said, "I told myself this guy is a complete flake, and he doesn't have a chance of succeeding... I was half right" (Wilson p. 42).

INSECURITY & PASSION

INSECURE RENEGADE

Prior to starting Oracle, Ellison did a stint at Ampex. It was there that he met the key individuals that would make Oracle a success. Testimony to Ellison's bizarre approach to life was when he was assigned a boss he refused to work for him and told the firm, ""I'll work for Bob Miner. He's the best guy. I'll work for him." When he started Oracle Bob Miner became his chief operating executive. It is no accident that Ellison's best friend today is Steve Jobs, of Apple Computer lore. Jobs was also an orphan and disenchanted with his parental upbringing, an iconoclast, and very insecure. Both are overcompensating billionaires who made their fortune in the high tech world of Silicon Valley, and use conquests to prove their self-worth.

First wife Adda Quinn says, "Larry wants desperately to be loved." He admits, "I don't' understand love or people bonding." Such a dichotomy has led to a steady stream of female companions to share his flamboyant lifestyle. What drives him? Proving his step-father Louis was wrong in calling him a loser. He also is out to validate his manhood by being the very best at anything he deems important, which at this writing is the destruction of Bill Gates. Third wife Barbara Boothe says, "He just needs to feel secure." Ellison says his early defiance was critical to his success. "I never accepted conventional wisdom. It served me well later in life."

EARLY LIFE EXPERIENCES

Childhood friend Steve Abramowitz, now a clinical psychologist, said that in his teens, "Ellison had an unending thirst for attention, but on some fundamental level he felt inadequate" (Wilson p. 31). A renegade from his youth, he called the Jewish rituals a "sham." He already hated his stepfather Louis even before he was told was not a blood relative when twelve. Larry was a loner and escaped into books. But the books were not textbooks. They were always those of his choice never those of his teachers. Rich Rosenfield said, "I don't think he did anything with his parents." At 6' 4" he was a natural at basketball, but as in most things he was never willing to listen to a coach, and that kept from ever excelling at any team sport.

The valedictorian of Ellison's high school class said, "He was very quiet, very withdrawn, not at all in the mainstream" (Wilson p. 22). Accounts of the Ellison late teens and college years are partially true, but more fiction than fact. Ellison seldom lets the truth interfere with a good story. Records indicate that he flunked out of medical school at the University of Illinois. Close friends of the time say that he was never there. His SAT's got him in but once again he wasn't about to conform to any schedule or regimen. Ellison's formal education has an eerie resemblance to that of his closest friend Steve Jobs and archenemy Bill Gates. All three high-tech billionaires had the talent tog et accepted by institutions of higher learning but were never interested in the demands of a classroom environment. Regurgitating vast amounts of data was never interesting enough to show up. All were more interested in life's opportunities and possibilities. Their take on education could be summed up in Ellison's statement, "Once I had learned everything on the menu, I saw no other reason to learn French." (Wilson p. 32).

PSYCHOSEXUAL ENERGY & RISK-TAKING

Passion dominated Ellison's life. When he arrived in the land of fruits and nuts, the San Francisco Bay Area he fit right in. Despite being enrolled in Berkeley, he could be found strumming a guitar in Yosemite, or just hanging out and sailing on the Bay. He met and married his first wife Adda Quinn, a secondary education teacher. She worked to keep him in his champagne lifestyle while he just played. She described his attention span as about "three seconds." During their breakup he agreed to see a psychotherapist and Quinn says something happened. He suddenly had a clear vision for his life. He told her, "If you stay with me, I will become a millionaire."

Adda Quinn describes Ellison as a man who always went for broke. Always wanting the bigger sailboat and more exotic car. He would buy them long before his income justified the purchase and in that way he forced himself to earn the money to pay them off. Later he would almost die body-surfing in Hawaii, take chances few would take in a wind-ravaged ocean race, or fly jets like a man trained for such a precarious hobby. Ellison would always bet on a new untried product and then force its success through sheer drive.

When the Oracle stock dropped precipitously in 1990 and the firm was close to insolvency, and Ellison about to lose a fortune, he was typically cavalier about the danger of starting over. He told a journalist, "Its exciting. It was a rush man" (Wilson p. 228). He had not sold a single share of stock to hedge his bet against such a calamity. His style has always been all or nothing. Living on the edge was a challenge and thrill in contrast to most businessmen. He leveraged his stock to finance an opulent lifestyle. Like many such entrepreneurial personalities he acted rich and famous long before he was. He played with stock as if it were blackjack chips. The stock was only a score-keeping device. They were chips in the game of life, and the money itself was never important except to allow him to buy the toys that made him happy. In 1998, when biographer Wilson asked him about the possibility of losing it all, he told him, "Sometimes I do things that are self-destructive" (p. 291). Such behavior is consistent with the Big T – risk-taking personality whose ego is tightly wrapped up in feelings of self-worth. He is the typical Type A, a man driven to succeed, not for others, but for his own feelings of self-worth. He says, "I'm a Type A, high energy guy."

HYPER-MANIC. An ex-associate said, "Ellison speaks with no commas or hyphens, fast like a search engine. He has an attention span of three seconds." First wife Adda Quinn said, "He has incredible intelligence, and he applies it with incredible intensity. And that intensity never lets up" (Wilson p. 39). Third wife and mother of his two children, Barbara Boothe says, "I've never met anyone like him. When courting he talked constantly. He was like riding a roller coaster" (Wilson p. 108). When the attractive blonde was asked why she was still single she responded, "Once you've gone vertical in a fighter jet, who wants to chug along in a biplane" (p. 155). A board member of Oracle describes him as "wildly enthusiastic and electric." Joe Costello describes his carnal energy. "It's that native curiosity, energy, intensity, enthusiasm…I mean it's infectious. He's just like, whoa. When he's into something, man, there's energy around it and he drags people along in his wake." (p. 232).

ARROGANT EGOTIST. Ellison is self-confident to a fault. Most associates describe him as arrogant, but in the same breath as an iconoclast. He frenetically searches for love, but usually in all the wrong places. He is obsessive and intense to the extent he just wears people out. He believes in his own decisions even when there is no precedent to do so. When the Internet appeared to be the ticket to worldwide leadership, he arrogantly announced to the world that he, not Gates, would dominate the arena with a new device he called a NT product. This was a PC sans the memory and operating software, all of which would be downloaded off the Internet. Naturally, Oracle would be the firm with the power and tools to do the downloading. His NIC product was launched within two years to sell at $199 retail. He personally financed the New Internet Computer Company. At the same time he totally altered Oracle's marketing strategy to sales via the Internet. Nothing he does is safe or without flare.

Ellison's motto is, "Life is the enlightened pursuit of happiness," but passion is the fuel that drives him. It has armed him with a Marchetti S.211 jet fighter, Armani suits, Cessna Citation, Maserrati sports car, exotic Japanese in posh Atherton, California. He sails the oceans and races in his 78-foot yacht *Sayonara*. Ellison needs wealth to finance his toys and the toys are necessary to feed his ego. He must own the fastest car, most exotic homes, finest clothes money can buy, and walk into the room with the most gorgeous blond on his arm. His passion finally paid dividends in April of 2000. That was the day he when Microsoft stock dropped and Oracle went up making Ellison richer than his self-proclaimed adversary Bill Gates. He was worth in excess of $50 billion making him the world's richest man.

With the approaching millennium Ellison had been single for some years despite three disastrous marriages. He announced on the Oprah show that he was looking for Miss Right. He has two children by third wife Barbara Boothe - a boy David and a daughter Megan. He has been infamous for dating any attractive female at Oracle, a no-no at most firms, but a place that is considered a fertile hunting ground for the maverick CEO. One of the many stories on Ellison's elicit moves was about his purchased of a San Francisco Marian mansion. He was purportedly driving with a new female acquaintance in the city when he noticed an attractive house. It was 2:00 a.m. and the story goes that he stopped, banged on the door, and offered the owner $4 million in cash for the house. The story has him making the deal, taking the money out of his trunk to pay off the owner, and then escorting the astonished girl into the bedroom to christen his new acquisition. When asked to confirm the story he just smiled.

Ex-wife Barbara Boothe never remarried. When asked why, she responded, "Once you've gone vertical in a fighter jet, who wants to chug along in a biplane? I've never met anyone like him, ever. Not even close. Others pale in comparison" (Wilson p. 155). But in the next sentence she says compared to life with Larry other problems are just a piece of cake.

INSATIABLE BILLIONAIRE

Ellison is infamous for dating his employees. At times he would date three at the same time. One female turned out to be as Machiavellian as Ellison. Adalyn Lee made goo-goo eyes at Ellsion in the Oracle elevator. It turned out her moves her premeditated with the expectation of a million dollar payday on the grounds of sexual discrimination. At the time Ellison was involved with two other employees - Kathleen O'Rourke, the woman with him when he broke his neck body-surfing in Hawaii, and a young biking enthusiast Adrea Zeman. Lee suggested a ride in the boss's Ferrari and then willingly went home with him. Lee's boss was about to fire her for incompetence, but Ellsion was never a hands-on manager and was not aware of her operating skills, or lack of. Her boss became alarmed when he discovered the boss was sleeping with a woman he was about to terminate. After a conversation with Ellison he was told the relationship should not interfere with her work and the manager should proceed with the firing. Lee then very adroitly, or so she thought, used the firm's e-mail to create a trail of memos suggesting that her firing was a cover up for her affair with Ellison. She filed a multi-million dollar lawsuit. Ellison was incriminated and forced to pay Lee $100,000.

Ellison had been duped and was never a man to avoid a fight. He went for the jugular, hired a private investigator, put together a case, and filed a lawsuit for extortion and asked for criminal charges to be brought against Lee. The investigator didn't like Elilson in any way, but saw that he had been taken advantage of and brought the case to trial. Lee was found guilty of perjury and extortion, forced to return the $100,000, and spent one year in jail.

Ellison biography says it all about his approach to life. Mike Wilson titled his work, *The only difference between God and Larry Ellison - God doesn't think he is Ellison*"(1997). Wilson describes Ellison as "brash, swaggering, combative, flashy, visionary iconoclast, and a man who takes few prisoners." The account says, The subject Ellison likes best is himself," offering confirmation of Adler's adage, "The more intense the inferiority the more violent the superiority."

CHARISMATIC

The charismatic tends to be highly effective at communicating a vision. Ellison is the wizard in this arena. When he gets an idea he becomes super-charged and is unstoppable. The electricity and enthusiastic approach has made him rich and famous. Ellison has all the qualities that make up a charismatic personality. He has confidence, style, eloquence, hyper-activity, and is fearless. Teenage friends in Chicago describe Ellison's uncanny ability to talk his way out of jams. When stopped for speeding he would make up wild stories so unbelievable they had to be believed. First wife Quinn says, "He was electrifying. There was an aura about him." One past engineer associate who didn't really like him, commented, "He's wildly enthusiastic and it's infectious. He has a powerful sense of possibility. He was the kind of person you would like to follow" (Wilson p. 40). Another said, "He dazzled people with insights and maddened them with lies."

LIVE-ON-THE-EDGE MENTALITY

Childhood friend Dennis Coleman told the media, "Larry was always the kind of guy who would take it to the limit, bet the house, and then bet it again. If he lost a hand in a poker game he would double up on his next hand." He never changed once in Silicon Valley where such behavior is more the norm than the exception. Everything decision is aimed at hitting a home run.

Singles are not his style, so if he strikes out so be it. How many people have a hobby that entails jet dogfights over the open ocean with their teenage sons? Not many! But Ellison and son David do it regularly. Ellison almost died in a yacht race off the Australian shore in late 1999 but he took the danger in stride, to the amazement of journalists.

Larry Ellison lives life on the edge and that is the excitement. He won that 1999 Sydney to Hobart yacht race, but in so doing had jeopardized his life and that of his crew. Four participants died, and fifty were seriously injured. Six lost their boats winds that reached hurricane force of 90 mph. Waves were four stories high but the intrepid Ellison sailed straight into the eye of the hurricane, never considering the chance of sinking, only thinking about the win. Such a devil-may-care attitude has made him a billionaire. That same style has made him an enigma to female companions.

The news media has described him as "a reckless CEO." In earlier days he often broke his nose playing pickup basketball games. Friends say he played as if the world depended on the outcome. In 1991 while bodysurfing on the Big Island in Hawaii he broke his neck and came precarious close ending it all. Just one year later he once again flirted with disaster on a bike trip in Napa Valley. He was trying to work out problems with long-term girlfriend Kathleen O'Rourke when his bike flipped on railroad tracks and shattered his elbow. His arm healed but the relationship soon ended.

PERSONAL VS PROFESSIONAL. Like many entrepreneurs Ellison is prone to confusing his personal and professional agendas. He has an office and conference room in his home where he regularly conducts business. If a business meeting in his home includes an attractive female so much the better. Females are fair game whether interviewing him or working for him. Female employees have never been off-limits regardless the sexual discrimination statutes that his HRS managers warn him about.

STYLE & GRACE. Ellison definitely has style. He divides his time between three exotic Japanese estates worth 100's of millions. He bets big and expects to win big. He uses the identical tactics in business and pleasure. Ellison says emphatically, "Oracle will live or die with a Net strategy." By this he means that operating systems like MS-DOS are history and his approach will ultimately win out. He is willing to bet the company on his beliefs and doesn't hedge his bets. At Oracle, it is Larry's way or the highway. He told CNN, "All of our sales reps *will* be forced to demo our systems via the Internet." One employee describes Oracle as "Larryland." Another calls it a "one-man amusement park." Biographer Wilson says in summing up the essence of Larry Ellison, "He sacrificed everything – love, family, friendships, all for business" (Wilson p. 48).

VISIONARY GENIUS

One business associate described Ellison's business style as "always looking at the horizon. He lives in the future and has a serious problem with verb tenses." Another describes him as "intensely active." There is no question he is highly impulsive, intolerant, and impatient. He agrees "I am not terribly forgiving of mediocrity." His long-time secretary, Jenny Overstreet, described his eccentric style as, "He doesn't live in today. There are problems today, there are solutions tomorrow." She described him as preferring a fantasy future to the present that may be safe bout fraught with realism.

A Vice President of sales at Oracle called Ellison "wildly ambitious and optimistic who demanded we double sales every year." A Silicon Valley venture capitalist characterized him as "requiring a forklift to carry around his ego." Testimony to his arrogance was a 1997 statement to the press, "IBM is the past, Microsoft is the present, and Oracle is the future." Mathew Benjamin of *Investors Business Daily* (March 30, 2000) wrote, "Financial analysts discounted Ellison's claims as the ravings of a delusional egoist." But he added, "they're not sure anymore." In April 2000, the brash, flashy, billionaire passed up the nerdy Gates as the richest man in the world.

RENEGADE WARRIOR

A former sales manager described his style. "It is not enough to succeed with Larry. Everyone else must fail." Sales were godly for Ellison who couldn't stand not being first. He couldn't stand to lose just one deal. Sales Vice President Gary Kennedy described working for the mercurial Ellison as precarious. He said, "Working for Larry is like riding a tiger. You had to keep clinging to the tiger's back because if you fell off he would eat you." When queried about his role as entrepreneur, Ellison replied, "I knew I had to do this (Oracle), because I knew I couldn't survive inside a conventional corporation." Quite introspective, since such a maverick is seldom tolerated in a more prudent organization.

For the renegade Ellison rules are irrelevant, the truth is but what works, and authority is for the taking. Such a non-conformist would have never fit in no matter his talent. But Ellison is convinced his iconoclastic approach is just what the world of high tech needs to move forward. He told the media, "I never accepted conventional wisdom. It served me well in later life." Ellison lives outside the box, but in his defense, no one ever accused him of mediocrity. He is loved or hated but is never treated with indifference.

INNOVATIVE CONTRIBUTIONS

Larry grew Oracle from nothing in 1977 to $10 billion at the turn of the century. After failing to fit in at firms like Amdahl and Ampex he founded Oracle. In a style reminiscent of Gates he borrowed extensively from IBM's relational database to become the third largest supplier of operating software systems in the world. Few are aware friend Steve Jobs did the same when he borrowed the graphic interface programs from Xerox's Parc Labs to create the Apple Macintosh.

1993 Ellison made the cover of *Fortune* for his success in developing and marketing relational databases. By 2000 Oracle databases were being used on the top ten largest web sites, on 93 percent of all public Internet firms, and in more than 100,000 business organizations. Oracle was now in a position to challenge both IBM and Microsoft for leadership. He was voted the Entrepreneur of the Year in 1990 and in 1999 won the prestigious Innovative Leadership Award. By the Spring of 2000 Oracle stock skyrocketed to $75.56 and he was no longer looked on as an eccentric entrepreneur.

On his trek to the top Ellison took few prisoners. He was single-focused to a fault, and found the pack and went elsewhere. Sales and Marketing Management (June 2000) quoted a former employee on his success. Tom Siebel who is now a competitor said of his former boss, "Larry wants to be the world's best marathon runner and the way he wants to do that is to sever the Achilles tendon of everyone else in the race, so he's the only one left. That doesn't seem to be the most fulfilling way to win the race." Such is the Machiavellian approach to business of a man who continues to overcompensate for a raging inner insecurity that propels him to success after success between flirtations with disaster. Passion is his forte. It has made him great and left a trail of corpses in his wake.

4

SEX APPEAL & SUCCESS

Oscar Wilde	Madonna
"Nothing succeeds like excess"	"I want to rule the world"

"Innovative people are sensuous"
Psychologist Frederick Herzberg

"Sex & Power are inextricably intertwined"
Michael Hutchison, *The Anatomy of Sex & Power* (1990)

"Sex energy is the creative energy of all geniuses"
Napoleon Hill, *Think and Grow Rich* (1960)

OSCAR O'FLAHARTIE WILLS WILDE
BISEXUAL IRISH WIT & PLAYWRIGHT
b. Dublin, Ireland, 1856
d. Paris, France November 30, 1900

NOTABLE TRAIT: ARROGANCE & ARTICULATION – DUBLIN SNOB

PHILOSOPHY: "THE WAY TO GET RID OF TEMPTATION IS TO YIELD TO IT"

SELF-ANALYSIS: "I WAS THE LORD OF LANGUAGE. I AM A PERVERSE AND IMPOSSIBLE PERSON"

MOTTO: "THERE ARE ONLY TWO TRAGEDIES IN LIFE. ONE IS NOT GETTING WHAT ONE WANTS, THE OTHER IS GETTING IT"

MARITAL STATUS: CONSTANCE LLOYD (1884) TWO SONS CYRIL AND VYVYAN

RELIGION: ROMAN CATHOLIC WITH LITTLE DOGMA

INNOVATIONS: *THE PICTURE OF DORIAN GRAY* (1891), A STUDY OF ALTERNATIVE L IFESTYLES

PASSIONS: "NOTHING IS SERIOUS EXCEPT PASSION"

AGGRESSIVENESS: "I HAVE A LOATHSOME EROTOMANIA"

THRILL-SEEKING: "AN IDEA THAT IS NOT DANGEROUS IS UNWORTHY OF BEING CALLED AN IDEA"

CHARM: DASHING ROCONTEUR – DOUGLAS SAID, "HE WAS THE GREATEST TALKER WHO EVER LIVED"

EGOISM: "I'LL BE FAMOUS, IF NOT I'LL BE NOTORIOUS"

ECCENTRICITIES: AFFECTED DANDY IN CLOTHES, TASTE, AND SEX

MANIAS: "I THOUGHT LIFE WAS GOING TO BE A BRILLIANT COMEDY; I FOUND IT TO BE A REVOLTING AND REPELLENT TRAGEDY"

MADONNA LOUISE CICCONE
SHOCK-MISTRESS OF ENTERTAINMENT
b. Bay City, Michigan August 16, 1958

NOTABLE TRAIT: MISENTHROPIC USE OF SEX FOR POWER

PHILOSOPHY: "HOW COULD I HAVE ENDED UP ANYTHING ELSE WITH THE NAME MADONNA"

SELF-ANALYSIS: "I'M A CONTROL FREAK. THAT'S WHY I'M NOT MARRIED. WHO COULD STAND ME"

MOTTO: "THE ESSENCE OF MY SUCCESS IS PUSSY POWER"

MARITAL STATUS: MARRIED TO SEAN PENN AT 27 DIVORCED DAUGHTER LOURDES BY CARLOS LEON AT 38 SON ROCCO BY GUY RITCHIE AT 42

RELIGION: NON-PRACTICING CATHOLIC

INNOVATIONS: DEMYSTIFIED SEX THROUGH BOOK & PERFORMANCES; WOMAN OF YEAR 1990

PASSIONS: "PUSSY RULES THE WORLD"

AGGRESSIVENESS: "I'M NOT INTERESTED IN ANYONE I CAN'T COMPETE WITH. THERE'S GOT TO BE A FIGHT"

THRILL-SEEKING: A FEARLESS INDEPENDENT SPIRIT

CHARM: THE MISTRESS OF HYPE

EGOISM: "I WANT TO RULE THE WORLD"

ECCENTRICITIES: RADICAL WHO HITCHIKED NUDE, HAD SEX ON ELEVATORS & SHOCKED WORLD WITH *SEX* BOOK

MANIAS: "I'M A WORKAHOLIC. I HAVE INSOMNIA, AND I'M A CONTROL FREAK"

SEX APPEAL & SUCCESS

SEX APPEAL CAN MOVE MOUNTAINS

That certain chemistry that attracts you to another person can be magical if not addictive. Some people have it. Others want it. And no one seems to know where it comes from. From the study of these individuals it is apparent it emanates from within a special person, one who sparkles and radiates energy. Such people have flare and a glow that attracts disciples to their side. Jesus had it. Mohammad had it. Casanova had it and so did Joan of Arc and Catherine the Great. Napoleon had it as well as all those cult leaders who mesmerized thousands.

Think of the appeal of an Isadora whose magical presence led Auguste Rodin to call her "the greatest female who ever lived." A Hollywood journalist described President John F. Kennedy "the most appealing human being I have ever met." Freud called turncoat friend Carl Jung "an Aryan Christ." Coco Channel didn't even like Picasso but was still, "swept up by a passion for him." Do such comments allow these individuals special privileges? You bet! Can such magnetism open important doors? It sure can. Such magnetic appeal is the reason many of these subjects were able to seduce so many. Dramatist Oscar Wilde and flamboyant entertainer Madonn are the two who personify sex appeal for this work.

The sexual energy exuded by Oscar Wilde was without limit but it was embellished by his awesome wit and flamboyant style. When he walked in everyone took notice as he was dressed in sartorial splendor with top hat and cane and an arrogance to match. Then when he spoke he had few peers for turning a phrase and double entendres. He was an effete snob but his dashing elegance and intellectual insights both amused and bemuse friends and adversaries. The Irish dramatist had a gift for words that he used to amuse and to destroy with cynical brutality. His appeal opened doors and then closed them with a bang. As in most creative genius Wilde's strength was his greatest curse. He drew the precocious and attractive, and when the young college set wanted to spend time with him he was incapable of stopping at verbal dialogue. Wilde was enthralled with the beautiful and it proved to be his undoing. Biographer Schmidgal (1994 p. 20) "Oscar was hopelessly and ruinously infatuated with beautiful young men."

Wilde became a celebrity soon after leaving the university based on his unique ability to entertain with a disarming radical repartee. Before long he was the toast of London and no salon could be without his presence. Had Wilde's lusts been restricted to females he would certainly have become one of history's great dramatists. He may even have made it to Parliament. But falling in love with the attractive son of the Marquess de Queensberry, Lord Alfred Douglas, proved his undoing. Bosie's youth, vitality, and intellectual precocity appealed to Wilde. As he was want to do Wilde followed his own advice and "yielded to temptation" as a means of "getting rid of it."

Madonna hit the headlines one hundred years after Wilde but did so with an equal amount of radical panache and renegade style that would make her both loved and hated as Wilde. The Material Girl, with tongue in cheek, saw it her duty to put on a world steeped in sexual Puritanism. It appealed to the teeny set, titillated the young adults, and infuriated parents and the religious right. Did she care? Not one bit. In fact saw herself a Joan of Arc like heroine armed with sexual metaphors and erotic lyrics aimed at shocking the uptight and breaking down religious dogmas. Her dress and blasphemous acts were idealized and seen as groovy by the teeny-boppers and the *avant garde*. They made her rich and famous while their elders saw her as a venomous monster.

When parents saw their teenage daughters dressing Like a Virgin, they were less than thrilled. Shock became her ammunition and the more she was demeaned the more radical she got. Bustiers and scanty outfits shocked and titillated even thought to her they were merely props to send a message, "Get hip or get shocked to the puritanical tyrants. The only reason she thrived for far greater sacrileges than Wilde was a changed world. For Madonna sex was but a prop, albeit a fun and exciting prop, but it was still a prop for her use. She used it to dupe an unsuspecting public into buying her records and then to make millions in the release of her SEX book (1991). During the media furor over her book she said, "My behavior, videos, Sex book, are all aimed at changing the mores of society." Why did she take on the world in a battle she was not about to win? Because she was incensed over the fear of skin and other accoutrements that were harmless compared to bad stuff like drugs and AIDS. She felt her props were both natural and victimless and when others didn't see it she went for the jugular. Through shock she felt she could communicate a message aimed at defusing antiquated prejudices and fears. Did she succeed? The jury is still out, but her message made her rich and famous as it drew a line in the sand between the young and old. The youth loved and admired her work. Older people saw her as disgusting.

WHAT IS CHEMISTRY? It is those goosebumps you get when around someone with magical appeal. It is what Freud described as libidinal energy. It is finding a soul mate with a similar view of the world. It is that gnawing hurt in the groin for someone you adore. It is passion with a purpose.

SEX APPEAL & SUCCESS

Chemistry is what happened to a young man who heard an aging Margaret Mead deliver a speech. The man was thirty years her junior, but hearing her speak he became so excited it alarmed him and he told a reporter, "The sex appeal of her mind was absolutely captivating. If she had pointed to me and said, You! You're the one I choose! Come off with me. I would have gone with her, anywhere" (Howard p. 1984). Such attraction is not sexual, and it is not emotional. It is seen as such however, and therefore we use sexual terms to describe our feelings of excitement.

Sex appeal is a cousin of sex drive. It is what Freud called the Pleasure Principle and at times psychic energy. Others have called it a Life Force. The ancient Chinese called it *feng shui* or a *life energy* of design and placement that was steeped in serenity, or what Joseph Campbell called *bliss*. A person knows when they have it as they are in the zone and so excited are unable to sleep or concentrate effectively. Cult leaders have it. Why? Because they have a cause that supercedes all things including reason. They are willing to die for their cause and that draws disciples to such passion. Without such ardor Napoleon and Hitler would never have been able to take over the French and German nations. It is what allowed Jim Jones to set up Jonestown and David Koresh to cause the immolation in Waco. Such passion is not always rational but it is always appealing and captivating.

Cult leaders like Charles Manson seduce the minds, bodies, and souls of needy women. When they have the women under their influence, they tend to test the limits of their powers. Such men exude a kind of emotional appeal that ultimately evolves into total control. Once in control of the flock they often justify their sexual fantasies in the name of perverse rituals. Sex orgies proliferate among the cultists, but it is a function of fear and control aimed at a common dogma. Such uses of sex appeal give it a bad name although it also can be very positive when bringing together people with a common purpose. Most in this book used sex appeal in the positive sense although the exceptions were Chaplin, Hughes, and Picasso, and at times Carl Jung.

CHARISMA – A TRANSCENDENT POWER

Love and lust are second cousins of charisma. As discussed above many cultists use their charismatic powers for personal self-gratification. Babe Ruth used his immense appeal to seduce young women, Picasso did the same, as did Jack Kennedy. Charlie Chaplin and Howard Hughes attracted legions of beautiful young women who were easy marks due to their dream of stardom. Both men took advantage of their roles as head of a studio, but without question both were highly charismatic.

CULT SEDUCTIONS. Cultists pick on the lonely, mostly women who have been disenfranchised. They threaten them with a common enemy, hell if you will, and then promise them salvation, with themselves as messiah. One important element is the creation of a common bond. Most successful ventures develop a *esprit de corps* among their followers. Each year thousands of attractive young people, especially runaway girls become victims of such men promising a *cause celebre*. Such leaders often use sexual coercion to entice new members, often emotionally vulnerable females become the "happy hookers" to embark on "flirty fishing" expeditions.

A find line separates those who use their charismatic powers for personal gratification or for a noble cause. Chaplin, Hughes, and Picasso definitely abused their charisma, as did Colette. But many times some incredibly seductive women on their own part have fallen prey to the truly powerful. Marilyn Monroe was incapable of resisting the charms of Jack Kennedy. She actually believed he might marry her. As President his position just added to his personal magnetism. Kennedy offered Marilyn an opportunity to fly on Air Force One, have sex in the White House pool, and other dalliances that were irresistible to this *femme fatale*.

Cultists offer a different form of power, usually a chance for enlightenment, religious purging, or a promise at salvation. Picasso offered women a chance to be immortalized in one of his paintings. Charlie Chaplin and Howard Hughes offered the chance at movie stardom. Larry Ellison would take new female acquaintances for a ride in his jet fighter. But whatever the offer these power brokers saw their seductions as a right of passage. They were special and if women were willing so were they. Marilyn Monroe was deluded in thinking that Jack would divorce Jackie and marry her. For him she was a one-night-stand to satisfy his lust. To her it was love and romance.

Women like Marilyn have been known to give sex to get love. Men have forever given love to get sex. That is the way of the world. Consequently, many women use their sexual attraction to gain power over a male while men in power will often use their power to get sex. The sexual machinations of Howard Hughes during his heyday were mind-boggling. For years he bedded the most beautiful women in the world, women like Rita Hayworth, Lana Turner, Susan Hayward, Katherine Hepburn, and Ginger Rogers. Most came away in shock. They had been used, abused, and discarded by a dirty man.

"Power," as Kissinger so eloquently said, is "the ultimate aphrodisiac." Just look at the number of paternity suits that haunted Chaplin, Russell, Jung, Hughes, Ruth, Kennedy, Camus and Ellison. All used their power to seduce and were surprised to find that their female conquests saw the liaison as more than just a quickie fling. The men saw the event as a momentary tryst. The women viewed it as a romantic adventure with a potential future.

ATTRACTION TO BEAUTY

Emotional attraction, especially to beauty, can addictive. Stanton Peele wrote a book titled "Love & Addiction" (1975). He described addiction as an "experience which grows out of an individual's routinized subjective response to something that has special meaning." That *something* is arousal. We call it chemistry, passion, and inner-tingling, or one's hot button. When turned on people have been known to do stupid things that in the light of rationality are quite illogical. But in the name of love many bizarre actions have occurred.

Futurist Robert Anton Wilson outlined a highly refined system with lust and love defined as a "socio-sexual circuit imprint." This circuit is #4 on his hierarchy of reaching physical Utopia, a place he defines as the genesis of beauty. In his words, "People who take their heaviest imprint on this circuit are *beautiful*," with the attraction to beautiful people defined as:

> *Beautiful people have received so many sexual neurotransmitters from the brain that they are constantly radiating the attractive mating signals that make up our perception of what is beautiful in a human being – an explosive mixture of egotism and sexuality"* (*Prometheus Rising* 1983 p. 132-135).

OSCAR WILDE – FLAMBOYANT PLAYRIGHT

To say Wilde was wild would be a gross understatement. He amused the world with his unmatched wit, shocked them with an iconoclastic morality, mesmerized them with his sartorial splendor, and incensed them by A pompous attitude. He blatantly pursued young men in London until his bubble burst. His wife Constance was but a foil in his alternative lifestyle, although he truly loved his two boys, but his passions were too great and led to his destruction. He was not even aware of his own desires until one night when a young Canadian houseguest Robert Ross, forcing him to confront his true desires, and after the liaison he would never be the same.

Wilde lived within the social decorum of Victorian England for some years. He had always been the renegade spirit, but it only surfaced in his with and iconoclastic dramas. Charm and style won him legions of fans including such erudite Londoners as George Bernard Shaw. Shaw was also one of the world's great wits as well as a rebellious dramatist. He said of Wilde, "If I craved for entertaining conversation by a first class raconteur I should choose Oscar Wilde" (Schmidgall p. 9). Politician Max Beerbohm wrote, "Oscar in his way was the greatest speaker I have had the privilege of hearing." Wilde's lover Bosie, aka Lord Alfred Douglas, said after Wilde's death, "He was the greatest talker who ever lived."

A WALK ON THE WILDE-SIDE. The Irish playwright has become the poster boy for gay intellectuals in America. The San Francisco and New York communities see him as symbol of rebellion, a man before his time, who dared live life on his terms regardless the price. Wilde certainly bet everything on his live and love as he pleased. His most flagrant error was in believing in his own phenomenal powers of persuasion. He was so articulate and so mesmerizing a dandy he actually believed he could convince the courts that the laws were wrong and he was right. He may have been correct in his right to live life as he saw fit, but when he chose to fight a member of the royalty on a matter of legality he was out of his element and it cost him dearly. Socialite Mrs. Patrick Campbell offered a cynical but accurate assessment of the Wilde debacle, "It doesn't matter what you do in the bedroom as long as you don't do it in the street and frighten the horses."

At the time of his 1895 scandal Wilde had just enjoyed the triumphant first night of his play *The Importance of Being Ernest* (1895). Ironically, the play's moral message was on the right of man to live a lie and refusing to change no matter the consequences. The play was a cathartic reprisal of

SEX APPEAL & SUCCESS

Wilde's double life. To the public he was an Oxford trained family man with a beautiful wife and two sons. He was expected to run for Parliament, since he was a highly regarded debater with political savvy, connections, and unparalleled wit. Only his most intimate friends knew he was a closet homosexual. Even his wife Constance was unaware of his preference for young boys until his infamous trail for taking a lover from the upper class.

Within a year of his celebrated play, Wilde had become a household name. Headlines screamed of his love life with a young Oxford lad – Lord Douglas. His trial for sodomy with the son of the Marquees of Queensberry resulted in a two-year prison sentence that reduced him from a theater idol to a criminal who would never again live in London. He has since become a martyr for his daring, the temerity to fight the establishment for his inalienable right to make love on his terms. But he was his own worst enemy. No one had ever been tried for sodomy in England. The law was on the books as if often the case but was summarily ignored. Wilde's ego got in the way of his common sense. When Bosie's father, the volatile Marquess, called him as a "sodomite," Oscar filed the lawsuit that precipitated his downfall. In that era, the term was equivalent to the modern day word *faggot*. The Marquees was attempting to free his son from the influence of Wilde, but the combative playwright was unable to control his furor, and filed a libel suit. This proved to be the biggest mistake of his life as it led to his trial for sodomy.

Wilde served his sentence. On his release he was forced to flee the England for the Continent. His final work was a letter-essay written in jail to his wayward lover Lord Douglas – *De Profundis* (From the Depths), "In this world there are only two tragedies. One is not getting what one wants. The other is getting it." He had gotten what he wanted, a lover and a trial to validate his right to him, but he also paid the price for his daring to fight the system. Passion dominated his life. It made him great and it destroyed him. His infamy was so widespread he was forced to live out his life under the alias Sebastian Melmoth in Paris. He died a broken man in France at forty-six.

Wilde was a man of vast talent and potential squandered on an emotional act. The London dandy ended up a vagrant living by his wits on the decadent streets of Paris. He was a sorry sight picking up young boys and paying for their services when he had not enough money to eat. In the end he had succumbed to his own aphorism, "Behind every exquisite thing that existed is something tragic" (Schmidgall p. 257). His life on the edge had come back to haunt him. On leaving prison he wrote, "I thought life was going to be a brilliant comedy; I found it to be a revolting and repellant tragedy"

(Schmidgall p. 20). French friend, confidant, and lover Andre Gide described the fate of Oscars, "Wilde! What life is more tragic?"

A PASSIONATE BEING

Passion pervaded the soul of Wilde. One writer described his life as "love, passion, obsession and loneliness combined to defeat prudence and discretion." He knew he was driven from something inside that was beyond his understanding or ability to control. In a moment of introspection he said, "I have loathsome modes of erotomania – passions and obscene fancies that defile, desecrate and destroy" (Schmidgall p. 171). Like his friend Bernard Shaw he used wit to disarm his adversaries and to get away with radical rhetoric. Wilde wrote often about the disharmony of marriage. "Bigamy is having one wife too may. Monogamy is the same." His hedonism knew no limits. He just wanted to play and live life on his terms like some big precocious kid. He didn't know whether to give in to his passions or respect social decorum. He gave in. In the *Picture of Dorian Gray* (1895) he spoke of the possibility of escaping into a fantasy existence and remaining as one is seen in a portrait. Wilde would have preferred time to have entered a time warp and become permanently fixated as a young virile Basil Hayward:

> *An ethical sympathy in an artist is an unpardonable mannerism of style...Each time that one loves is the only time one has ever loved. Differences of object, does not alter singleness of passion. It merely intensifies it. We can have but one great experience at best, and the secret of life is to reproduce that experience as often as possible.*

EARLY LIFE EXPERIENCES

Oscar O'Flahertie Wills Wilde was born in Dublin, Ireland the middle son of an eccentric poet, Jane Speraza Francesca, and a philandering physician, Sir Robert Wilde. His mother was a liberated six-foot tall author who would be a dominant influence on his life. His father was an eye surgeon once sued for raping a female patient on his operating table after chloroforming her. The father was far more incorrigible than his infamous son. Sir Robert sired three illegitimate children before his marriage to Lady Wilde. His mother admitted to treating her middle son as a girl for the first ten years of his life clothing him in dresses and pretending that he was her daughter.

At age nine Oscar and his two-year older brother Willie were sent to the Portola Royal, a boarding prep school in Dublin. Oscar excelled in school partially due to an unusual talent for speed-reading. According to biographer Ellman (1987) Wilde was able to read a three-volume novel in half an hour. By reading both pages of text at one time he was able to finish a small book in minutes leaving the other children dumbfounded. He had a profound love for aesthetics and the Greek classics. His heroes were Keats in poetry and Balzac in novels prompting a comment, "I cannot travel without Balzac. Young Oscar devoured the *Humaine Comedie*is saying, "Balzac's work is the greatest monument that literature has produced" (Schmidgall p. 30). He loved to quote from *Agememnon.* Wilde graduated from Trinity College in Dublin with a degree in the classics and then went on to Magdalen College at Oxford where he graduated with a BA in the Classics in 1878.

Despite affected speech and erudite words that left his peers in awe or searching for a dictionary, Wilde was a man's man who once took on four young upstarts who were intent on destroying his Oxford quarters. He was a huge man who dispatched them all without injury to his person. Once while a student at Trinity a bully sneered at one of his poems and Wilde went after the ruffian and punched him. He was a dandy, but not one to be taken lightly.

Between 1884 and 1887 Wilde earned his living as a journalist and book reviewer in London. He toured the British Isles and America lecturing on the Greek Classics and other scholarly subjects. He was named editor of *Woman's World* magazine in 1887. Wilde was a brilliant wit that endeared him to the London's literary set. Every salon vied for his presence, and when he arrived elegantly attired with long hair, velvet knee britches, pearl-handled cane – the epitome of dashing allure. At 6" 3" he was a dominating presence capable of regaling an audience with insightful witticisms and intellectual repartee. Many saw him as an effete snob, but even his worst critics acknowledged he had a way with words that were without peer. He soon had a huge following of intellectual disciples including Whistler, Shaw, John Ruskin, Aubrey Beardsley and entertainer Lillie Langtry.

Wilde met and fell in love with Florence Balcombe in 1878. But she spurned him for Bram Stoker, author of Dracula. He toured America and returned at thirty to marry a wealthy Irish woman Constance Mary Lloyd in 1884. Constance had been educated in America. She bore him two sons, Cyril and Vyvyan, for whom he wrote the children's classic fairy tale, *The Happy Prince & Other Tales* (1888). On the surface the couple were a happy duo with his wife tolerating his flippant soirees. She assumed he was having female liaisons and had no idea of his double life with young boys. Wilde wrote, "I was bored to death with the married life." But an indication of his allegiance to family life can be found in his cynical comment, "One can always be kind to people about whom one cares nothing. That is why English family life is so pleasant" (Schmidgall p. 123).

CRISES & AN EPIPHANY

Oscar lost his sister Isola when thirteen. His controversial father died while he was at Oxford. While in school he contracted syphilis a perilous infection in the 19th century, one that had destroyed a man with a similar penchant for erudite expressions, Frederick Nietzsche. Paradoxically, both would die in 1900, Nietzsche from a syphilis infection, Wilde from despair.

Wilde first began to question his choice of lifestyle just a few months into his marriage to Constance. He was waiting for her in front of a downtown London department store when he was suddenly attracted to a beautiful young man who happened by causing him to write, "an icy hand immediately clutched my heart." From that moment he knew he was "predestined for folly, misery, and ruin." He admitted that his attractive wife was suddenly "disgusting," and looked for an excuse to stop sleeping with her. He told her that his syphilis had returned and he feared infecting her. She bought into the ruse and would not suspect the real reason until his trial.

PSYCHOSEXUAL ENERGY

The protagonist in *Woman of No Importance* (1893) says, "Nothing is serious except passion," offering insight into Wilde's psyche. Another indication of his fervor in *De Profundis*, "Every thing to be true must become a religion." For Wilde, religion was synonymous with ardor. It pervaded his mind, soul, and spirit. It would come to dominate his every waking moment until he would say, "The only way to get rid of temptation is to yield to it." The irony is that once he allowed full reign to his passion, it would destroy him, since he was incapable of moderation in anything, least of all sex.

Wilde had utter contempt for morality. His essay from prison was a last attempt to demonstrate frustration with living life to someone else's moral standards. Living a lie was unworthy of the thinking man according to Wilde. He would be better off dead. In his only novel *The Picture of Dorian Gray* (1895) he touched on the subject by attempting to alter reality via surreal imagery. It was a work of psychological genius, if not literary genius, aimed at refuting the façade we often hide behind to maintain our social position and personal integrity. Conservatives, what Wilde called "the prurient" typed the book "immoral" and "decadent." He disagreed saying it "has a terrible moral only revealed to all whose minds are healthy" *Contemporary Authors* p. 411).

The story was aimed at elevating man above the ritualistic moral standards of the masses. It was about a hedonistic aristocrat living a lie and the price of such a life. As with most authors, Oscar was that hedonist hero attempting to convince a Victorian world to see his right to live life on his terms.

After much travail Wilde finally realized, "I am a perverse and impossible person" (Schmidgall p. 37). He believed "Disobedience is man's original virtue," but even so was unable to constrain his passions. He only had eyes for Bosie, the handsome and dashing Oxford undergraduate. Both embraced an alternative lifestyle, bright lights, travel, and the good life lived on the edge. They became caught up with renting young boys of the night to fulfill their wildest fantasies. Wilde was discrete with his assignations, after all he had a wife and two young sons, Bosie was not. Boise detested his domineering father and relished the chance to flaunt his lifestyle to enrage him. Unfortunately, his father's rage was directed at his lover Wilde.

One night the Marquees stormed into Wilde's club, The Albermarle, and left him a note addressed, "Oscar Wilde – posing Sodomite." That incensed Wilde and the battle was on. Homosexuality was illegal in England at the time and that worked to the Marquees' legal advantage. He called some of their "rent boys" as witnesses to testify for the defense. Wilde lost the case and was arrested and found guilty of sodomy. The resulting trial was scandalous and ended Wilde's career. It also ended the relationship with Bosie. Wilde fled England for fear of further imprisonment. Paris was not so severe as more than half of Paris was bisexual. Constance left with his boys for southern Europe. Wilde never saw them again.

DIVERGENT THINKING

Wilde had total contempt for convention. Eccentricity defined him. He was a renegade who loved being the center of attention and was constantly making comments like, "Disobedience is man's original virtue." Here was an unorthodox rake with a flare for the dramatic. He said, "Art is individualism" and defended his natural right to live life on his terms and refused to believe any society had the right to interfere with the free flow of ideas.

Wilde believed he was above societal standards of conduct. He also had the romantic notion that love conquers all. Alternative lifestyle flourishes today in cities like San Francisco, Key West and New Orleans, but they were considered unacceptable in 1895 London. Wilde, like his protagonist in Dorian Gray desperately wanted to become as he saw himself rather than as the world saw him. He wanted to be reincarnated into a fashionable but acceptable symbol of male love. He had become caught up in his own deluded reverie, and actually believed he was above prosecution. What he saw as love, the establishment deemed perverse. Wilde had always seen himself as different from ordinary mortals. He was brighter, better dressed, more articulate, and wittier. Why didn't that allow him to behave differently? That appears to have been his rationale. It may have played well in his inner script, but it didn't play at all in court or salons of London.

Theater mavens considered *The Importance of Being Ernest* (1895) without equal. Allan Aynesworth, the actor who played Algernon in the first performance, said, "In my fifty-three years of acting I never remember a greater triumph than the first night of *Ernest*. The audience rose in their seats and cheered and cheered again" (Melmoth p. 412). Six months later the play closed, not for its entertainment merit, but due to the despicable reputation of its author. Ironically, he was in many respects the protagonist recast metaphorically as a man trying to live a double life. Wilde had written about his own duplicity. No one had been hurt by gay lifestyle so why the big deal. *Ernest* was farcical and witty fantasy. In many respects Wilde was the Auntie Mame of 19th century London, but to the establishment he was scandalous and deserved to be punished for flaunting his lifestyle.

Wilde's final words in *De Profundis*, offers insight into a renegade nature:

> *I am one of those who are made for exceptions, not for laws. But while I see that there is nothing wrong in what one does, I see that there is something wrong in what one becomes. Reason does not help me. It tells me that the laws under which I am convicted are wrong and unjust laws, and the system under which I have suffered is a wrong and unjust system.*

CREATIVE INSPIRATIONS

Few writers have been as erudite or witty. Wilde used words to inform and amuse, but more importantly to couch his inner passions. Like the Russian radical Ayn Rand he learned in reverse. He wrote, "The end in art is the beginning." All creativity has such a genesis. To be creative one must begin with an idea and work back to prove it or to demonstrate its essence. Such a process ultimately matriculates into art. In simpler terms, one must see the end to devise a logical beginning in anything.

Contemporary Authors (Vol. 119) wrote, "No name is more inextricably bound to the aesthetic movement." One reason is that he dared write of things imaginatively like a child, whether politically correct or not. His words were majestic and funny while he was in vogue. The minute he was *persona non grata* he was not nearly so funny. His words suddenly had hit home. The truth of what he was saying when heard through the voice of a fantasy protagonist were just more theater. When the words portrayed a philosophy of life to live by they were not funny, in fact, they frightened the average man.

Political correctness had never been important to Wilde, especially when he wrote things like, "Work is the curse of the drinking classes," or "Beautiful sins, like beautiful things, are the privilege of the rich." But he was expressing his own perception of how to live life. In levity they are amusing when they are preachments for teenage children they are viewed in a different light. He said of America, "We have really everything in common with America except language." This is hilarious in the theater but could rouse anger when debated in college English class. His perspective on the English marriage contract – don't be too nice to your wife - in contrast to the French way is delightful rhetoric on stage but something else in marital arguments:

> *Great men in France have loved women too much. Women don't like that. They take advantage of that weakness. Moliere, Louis XIV, Napoleon, Victor Hugo,and Balzac – all cuckholds...In England great men love nothing, neither art, nor wealth, nor glory, nor women. It's an advantage you can be sure* (Ellmann p. 217).

Wilde's work was constantly bashing the establishment or justifying his own alternative lifestyle. To him, a wife and children, were more possessions than treasures. In *An Ideal Husband* (1895) he wrote "Lady Chiltern has to reconcile herself to the fact that behind every ideal husband is a real secret." His secret was kept until just before his trial when Constance caught he and his lover Bosie in a compromising situation. Other articulate wit went:

- *The happiness of a married man depends on the people he did not marry*
- *Women have a wonderful instinct about things. They can discover everything except the obvious.*
- *A woman with a past has no future.*
- *The real drawback to marriage is that it makes one unselfish, and unselfish people are colorless. They lack individuality.*
- *How marriage ruins a man. It is as demoralizing as cigarettes and far more expensive.*
- *Women are a decorative sex. They never have anything to say, but say it charmingly*

SYBARITIC GENIUS

TRAGIC INNOVATOR. In one introspective moment Wilde offered insight into how his passions proved inspirational to his creativity writing, "We are all in the gutter, but some of us are looking at the stars." It was his way of justifying licentious acts in the name of creative expression. An overzealous ego and intellectual precocity led him to not only justify his lifestyle but to dare anyone to restrict his right to it. He believed some people to be more equal and above the law. Why should a person with his special gifts be forced to adhere to pedestrian standards? It so infuriated him he wrote plays about it that was lost on the audience who saw his wit as theater, not anything he really believed. *Au contraire!* Wilde, as do most people, never saw himself as others saw him. He had become so engrossed in his own reality it was truth, but to others it was a deluded fantasy. He should have looked into the mirror of Dorian Wilde living in a Victorian world, instead of the mythical portrait of his own passions.

Many of his sophisticated Oxford buddies, dramatists, and intellectuals of the time agreed with his right to live outside the bounds of social decorum and not have to be punished for it. Most disagreed with his lifestyle but would have agreed it was his right, but few came to his defense when the trial became so heated. Not one appeared to defend him at his trial. All watched from a distance as Wilde defended himself in a battle was destined to fail from the beginning. George Bernard Shaw was a radical friend who made a feeble attempt to help him. Shaw hated the Victorian laws as much as the establishment. He detested what he called "Wilde's debaucheries," but wrote to the authorities calling the antiquated laws an "Act of Gross Indecency."

At 41 Wilde was at the very height of his powers of articulation and it is one of the travesties of history that he would never again write a play. Shaw's strong letter assaulting Section 11 of the law, said, "I appeal to the champion of individual rights ...to join me in a protest against a law that is an insidious intrusion into the private lives of citizens." It was ignored, as was Wilde's ardent appeal to the rights of man. He was tried and convicted of sodomy, and went to prison. He never saw his family again as they fled the country. On his release he was an altered man and fled to the continent where he lived out his short life a under an assumed name and died a broken man, destroyed by his passions.

MADONNA – SHOCK MISTRESS OF ROCK

Our Lady of Perverted Promotion seduced the public and countless lovers on her methodical march to the top. Madonna was a woman who made up for her lack of talent with unmatched zeal. This was a mediocre singer, journeyman dancer, inept actress - having been voted the world's worst in 1993, but a woman on a mission that would not be denied. Despite her mediocre talents the Material Girl would go on to accumulate $200 million in a profession where women with far more talent could be found on welfare or at best waiting on tables.

How did Madonna achieve such success with so little talent? Guts and chutzpah were her fuel to the top. She learned that shock could lead to success while in middle school in Michigan. At nine she entered a talent contest at St. Francis and in a bold move came on stage dressed in a skin colored bikini that mortified her conservative father and caused the nuns to grab their rosaries. The intrepid Madonna would be transformed that night when she received a standing ovation by the student body and won a contest that would mold her into the Mistress of Shock. She had been imprinted with the unconscious knowledge that *shock is success.* Her pathway to the top was formed that evening, one that has little to do with real talent but is based on being different.

Later when Madonna got her chance to appear on MTV, in rock concerts, and even in movies she turned to what worked. She gave fans what they wanted, titillation and unabashed style. They flocked to see what new sacrilege or weird outfit she would dare wear on stage. She was soon seen as defying all decorum in show business. Her video-musicals were banned from TV, concerts in Europe and Canada were attacked as banal, her *SEX* book was boycotted, and her clothes and jewelry were from outer space. Everything she did was shocking to parents and middle age adults. What they hated their teens found wonderful. Here was a woman to worship for daring what they could not. Her target audience were teeny-boppers. They came in droves and bought her records by the millions. Soon she was a trendsetter and would be mimicked by the Rappers.

Madonna came out of the 80's with twenty-one consecutive #1 hit records. In just a few years she had broken the Beatles all-time record of #1 hit singles. By 1990 she was the highest paid entertainer at $39 million in earnings. *US* magazine ranked her #1 in the top 100 "Most Powerful People in Entertainment." Madonna had surpassed her wildest fantasies. She has surpassed Michael Jackson, Bruce Springsteen, and Prince. Her business acumen and entrepreneurial talent became legend when *Forbes* (October 1990) named her "America's Smartest Business Woman." They portrayed her as a woman with a "brain for sin and a bod for business." By her mid-30's this no-talent had made more money than she could spend. How did someone with no talent fare so well? Because talent is way down the list of necessary qualities to make it to the very top in almost any discipline. Far more important are those things she did have: passion, high self-esteem, an indomitable will, sex appeal, charisma, temerity, ego, intuition, and tenacity.

Despite her bad rap as an actress, Madonna managed to land the role as Eva Peron in the 1998 movie *Evita*. She reprised the role of Maggie in Tennessee Williams classic *Cat on a Hot Tin Roof* in the London theatre, where she met and fell in love with a young director Guy Ritchie who sired her son Rocco. Why did Madonna want this part? Because Maggie the Cat is a sexually voracious woman, the very personification of Madonna's International image as a vixen with a penchant for seduction. Madonna had prevailed one more time in a role that she took from far more talented actresses. How does she do it? With unmitigated gall, uncompromising sex appeal, and unequaled intensity. She told the media in 1985, "Even when I was a little girl I knew I wanted the whole world to know who I was, to love me and be affected by me." But even more importantly she said, "I don't conform to any stereotypes."

RENEGADE ON A MISSION. The Material Girl is a renegade and flagrant self-promoter who often manipulates the media like a puppeteer with a Midas touch. She prides herself on violating convention and especially enjoys destroying social and religious dogmas. *Time* wrote in 1999 "It's almost as if Madonna can't leave the stage until someone has been offended." This was an editorial in response to her appearance on the 1999 MTV Awards dressed as Shiva, a Hindu god she portrayed as a sexual avatar. The Hindu world was not pleased. But that has been her *modus* operandi. She has risen on the dead bodies of many managers, friends, and lovers. In the mid-eighties she could be found dancing on Christian icons like crucifixes, rosaries, and bibles. Her props were equally blasphemous. When she shocked the world with the *SEX* Book (1992) she said it was but an attempt at "changing the mores of society." But the philosophical stance was lost on the contents that included such societal taboos as incest, bi-sexuality and bestiality. Her rebellion knows no bounds.

The woman known as the Bimbo of Babylon has allowed her perverse sense of humor to invade her business dealings. Her corporations have names like Boy Toy, Inc., Siren Films, and Slutco, Inc. The titles of her songs were equally diabolical, "Material Girl", "Papa Don't Preach", "Like a Virgin" and "Express Yourself." Her self-financed movie *Truth or Dare* (1991) pushed the limits in homosexuality, language, nudity, and religious blasphemy.

SEX APPEAL & SUCCESS

PERSONAL BACKGROUND

Madonna came into this world as Madonna Louise Veronica Ciccone in Bay City, Michigan on August 16, 1958. Her father, Tony Ciccone was a first generation Italian immigrant. She was named for her mother Madonna, a woman of French Canadian ancestry. She had two older brothers, Anthony and Martin, two younger half-sisters Paula and Melanie, and a half-brother Christopher. As the oldest girl she idolized her mother who died when Madonna was five. In a 1992 MTV interview Madonna said, "My mother is like a fantasy to me. She is the perfect picture of a human being, like Jesus Christ." When queried about her success, she told a *Vanity Fair* (Oct. 1992) reporter:

> *I didn't have a mother and I was left on my own a lot, and I think that probably gave me courage to do things. I think when you go through something really traumatic in your childhood you choose one of two things - you either overcompensate and pull yourself up and make yourself stand tall, and become a real attention getter, or you become terribly introverted and you have real personality problems.*

Growing up Madonna was bombarded with religious icons. She says, "The Singing Nun was my favorite show. Nuns were all powerful and perfect and I was obsessed with being a nun." Friend Karen Craven told the media, "She was always out to shock, she was absolutely fearless and would flip to the top of a human pyramid without panties causing sheer havoc among the male members." When asked about that talent show she won at St. Francis, she said, "I was practically naked, but the talent show was my one night of the year to show them who I really was and what I could really be." Her future was set with the emotional imprint made when she won that contest.

A flamboyant dance instructor named Chris Flynn would be the major influence on her high school years. Flynn taught her to dance and how to cope in a diverse world. Flynn was a homosexual who would later die of AIDS. He took her to gay clubs and nurtured her. She found it necessary to seduce him but it was just another conquest for a woman already on target for the fast lane. Madonna admitted, "I saw losing my virginity as a career move." Madonna scored 140 on a high school IQ test. A school counselor was instrumental in getting her a one-year scholarship at the University of Michigan music school. Madonna spent one year studying dance at Ann Arbor before getting on a bus for Manhattan to pursue her destiny. She got off in July 1978 with $37 in her purse, dance shoes, and a dream to become rich and famous.

SYBARITIC GENIUS

A MACHIAVELLIAN IN TRAINING

Madonna almost starved in New York City in July 1978 at age twenty. She was already armed with strong opinions. One was a vegetarian diet, a tough regimen for those times when she was forced to find food by foraging in the refuse of fast food parlors. She was lonely, hungry, and often emaciated. Many times she questioned her ability to make it, but she never gave up the ghost. Reminiscing on the period she said, "I'd write in my journal, pray to have even one friend ... But never once did it occur to me to go back home. Never!" To earn some much needed cash she mimicked Marilyn of an earlier period by posing nude. In a similar manner it would come back to haunt her once she was in the bright lights. Her nudie shots would find their way into both *Playboy* and *Penthouse*. She auditioned for musicals and films and a plethora of chorus lines. She survived by living with young musicians, which turned out to be her ticket to the top. One taught her to play the guitar, another how to play the drums, and one band allowed her to become part of their group.

In May of 1979 Patrick Hernandez, a minor disco star, had a hit called, "Born to be Alive" which grossed $25 million. French producers were scouring Manhattan for new young faces. One discovered Madonna and offered her a trip to Paris. The three-month soiree proved to be a low point in Madonna's budding career. According to the producers she did little else but sleep her way through the Left Bank. One of the producer's wives described her wayward ways. "She was very beautiful and dated a lot of French boys. But she thought they were very old fashioned, and she was very free. Very liberal! She wanted a lot of boys." Madonna's take on the period, "I'm attracted to bums." When terminated she told them, "Success is yours today, but it will be mine tomorrow."

Back in New York, Madonna met Carmille Barbonne, a woman who became her mentor, lover, and manager. They would eventually end up in court but Borbonne opened many doors for Madonna. During long vigils alone in an apartment, Madonna wrote fourteen songs. Camille then introduced her to Mark Kamins, who signed her for Sire Records, a Warner studio that took on struggling young artists. Seymour Stein was the president of Sire. He told *People* magazine, "When she walked into the room, she filled it with her exuberance and determination. It hit me right away. I could tell she had the drive to match her talent" (Anderson 1982).

Her first album by Warner was titled appropriately *Madonna*. It was released in July 1983 with her own songs. *Borderline* became a hit. Mark Kamins said, "She had this incredible sense of style. She had an aura." She was on a roll and by 1984 *Rolling Stone* had named her the #2 "Best New Artist" behind Cyndi

Lauper. In 1985 *Rolling Stone* listed her the second best in categories: Best Female Singer, Sexiest Female, and Best Dressed Female. Her second album *Like a Virgin* was cut in 1984. The music video of the same name, catapulted Madonna into the spotlight and elevated her to pop icon status. Her hit songs *Like a Virgin, Touched,* and *Material Girl* dominated the record charts and airwaves in late 1984 and early 1985. Her *Material Girl* video had a hit song from *Gentlemen Prefer Blonde"* called *Diamonds are a Girl's Best Friend.*

Her first concert tour was called the Virgin Tour, a name that was supposed to attract the teeny-boppers, whom Madonna correctly identified as her audience. They saw her as a renegade role model and flocked to her concert and bought her records in record numbers. Madonna was a symbol of defiance to that era and dressed to fit the part. Then she married the Brat Pack teen idol Sean Penn in 1985. He was five years younger, but the relationship only served to cement her to the teen set. The marriage did little for her career and it was short lived as the two got along like oil and water.

MATERIAL GIRL BORN. Madonna correctly branded herself as a blond *femme fatale* in the imagery of past heroines. Her songs all gave validity to such a persona, songs like *Express Yourself, Like a Virgin, Breathless Mahoney,* and *Material Girl.* She was now committed to look like Jean Harlow, Marilyn Monroe, and Carole Lombard. By 1990 she had moved further off center culminating in her personally financed provocative movie *Truth or Dare.* She had it filmed during her *Blonde Ambition* tour. It would become a cult film for the gay community and all alternative lifestyle types. *Truth or Dare* became the highest grossing theatrically produced documentary of all time. She had boldly put up $4 million to have it produced and the industry experts thought her nuts but were blown away when it grossed $15 million in the first few months. The success only added to her rebellious attitude and refusal to adapt. She moved further and further out of the mainstream, but was smart enough to reinvent herself for each defiant move.

When the Material Girl announced her *SEX* book in 1992 she succeeded in pissing off every facet of the establishment. Middle age women were up in arms at what she was doing to America's youth and they hated her. The book hit newsstands with unbelievable fanfare. Its explicit sexual content, complete with scenes of bi-sexuality, bestiality, masturbation, multi-racial sex, and dialogue to match only confirmed her detractor's claims. The book even shocked readers of *Penthouse.* The *London Times* called it "the desperate confection of an aging scandal addict." Once again she had outfoxed the experts. *SEX* earned $50 million in the first month at $49.95 a copy. Profit on the first printing was $20 million. One fan told the media, "She's the most sick, twisted psycho that ever existed. I will buy the book when I get paid Friday. It turns me on." Madonna admitted that it was a tongue-in-cheek means of pulling the chains of the uptight. She rationalized her work on MTV. "The book is more fiction than fact, besides, reading and watching are the safest kind of sex anyway."

The launch of the book was the most extensive introduction in history. Over 750,000 copies went on sale simultaneously in Japan, Great Britain, France, Germany, and the United States. The $20 million in profits is the consummate example of SEXCESS. Japan banned the book and in a national poll in 1993 a United States audience said Madonna had gone too far. But her adoring fans backed her. Seventy-nine percent were in favor of the book with only 21 percent opposed to it. Madonna told a reporter that S & M meant "Sex and Money" a typical tongue-in-cheek response to the public furor. She said, "The best way to seduce someone is by making yourself unavailable." Her philosophy of life is described best in her MTV interview on October 21, 1992:

> *I would like to offset the sexual mores of society. My behavior, videos, book, are all aimed at changing those behaviors. Our society is beset by an evangelic scrutiny of what's right and wrong. I am determined to change it if I can.*

VIXEN ON A MISSION

Madonna admits, "I never take time off if I can help it." Publicist Liz Rosenberg concurs saying, "She isn't big on wasting time." Madonna is frugal and often does her own laundry when on the road. Intensity is her trademark. Backup singer Donna Delory says, "She works very hard." Prior agent Freddie Demann said, "I don't believe Madonna's taken a full week off in nine years." In her own egoistic self-analysis Madonna says, "I am ambitious, but if I weren't as talented as I am ambitious, I would be a gross monstrosity." Demann said, "She has the most unbelievable physicality I've ever seen in any human."

PERVERSITY. Madonna loves fine art and at times her taste is arcane. An example is a bizarre painting she had hanging in the entrance to her home for many years. It was titled *My Birth,* a birth scene replete with blood in variegated color depicting the artist's head protruding from a mother's spread-eagled legs. Madonna's defense, "If somebody doesn't like this painting, then I know they can't be my friend." Once again it is shock aimed at innervating her audience.

SEX ORGIES, MARRIAGE & BABY

Erica Bell, a black dancer, was a close friend of Madonna's in the early days. She said, "Madonna's not afraid of anything. We'd get all dressed up and drive in her limousine to Avenue D. (Manhattan), when she spotted some good-looking Puerto-Rican boy, she'd order the driver to stop the car, then roll down the window and call out, `Hey, Cutie, want a ride?" (Anderson 1991). Bell described parties in Madonna's apartment with "Madonna sleeping with three or four guys at once." One of the games they played when bored in the city was an "elevator game" where unsuspecting young men were seduced between floors. Bell said the guys would leave, "cross-eyed." Barbonne estimated that Madonna had slept with at least one hundred different men between 1979 and 1983.

Madonna married Sean Penn to huge fanfare on her birthday - August 16, 1985. Sean was her match for volatility but they were in no way compatible. But he fit her ideal in a man, which is slight of build, dark, introverted, and aggressive. The media labeled them correctly as the "Poison Penns." Sean had a mercurial temper and scandal was the highlight of their brief marriage. He once threw her fully clothed into the pool, through chairs through windows, and once stuck her head in a gas oven. Sean reached the peak of his maniacal behavior in 1989, breaking into her Malibu house, beating her for two hours, and tying her to a chair for nine hours. The next week Madonna had had enough and filed for divorce, bequeathing their $4 million mansion to him.

Madonna had two abortions during her 20's. As she aged she became more aware of her biological time clock. Ex-manager Barbonne told a reporter:

> *She loves sex. There's a strong maleness in Madonna. She seduces men the way men seduce women. She's a sexual human being. She can only communicate in that way. It's all she knows. It's got her everything. At the same time, sex means nothing to Madonna. It's a means to an end. She thinks of sex in the same way as some men -very promiscuous men (Anderson 1991).*

In 1998 when approaching forty Madonna had a baby by her physical trainer Carlos Leon. But as in all things it was on terms. She carefully planned the event and made sure Leon and the world knew she intended to be a single mother raising her daughter Lourdes. Motherhood appeared to have altered her. She went into seclusion, protected the child, and spent many months on sabbatical from show business. She sold her Miami Beach home to remove herself from the South Beach scene. By the millennium she bought a home in London where she felt Lourdes could be raised with less fanfare. Then she fell for a ten-year younger British director Guy Ritchie. He would be the father of her second child Rocco at age forty-two in 2000.

LIBIDINAL SEXCESS

Madonna has admitted to having an Electra and Oedipal Complex. She said, "Like all young girls, I was in love with my father. I kept saying, if you die, I'm going to get buried in the casket with you." A testimony to this emotionally charged hang-up can be found in her movie *Truth or Dare*. She had a line, "I fell right to sleep [with my father] after he fucked me. Just kidding." In April 1990 she told *Vanity Fair*:

> *I have not resolved my electra complex. The end of the `Oh Father' video, where I'm dancing on my mother's grave, is an attempt to embrace and accept my mother's death. I had to deal with the loss of my mother and then I had to deal with the guilt of her being gone and the then I had to deal with the loss of my father when he married my stepmother. So I was just one angry, abandoned little girl. I'm still angry.*

Madonna summed up her libidinal nature by telling *Vanity Fair* in 1992, "I love my pussy. I think it's the complete summation of my life." Earlier when asked about her music video *Express Yourself* she said, "Pussy rules the world." Madonna is a passionate woman with a penchant for living right on the edge without exceeding those bounds that could have destroyed her. She has spent her life seducing personally and professionally. She admits that part of it hs to do with what she sees as "America's sexual repression." Love her or hate her, she has raised sexual props to a new level in the world of entertainment.

Madonna is nothing if not introspective about her role in life. She told a talk show host, "I know I'm not the best dancer. I know I'm not the best singer. But I'm not interested in that. I'm interested in pushing people's buttons."

5

PASSIONATE THRILL-SEEKERS

Buckminster Fuller — Pablo Picasso

"I am a design science revolutionary"

"Art exists to use against the established order"

"I will not live a conventional life. I want to dare what any man will dare" Amelia Earhart

"If a man hasn't discovered something he is willing to die for he isn't fit to live" Martin Luther King, Jr.

"Sex on Wall Street is unbelievable. People who choose that kind of work are thrill-seekers. When they come out of there they are jacked" *Fortune* (May 10, 1999)

"Type T's are thrill-seekers; they created the modern world. They like a lot of sex, a lot of variety and tend to start sex early in life" Psychologist Frank Farley

THRILL-SEEKING PASSION

PABLO PICASSO
20TH CENTURY'S GREATEST ARTIST
b. Malaga, Spain Oct. 25, 1881
d. Paris, France April 8, 1973

NOTABLE TRAIT: INEXHAUSTIBLE PASSION FOR WORK AND SEX

PHILOSOPHY: "I CAN'T HAVE FRIENDS UNLESS THEY ARE CAPABLE OF SLEEPING WITH ME"

SELF-ANALYSIS: "I HAVE NO TRUE FRIENDS, I HAVE ONLY LOVERS"

MOTTO: "THERE ARE ONLY TWO KINDS OF WOMEN – GODDESSES AND DOORMATS"

MARITAL STATUS: OLGA KOKLOVA, RUSSIAN DANCER AT 36 JACQUELINE ROQUE AT 80; FOUR CHILDREN

RELIGION: ROMAN CATHOLIC TURNED ARDENT ATHEIST

INNOVATIONS: CUBISM: *Les Demoiselles d'Avignon* (1907) SURREALISM: *Guernica* (1937)

PASSIONS: VITALITY AND SADISTIC TENDENCIES

AGGRESSIVENESS: "ART EXISTS TO USE AGAINST THE ESTABLISHED ORDER"

THRILL-SEEKING: "IF YOU'RE NOT WILLING TO TAKE THE RISK OF BREAKING YOUR NECK, WHAT GOOD IS LIFE"

CHARM: "HE HAD A MAGNETIC RADIANCE" (COCTEAU)

EGOISM: "AN IRRESISTIBLE SELF-CONFIDENCE" - PAINTED *I THE KING* FOR MOTHER AT AGE 19

ECCENTRICITIES: RADICAL ATHIEST, COMMUNIST; "HE HAD AN "ALL CONSUMING URGE TO CHALLENGE, SHOCK & DESTROY" (MATISSE)

MANIAS: "I NEVER GET TIRED AND I SACRIFICE EVERY-THING TO MY PAINTING, YOU (FRANCOISE GILOT) AND EVERYONE, MYSELF INCLUDED"

RICHARD BUCKMINSTER FULLER
FUTURIST, ARCHITECT, INVENTOR, POET
b. Milton, Massachusetts July 12, 1895
d. Los Angeles, California, July 1, 1983

NOTABLE TRAIT:	DRIVEN TO FIND MOVING FORCE IN WORLD
PHILOSOPHY:	"EPHEMERALIZATION – ACHIEVING MORE & MORE WITH LESS & LESS" & DYMAXION – A CONJUNCTION OF DYNAMIC & MAXIMUM
SELF-ANALYSIS:	"AN UNQUENCHABLE NEED FOR LOVE" (HATCH)
MOTTO:	"LOVE IS THE MOST IMPORTANT PRINCIPLE IN THE WORLD – DON'T LET UP"
MARITAL STATUS:	ANNE HEWLETT AT 22; TWO CHILDREN
RELIGION:	"THE NEXT MOST DANGEROUS THING TO THE ATOMIC BOMB IS ORGANIZED RELIGION"
INNOVATIONS:	GEODESIC DOME, DYMAXION HOUSE, CAR, MAP "OPERATON SPACESHIP EARTH"
PASSIONS:	DRANK ALL NIGHT & WORKED ALL DAY SOMETIMES WITHOUT PAY FOR VISION
AGGRESSIVENESS:	"PROGRESS = MOBILITY – SPEED IS CRITICAL TO ALL SUCCESS; DYMAXION SLEEP = 30 SECOND CATNAPS FOLLOWED BY SIX HOURS WORK
THRILL-SEEKING:	FAST CARS, FAST BOATS & FAST WOMEN
CHARM:	AWESOME ENTHUSIAM WAS CONTAGIOUS
EGOISM:	A RAGING OPTIMIST WITH ENORMOUS EGO
ECCENTRICITIES:	"ANTIESTABLSIHMENTARIANISM" LED TO A BOHEMIAN LIFESTYLE AND EPIPHANY
MANIAS:	"PROGRESS MEANS MOBILITY" – WOULD SPEAK NON-STOP FOR HOURS WEARING OUT EVERYONE

THRILL-SEEKING PASSION

SUCCESS COMES TO THOSE WILLING TO TAKE A CHANCE

No guts, no glory is the battle call for many in the military or competing in the sports arena. It may be trite but it is the pathway to success in virtually any venue including science, the arts, and even psychology. Bertrand Russell wrote, "Fear is at the bottom of all that is bad in the world. When once you are rid of fear you have freedom of the universe." A similar approach to politics was used by Kennedy to gain the Presidency of the United States. It was Babe Ruth's route to a Hall of Fame career in baseball, and the two individuals in this chapter Picasso and Bucky Fuller, two men who lived life right on the edge.

While serving in the Solomon Islands during WW-II, Jack Kennedy earned the nickname "crash Kennedy." Babe Ruth was infamous for swinging for the fences on every swing. It caused him to lead the league in strikeouts each year and also in homeruns. Ruth told reporters, "I could have hit .600 if I would hit singles. Architect Frank Lloyd Wright was so wild and in a hurry he would run cars off the road when in his 60's. He had a number of head-on crashes as did the Babe. Albert Camus died in a car accident due to a tempestuous lifestyle that was fearless. Bucky Fuller was notorious for driving twice the speed limit. Kennedy had a similar proclivity.

Many studies have shown that the world's great entrepreneurs receive double the speeding citations of more ordinary citizens. The woman who taught Amelia Earhart to fly said, "She scared me to death. I had to watch her all the time or she would try to fly between two high-tension wires eight feet apart" (Landrum 1996 p. 193). In a poem written just prior to her record breaking transatlantic flight she wrote, "Courage is the price life exacts for granting peace." Danger made her the darling of flight and led to her death. Larry Ellison nearly died in a yacht race, while bodysurfing, and on a bicycle. He loves driving fast sports cars and flies his own fighter jet. An on the edge lifestyle led young Isadora Duncan to using her first earnings for dance to buy a remote mountain in Athens, Greece to found a dance school. There are no great wins without great risks and no better examples exist than in the lives and work of Picasso and Fuller. Daring to risk it all led Picasso to found Cubism and Fuller to create the geodesic dome. Both thumbed their noses at convention and became societal outcasts by daring to be so different the establishment looked on them and their work as heresy. Posterity has now elevated both men to a position of deity.

DARING TO BE DIFFERENT

Great people take great risks. Average people take average risks. And those relegated to subordinate roles in life tend to take no risks at all. Risk is the demarcation between success and mediocrity. Fear is the pal of security, and danger the fuel for change masters. Those who change the world do so by daring to challenge and defy what exists. Picasso defied his father, an artist from the traditional school, who his son vowed to destroy. He showed the ultimate defiance by taking his mother's name Picasso when he was the only son left to carry on the family name Ruiz.

Picasso aroused the wrath of the art community with his breakthrough work *Les Demoislles d'Avignon*. The work that launched Cubism he called, "My first exorcism painting. Critics described it as "an orgy of destructiveness." His friend Matisse called it a "mockery" and described his fellow painter as a man with "an all-consuming urge to challenge, shock, to destroy and remake the world." Picasso admitted, "Every act of creation is first of all an act of destruction." He, like all great innovators, never look for guarantees, safety nets, or even acceptance. Such people are content to break new ground. Picasso was the quintessential example of a man on a mission to reinvent the world of art. Most experts agree, that he more than any other painter, documented 20th century's unconscious psyche through art. New paradigms are the hallmark of reckless personalities. Picasso qualified.

Fuller was equally the iconoclast. He was a man without fear. He loved fast boats, fast women, fast cars, and spoke, worked and thought at warp speed. If a concept was conventional it held no interest for him. He was convinced the problem with the world was that most people were too into security to do anything worthwhile. He spoke extensively about the deplorable self-serving. Speed was his god and speed demands temerity. He concocted a whole new philosophical concept around the word DYMAXION – a conjunction of Dynamic and Maximum. This concept was labeled *Ephemeralization.* It was his term for "achieving more and more with less and less." Fuller felt he was way out in front of the rest of society, in fact he believed he was about a half-century ahead of society. His theory was validated with his prediction of the Internet in the 1960's. He lived on the wild side, ignoring convention, and was kicked out of Harvard for taking a New York City chorus line to dinner instead of taking his mid-term exams.

Charlie Chaplin is another creative genius who risked big to create big. He became the greatest actor in the 20th century by refusing to listen to movie experts. Had he been more prudent and listened to his boss Max Sennett he would have become a journeyman actor and the *Little Tramp* would never have been born. During his first films he refused to be directed. Sennett was about to fire him for insubordination when Chaplin bet him his salary of $1500, a huge sum in 1914, that he could direct a better film on his own without direction. Sennett told the English upstart, "Okay, but if you fail, back to England you go Charlie" (Milton p. 69). Chaplin took the challenge and his gutsy act made him the greatest entertainer of the 20th century.

NEVER CHASE MONEY. The eminent never chase money. Money is only a vehicle to validate success. It is a way of keeping score on your journey to the top. Chasing money as a commodity can only result in failure and will keep one from success. Only the uninformed and mediocre chase money. Real success emanates from the pursuit of a dream, and if reasonably successful, the money will come. Picasso's paintings were worthless when first created and were priceless over time. Had he painted for money he would have been working for an art gallery.

Bucky Fuller said, "Wealth is not money. All money-making is undesirable" (Fuller 1981 p. 225). He said, "You have to make money or make sense, and the two are mutually exclusive." He believed money to be an "expediency" required to fund your dreams. In *Critical Path* (1981) he wrote, "I did not take out patents to make money. I have proven that an individual can be world-effective while eschewing money, besides I have showed they almost never pay off. The drive to make money is inherently entropic, for it seeks to monopolize order" (p. 149 & 276).

Were Picasso, Fuller and Chaplin rich and famous? Sure they were, but it had nothing to do with trying to get rich. There secret was a prescient vision followed by daring execution. Anyone who sets out to become rich and famous is setting themselves up for failure and incredible anxiety. People get rich, not because they chase money, but because they chase excellence. In capitalism the score is kept by money, which is little else than superior execution of a dream. And whether you hit homeruns like Ruth, paint masterpieces like Picasso, or make the funniest films like Chaplin, fame and fortune will come.

The Bambino understood the above axiom well. He went for broke in all things. He home runs because of his live on the edge mentality, in fact he hit more home runs than every other team in the league most years and once more than the whole league. And when the media learned that he was being paid $80,000 in 1931, more than President Hoover, they asked why? In typical Ruthian logic he responded, "I had a better year than he did." Hoover had just led the nation into the Great Depression making Ruth's line one of the more profound statements in the history of sports.

THE BIG T SYNDROME

Cleopatra, Casanova, Amelia Earhart, and Bill Clinton were Big T's. What is a Big T? The T stands for both testosterone and thrill-seeking. Such individuals are those with what psychologists call "high arousal" in contrast to "low arousal." In other words, passion! Big T's are the types who settled America. Why? Because they refused to be persecuted and set out to find their own nation leaving the Little t's in Europe. Researcher Frank Farley called Bill Clinton, "a sexy personality, the Type T." He said, "Such types created the modern world" (USA Today 6D 9-16-98). He wrote:

> *Big T's tend to be more creative and more extraverted, take more risks, have more experimental artistic preferences and prefer more variety in their sex lives than do Little t's. Men high is stimulation seeking also have rather high testosterone levels."* (Farley, May 1986)

The difference between the high risk-taking Big T's and the low-risking Little T's, according to Farley are:

TABLE 6

BIG T & LITTLE T PERSONALITIES

BIG T'S	LITTLE T'S
SEEK NOVELTY	SEEK FAMILIARITY
HIGH INTENSITY	LOW INTENSITY
LOVE AMBIGUITY	RESIST THE NEW
HIGH IN RISK TAKING	RISK-AVERSE
THRIVES ON CONFLICT	RESISTS CONFLICT
NEEDS VARIETY	NEEDS SIMPLICITY
HIGH SEX DRIVE	LOW SEX DRIVE

Although it is impossible to test the subjects in this book, they fit the above characteristics so well it is obvious they were Big T personalities. They met all of Farley's qualities, especially high risk-taking, intensity, and sex drive. All sought novelty and thrived on both conflict and ambiguity.

Buckminster Fuller admitted to driving twice the speed limit since that was his area of comfort. Picasso loved bullfights and ran with the bulls at Pamplona. Hughes, Chaplin, and JFK had numerous narrow escapes out of bedroom windows fleeing husbands of their conquests. Jack Kennedy was one of America's most brazen presidents. He constantly snuck women into the White House to the chagrin of his CIA security guards. Jackie was not pleased and seldom duped over his blatant philandering. She once found another woman's panties stuffed in her pillow. She walked into his bedroom holding the evidence and told him to find the girl that these fit, "They're not my size." The fearless president once made love to Blaze Starr in a closet while her fiancé, Governor Earl Long, was in the next room. Is that a Big T President? No wonder he didn't see Khrushchev as a threat.

RISK-REWARD CURVE – A ZERO-SUM GAME

Mitigating risk only suffices in reducing the opportunity. That is true for all disciplines including entertainment, sports, business or politics. Big T's tend to live high on the curve and consequently when they win they win big. And when they fail it is a blockbuster. Those less prone to risk will not suffer the same losses but will also never reach the same levels of success.

DANGER. Great achievement can never be achieved without great danger. The super-successful thrive on danger. When they lose, and they do lose occasionally, they chalk it up to experience and do not allow it to be debilitating. It is but part of the score keeping. When President Bill Clinton was caught in the Lewinsky cookie jar he was non-plussed. It was as if he only entered into the relationship because of the high risk, with his secretary and wife in the same building during his liaison. The titillation was tied to the risk without which he may not even have considered taking part. Such men pride themselves on having the temerity to go where lesser men fear to go. That sets them apart. Marilyn Monroe and Monica Lewinsky discovered this when they offered all they had to engage in an exciting relationship with a powerful man. Both women were devastated to find their powerbrokers off chasing other conquests once the thrill was gone.

Bertrand Russell wrote, "How dare we speak of the laws of chance? Is not chance the antithesis of all law?" He lived his life to prove his aphorism with comments like, "Fear is at the bottom of all that is bad in the world. When once you are rid of fear you have freedom of the universe" (Russell 1987 p. 317). During the same era, Oscar Wilde was writing plays of cynical witticism in direct opposition to Victorian morality. Wilde knew that creativity was pushing the very limits of propriety. He wrote, "An idea that is not dangerous is

114

unworthy of being called an idea" (Schmidgall p. 39). Howard Hughes personifies both Russell's and Wilde's theses. His movie and real estate empires were created out of pure daring. What is amazing is that he didn't have the first clue about how to make a movie when he fired both producer and director and took on those roles as a kid in his twenties. No one took him seriously until he succeeded. He would go on to revolutionize many aspects of the movie-making and airline industries through sheer bravado.

John F. Kennedy lived life on the edge. Few politicians would ever dare what he did, personally or professionally. Jack had always been a reckless driver, once overturning a car on the Riviera when he was twenty. Biographers described him as "reckless." Thomas Reeves said, "John Kennedy thrived on danger, risk, and intrigue" (Reeves p. 9). His reckless daring when it came to seduction had few peers including Bill Clinton. A friend who accompanied him in Arizona on a horseback riding vacation when he was supposed to be recouping from malaria and back problems said, "He was wild rider. He loved speed. He was a very daring fellow" (Reeves p. 74). His friend spoke of Jack charging down the mountain and "always taking chances."

PICASSO – PERVERSE RISK-TAKER

It is almost as if Picasso had a microscope into the unconscious of the 20th century. His art was a kind of Rorschach depicting the destructiveness, perversity, cruelty, and violence that pervaded the most brutal century in history. His life and work began at the turn of the century and continued until his death in 1873. By the end he had documented almost eighty years of torment and vileness and had a more incisive feel for the century than any other artist or write. He was intuitive enough to understand his therapeutic approach to art saying, "I have the revelation of the inner voice." He was far more insightful than he was aware although he certainly had an affinity for what was happening. Picasso was highly destructive in all aspects of his turbulent life. He admitted to "destroying one image to give it another life." Bullfights were part of his Spanish heritage. His art was closely aligned to this "dance of love ending in death." His idyllic life was Mass on Sunday mornings, bullfights in the afternoon, and a whorehouse that evening.

A DEFIANT & FEARLESS ARTIST. Defiance was his forte. It permeated his art and his lusts. Picasso lived right on the precipice in his art and romance. Nothing seemed to bother him, and the more cruelty and shock the better. The Father of Cubism would become the most prolific artist of all time as he refused to allow anyone or anything interfere with his passion for painting. Underlying his violence was a seething hatred of the beautiful, especially women. He never allowed taste or decorum to interfere with his mission. Shock and death permeated most of his work and it was completed with passion. He wrote, "Taste is the enemy of creativeness," as he set out to destroy the masters.

An indication of his belief in the radical and risk-taking to succeed was given with a metaphor on jumping rope. He said, "If you jump you might fall on the wrong side of the rope. But if you're not willing to take the risk of breaking your neck, what good is it? You don't jump at all." That was how he saw himself relative to the more conventional artisans of his era. To him not living on the edge was tantamount to mental masturbation – a kind of playing with your head instead of the guts to pursue your dreams.

In April, 1911, the *New York Review* wrote, "If Picasso is sincerely revealing in his studies the way he feels about nature, it is hard to see why he is not a raving maniac." Art historian William Rubin called him "perhaps the greatest psychologist of the 20th century." Quite the statement considering the contemptuous attitude Picasso held for all women, religion, society, and traditional artists. Art critic Waldemar George said, "Picasso has the cleverest expression of modern disquiet, corresponding the collective reality of the moment, to a modern neurosis."

The creator of Cubism offered the world a unique insight into societal shifts, ills and anxieties. Every masterpiece had an underlying psychological meaning that seemed to sense better than his peers. Nothing was sacred to his so he honed into the very essence of the prostitutes nature and death. Both are depicted with ferocity and sexual depravity in *Les Demoiselles d' Avignon* (1907). This opened the door and would become his trademark means of expression. It is not what it depicts in structure but what it depicts in essence. His was a kind of existential surrealist who explored the depths of the soul and the underlying meaning of actions. He wrote of his defiant expressionism. "Portraits should possess not physical, not spiritual, but psychological likeness." Apollinaire, the first leader of Surrealism, gave insight into Picasso's insight saying, "Picasso studies an object the way a surgeon dissects a cadaver." Biographer Huffington described his role as, "a painter fashioning weapons of combat against every emotion, against nature, and god" (p. 474).

PERVERSITY UNBOUND. As a free-spirited teenager in Barcelona, Spain Picasso frequented brothels more than church. Prostitutes intrigued him because of their ability to separate sex and romance, but also because of their defiance. They would dominate his thinking until he went to visit them in prison at Saint-Lazare to better depict them in his classic *Les Demoiselles d'Avignon*. This painting featured five prostitutes who were repellent rather than symbols of seductiveness. He attempted to go inside their psyches and depict them as they saw themselves rather than as their needy customers did. Satanic lust was their legacy rather than passionate seductiveness. Such an inner search for the meaning within came to the surface when he painted friend and supporter Gertrude Stein. She was wise to Picasso and found him both interesting but dangerous. When her lover Alice B. Toklas complained that his portrait of her looked nothing like her, Picasso responded cynically, "Don't worry it will."

The portrait of long-term mistress Dora Marr was one more example of how he depicted art replicating life. *Weeping Woman* (1937) showed her as an unstable woman – made that way due to his cruelty. She told him, "You've never loved anyone in your life. You don't know how to love." She was correct. He confessed, "I gave her a tortured appearance, not out of sadism, and without any pleasure on my part, but in obedience to a vision that had imposed itself upon me." Maar spent life in and out of institutions due to her allegiance to a man who got pleasure from females in love with him or in need of him.

Picasso's most provocative work of art, and most telling in respect to his perversity, was *The Minotaur Carries off a Woman* (1937). In this painting Picasso depicts himself as half-man and half-bull carrying off the nude nymph Marie-Therese, a young needy mistress who he kept for many years and used and abused. In the painting the perversity of Picasso surfaces when he has another mistress Dora Maar watching as he seduces the nymph Marie-Therese. He delighted in having women fight over him and often staged meetings guaranteed to enrage the adversaries. Picasso had to own a woman or destroy her. To him, women were either "goddesses or doormats" (Gilot p. 1964). For a woman to be part of Picasso's eccentric life she had to live by his perverse rules. They were to sacrifice their minds and bodies at the altar of Picasso. The amazing part of this psychodrama is that Picasso was not a sex-raved youth with a raging libido. He was 56 years old when he painted the *Minotaur*.

Picassso's most psychologically prophetic painting was *Jacqueline in a Rocking Chair*. This painting immortalized his housekeeper, turned lover, and ultimately second wife. Jacqueline was fifty years his junior. In this painting he had depicted her as his caretaker in his old age.

EGO, ART & SEXCESS. Arrogance, temerity, and lust defined him. Huffington in *Picasso – Creator & Destroyer* (p. 198) described him as possessing a "volcanic lust." Everyone in his life took second place to his work including his own well-being. When his mistress Francoise Gilot, the mother of his last two children Claude and Paloma, asked for more of his time he told her, "I sacrifice everything to my painting, you and everyone else, myself included." When the Germans occupied Paris, politicians and friends told him to leave for America. Picasso refused to leave saying, "I don't care to yield to either force or terror ... I prefer to be here, so I'll stay whatever the cost." One more example of his temerity in the face of imminent danger, since he was a Communist and the Nazi's occupying Paris hated the Reds more than the Jews.

Picasso had to have a woman in his life and bed at all times. If he decided to get rid of one he made sure to replace her prior to dumping her. He always had at least three mistresses during any period up until his late 60's. All had to worship at the Masters feet and perform in bed. Francoise Gilot was a beautiful young painter who became his mistress later in life. She was fifty years his junior. In her book about her life with Picasso she wrote, "He refused to discard anything he ever owned - property, women, art or clothes." What he was unable to control he wanted to destroy. "I'd rather see a woman die any day than see her happy with someone else" (Huffington p. 56).

Picasso's success emanated from an inner fire that burned deep. This strong sense of self armed him with a power not found in most people. He saw himself as special and outside the bounds of ordinary mortals. Picasso believed it was his destiny to "Destroy!" He said, "To create, I always try to be subversive. It's not what an artist does that counts, but what he is. Art is not truth. Art is a lie that makes us realize truth" (Gilot p. 1964). He believed he was omniscient when it came to art and nobody had better question his approach to the craft. His was an indomitable will and supreme self-confidence that said, "I do not seek! I find." These are the words of an egomaniac on a self-serving mission.

118

SYBARITIC GENIUS

EARLY LIFE EXPERIENCES & INFLUENCES

Pablo Picasso was a stillborn baby in Malaga, Spain in 1881. The first and only male in the family was not expected to live. He survived only to be doted on by the highly spiritual females who smothered him with affection. Women pervaded his life with the only man a father who was seldom home and the weak link in the home. An eerie likeness can be found in Picasso's early life and that of the Marquise de Sade. Both men were the only males in a household of adoring women who molded monsters who grew up with no respect for women. In the Ruiz home was Picasso, two younger sisters, four old-maid aunts, a grandmother, plus his indulgent mother. Everything he wanted he got. He was told he was godly and grew up arrogant with a belief the world was beholding to him. He wrote, "I was an angel and devil in beauty." He would ultimately compare all women to his beloved mother and he learned to hate his father.

Picasso learned art from his father, an art teacher. Don Jose Ruiz hung the works of the great masters over Pablo's crib in Malaga, Spain in hopes of an epiphany for his son. It worked! By the time Picasso was five his only words were *piz* for pencil. His two younger sisters were Concepcion and Conchita. When Picasso was three a devastating earthquake hit Malaga and Pablo was carried screaming from the burning house. Shortly after a famous master painter, Don Antonio, came to visit the family. He arrived coincidentally with a visit to Malaga by King Alphonso XII who came to inspect for earthquake damage. But Picasso equated the pomp and ceremony, not with danger, but with art. Art and royalty would always be inextricably tied together from that moment in Picasso's life. Artists were to be revered as an endowed species. He suddenly saw "painting as glory," as he remembered fifty years later.

Picasso was a horrible student. Painting was his only love. In elementary school he would purposely misbehave so he could be sent off with his beloved pencil and paper and without books. His first painting was the *Port of Malaga Lighthouse*. At six he painted *Hercules with His Club*. Later he said, "I never did any childish drawings like other children." When fourteen his eight year-old sister Conchita contracted diphtheria. This was a traumatic event for the teenager. He made a Faustian pact with God agreeing to stop painting if Conchita would be saved. It was psychologically devastating pact. Picasso loved to paint and was torn between her living and giving up art. She died and he blamed the whole event on god and from that point was anti-religion.

OEDIPAL COMPLEX. As a child Picasso adored his father but came to see him as an adversary by his teen years. In contrast his mother told him he could do anything. She said, "If you become a soldier, you'll be a general. If you become a monk, you'll end up Pope." He saw his mother as hope and his father as an old-fashioned ascetic steeped in tradition, something Pablo hated with a passion. Don Jose was everything that Picasso was not. He was tall, dark, trim and walked with an elegant gait. Picasso was short, squat, heavy and nothing about him was elegant or graceful. His father was a traditionalist. He was a radical. When his father refused to acknowledge his early work in Cubism the separation was complete and the Ruiz name was dropped and Picasso took its place. Picasso wrote, "Every time I draw a man I think of my father. To me, man is Don Jose." But it was his mother who idolized his every move. She told him he was special and would be the strength of his life.

PARIS & THE BLUE PERIOD

The rage within came to the fore in color for Picasso. He documented his moods in color. He spoke of the "secret of art is getting rid of internal sensations. I go for a walk to the forest of Fountainebleau and I get *green* indigestions. I must get rid of this sensation into a picture. Green rules it. A painter paints to unload himself of feelings into visions" (Boostin p. 728).

During those early years of despondency in Paris he painted everything in blue. He lost himself in work, producing a new painting every day, in an attempt to release all the turmoil in his head and the myriad of activity he saw on the frenetic streets of his adopted city Paris. The Blue Period is pervaded by images of beggars, prostitutes, sad couples and poor families. His *Two Sisters* depicts one sister as whore, the other as Madonna. The Blue Period had its genesis with the tragic death of his best friend, existentialist Spanish painter Carlos Casemegas. The two friends had moved to Paris together and Casemegas fell madly in love with a free-spirited Spanish model. Picasso slept with her during the travail with his friend. Then she jilted Casemegas, and in total despair he killed himself. His early masterpiece in blue was *La vie* (1903) that depicted his friend Casagemas with a womb on his temple being embraced by his lover.

With the Blue Period came Picasso's first mistress Fernande Olivier, a French woman five months his senior. She was Jewish but a free soul who had a child at 17, but soon after the father and son disappeared. Fernande was elegant, chic and beautiful. She would later write of his "drive towards everything tormented." She moved him out of the Blue into the Rose Period, but that would prove her demise. During this frenetic Blue Period he painted *The Tragedy*; *The Ascetic*; The Old Guitar; *The Poor Man's Meal*; and *Poor People at the Seashore*. Derelicts dominated the Blue Period.

THE ROSE PERIOD. Fernande proved to be the catalyst that pulled Picasso out of the Nihilism of the blues into the brighter roses. She never understood the seething negativity raging within his soul and art and it would ultimately end their relationship. In the Rose Period, Picasso painted with intense colors featuring harlequins, circus performers and clowns. His most noteworthy work was *Family of Saltimbanques* (1905). During the early years in Paris, Picasso struggled for survival. He had slept with homosexuals to eat and prostituted himself to make a name but that was short-lived. A major patron proved to be the gay Max Jacob. Bi-sexuality was not unusual in Paris at the beginning of the 20th century and it was not unusual for him to have flings with his admirers including poets Max Jacob, Guillaume Apollinaire, and Jean Cocteau. Nude boys came to dominant his work - *Nude Boys Leading a Horse, Nude Rider, Nude Boy on Horseback,* and *The Harem* featuring four nudes all Fernande in different poses. He met Gertrude Stein during this period and called her his only female friend. She was far more masculine than his male friends.

CUBISM – A PASSIONATE SURREALISM. Picasso was turning quickly into an existentialist where revolt and nihilism reigned supreme. Max Jacob had introduced him to Gertrude Stein. She was an intellectual lesbian and posed no threat to Picasso's manhood. Every other female in his life were either lovers or adversaries and all the lovers ultimately became adversaries. He frequented Stein's salon and painted and repainted her to get to the essence of Stein. The portrait ended in an obscure mask in dark brownish-grays. Alice B. Toklas was now living with Stein. She told him, "It is nothing like her. It's depressing." Picasso's famous response, "Don't worry. It will."

By twenty-five Picasso was on the verge of greatness. He said, "I must find the mask in a harmony with its God," and with Stein he had forced her into eighty sittings to find the inner source of her power until he finally admitted, "I can't see you any longer when I look." That would lead him beyond the real into the surreal and begin the renaissance in art. He was in a life and death struggle with the French master Henri Matisse. That was cause enough for Picasso to hate any work by Matisse, especially his traditional and colorful scenes. Picasso set out to destroy Matisse by creating his own original style. He chose the female psyche in all its complexity. Nowhere did he find *female terror* manifested more than in the prostitute and he would attempt to portray that in a work that would become his masterpiece, *Les Demoiselles d'Avignon.* But as in all radical creations, the world was not quite ready, especially for the barbaric destructiveness of the painting that would launch Cubism. Art dealers described it disgusting and scandalous and Matisse labeled it a "mockery." It was so denigrated by all, Picasso put it in a closet and didn't bring it out until he met Braque who also saw the world of art through a similar filter. It would not be until artist Georges Braque chose a similar path and the two iconoclasts would blaze the same trail in destroying traditional art forms.

Picasso's second mistress became associated with the Cubist Period. Eva Humbert was a nubile young aspiring artist who adored Picasso. He was devastated when she died of a congenital illness. During his mourning, he was introduced to a Russian dancer on tour with the Diaghilev Ballet. Olga Koklova was the featured ballerina. He already had a strong attachment to the Russian Revolution and began courting her. He was thirty-six when he married Olga on July 12, 1917. Their son Paulo was born in 1921 but would grow up to become an alcoholic. His mother would be driven insane by the duplicity of Picasso.

Picasso never gave compliments and saw few as peers. But Braque was seen as a co-conspirator against traditional art and would help him pave the way into a new era. He said, "Braque is the woman who has loved me the most." His basic gender insecurity can be seen in this remark. Braque had given legitimacy to his "illogical" and "antisocial" art. He brought back his *Les Demoiselles d'Avignon* of five prostitutes that would become known as his "orgy of destructiveness." Understandably, Matisse hated Picasso's "exorcism." Picasso was reborn into an irreverent renegade an image he liked. He would spend the rest of his long life perpetuating that image. *Demoiselles* defined his innermost turmoil and summed up a nihilistic philosophy:

> *The painter takes whatever it is and destroys it. At the same time he gives it another life. But he must pierce through what the others see - to the reality of it. He must destroy. He must demolish the framework itself* (Huffington p. 118).

PROLIFIC PERVERSITY

After *Les Demoilles d'Avignon* Picasso was no longer the struggling artist. His work was bizarre enough to find acceptance by the *avant garde* set and others looking for a change. By his early thirties Picasso was earning huge commissions. From age forty he was earning 1.5 million francs annually. He averaged about three hundred paintings a year, more than any other artist in history. In 1977 when his estate was finally settled a total of 50,000 works of art were counted including: 1885 paintings, 1228 sculptures, 2880 ceramic works, 18,095 engravings, 6112 lithographs, 3181 linocuts, 7089 drawings, 11 tapestries, 8 rugs, 149 notebooks filled with another 4659 drawings and sketches. Within twenty years these works had a value in excess of $1 billion. What had he achieved? According to friend and one time lover Jean Cocteau, "Picasso sanctified defects. That is for me, the only genius. Everything else is play."

A CHARISMATIC WITH UNABATED ZEAL. Picasso was mesmerizing. Coco Channel was in awe of him. She said, "I was swept up by a passion for him. He was wicked. He was fascinating like a sparrow hawk, he made me a little afraid ... He had a way of looking at me ... I trembled." Jean Cocteau characterized his magnetism saying, "discharge of electricity... rigor, flair, showmanship and magnetic radiance. He had an almost cosmic and irresistible self-confidence. Nothing seemed beyond him." The cynical Gertrude Stein confirmed his power as a "radiance, an inner fire one sensed in him, gave him a sort of magnetism which I was unable to resist."

Picasso enjoyed espousing the essence of his nihilism. He told the media, "Art is not truth. Art is a lie which makes us realize the truth." He created highly controversial and outrageous works portraying rebellion, violence, conflict, despondency, and tragedy. Dora Maar was the tragic muse in *Guenrica*. But the perversity of Picasso was in a torrid love affair with mistress Marie Therese while in the process of beginning a new life with Maar and used both in his work. During this middle period he created: *Three Dancers* (1925), *Nude on a Black Couch* (1932), *The Minotaur Carries off a Woman* (1936), *Guernica* (1937), *Weeping Woman* (1937), and *The Charnel House* (1945).

A PERVERSE GENIUS. Picasso kept a series of mistresses while married to Russian ballerina Olga. Their marriage was short-lived from a romantic perspective although they remained married for many years since they were unable to divorce in Roman Catholic France. As he aged Picasso took on ever-younger mistresses, one of whom was Marie-Therese Walter, an 18 year-old virgin when he seduced her at age forty-eight. Marie is immortalized in *Woman in an Armchair* - a work of "sexuality and horror." She bore him a daughter Maya when he was 53. This was the time he was beginning a new torrid relationship with artist Dora Maar. Howard Gardner said, "Picasso's mistresses served as a catalyst for fresh artistic experimentation" (Gardner p. 180).

Maar remained faithful to Picasso through many tortuous years of malicious treatment. This beautiful and brilliant artist became *The Peeing Woman* (1937). Destruction was not limited to females. He was empowered by the desecration of the German bombing of a Spanish town that inspired his most famous painting *Guernica* (1937). The painting portrayed in vivid color the desolation, destruction, and despair of a town where 1700 men, women and children died. The painting exposed the satanic nature of its creator. It portrayed a horse, bull and female as tragic symbols of a world gone mad. Art critic Herbert Read described *Guernica* as "Picasso's great fresco, a monument to destruction, a cry of outrage and horror amplified by the spirit of genius." Harvard psychologist Howard Gardner said it "harbors intimations of horrifying experiences from

Picasso's own life, particularly the memory of the chaos when his family had fled the earthquake when he was three." The work symbolizes his genius and his inner torment all exposed in this work that would become his legacy.

The inner evil of Picasso can be seen by his use and abuse of women. He once invited mistresses Marie-Therese and Dora Maar to his studio at the same time. His intent was to incite a jealous clash. When they showed up he provoked a fight between and the two women. They ended up on the floor in a fistfight. Picasso painted right through the fight smiling at his duplicity. He would later describe the event as one of his "choicest memories."

Picasso was a mixture of passion, perversity, rage, seduction and rape. His life-long mistress Marie-Therese Walter endured his charm and wrath longer than any other woman. When asked what made him happy she replied succinctly, "He first raped the woman, and then he worked." To Picasso, he was the Minotaur armed with metaphysical powers allowing him to seduce and rape and then to win out in the end. In *The Minotaur Carries off the Woman* Picasso enacts his sadism by having Dora Maar watch as he carries off the nude Marie-Therese. Olga is in the water ogling the whole affair. It offers insight into his need to subjugate adoring women to the master manipulator Picasso. Such destructive masterpieces led art critic Klinger to say, "He reminded me of a racehorse. There was something massive and supernatural about him."

LIBIDINAL DRIVE. Picasso had an obsessive need to seduce, not for sexual gratification, but for ego-gratification. Becoming a father had more to do with proving his manhood than the desire to have children. He had four by three different women. His son Paul was by first wife Olga Koklova. His mistress Marie-Therese Walter bore him a daughter Maya. Mistress Francoise Gilot bore him a son Claude and daughter Paloma. He found a perverse pleasure in pitting these women against each other and spent virtually no time with the children. His perversity knew no bounds. He would go on holiday and invite three different women all of whom he was involved and delighted at his ability to manipulate them to meet his own demands. On one vacation he invited his estranged wife Olga to visit the Cote d'Azur paying for her room in the same hotel where he was living with Dora Maar with mistress Marie-Therese ensconced in a nearby hotel. At age sixty he took up with the twenty-one year old Francoise Gilot while maintaining a relationship with Dora Maar and Marie-Therese. At age 69 when he seduced a 21 year-old college student, Gilot had had enough and split.

DESTRUCTIVENESS. Picasso reveled in destruction. He made Olga into an emotional cripple and did the same with Dora Maar. Both Marie-Therese and second wife Jacqueline committed suicide when he died. His life and work are one long series of destruction. His had a perverse need to create and a compulsion to destroy and admitted. "The painter must destroy and everything is the enemy - a good painting ought to bristle with razor blades." His attitude towards women was pernicious. "I would rather see a woman die any day than see her happy." This was never more apparent than his planned destruction of Francoise Gilot when she dared leave him before he could leave her. She married a young artist when Picasso proposed she return to him and he would adopt their two children. The insidious Picasso was already engaged to marry Jacqueline, but when he read of Gilot's marriage in the newspaper he was intent on her destruction. He enticed her into filing for divorce and during her divorce proceedings secretly married his housekeeper Jacqueline. Picasso was eighty during this diabolic act and was amused when he read of Francois divorce and then made sure his marriage was placed in the paper so she could read of it.

Francoise should have been aware of Picasso's ruthless chicanery. When she began labor pains with his daughter Paloma, she asked to have his driver Marcel to drive her to the hospital. Marcel was sitting reading a newspaper and Picasso said, "I need Marcel today. You will have to find other means. Why don't you call an ambulance?"

The Picasso personality was defined by Carl Jung who resorted to handwriting analysis based on a letter of his sent by poet Paul Eluard. The famous psychotherapist was not told who wrote the letter but was unbelievably correct in his analysis. Jung compared the writing to other schizophrenic patients and wrote back to Eluard, "This man expresses the recurring characteristic motif of the descent into hell, into the unconscious. It is ugly, sick, grotesque and incomprehensible. The man loves intensely and he kills what he loves. He is sad. Looks for an escape from his sadness through pure creation" (Huffington p. 202). Such passion gone amok is the legacy of a man who used it to create but also used it to destroy.

BUCKMINSTER FULLER – RENAISSANCE MAN

The inventor of the Geodesic Dome was a man fifty years ahead of his time. He was an intrepid renegade with passion that knew few bounds. An indication of his prescient vision was his prediction of the Internet forty years prior to its existence in the nineties. He wrote:

> *We must integrate the world's electrical-energy networks. Individuals will go shopping on Cable TV. I therefore predict that before the end of the 1980's the computer's politically unbiased problem-solving...The world electric grid, with its omni-integrated advantage, will deliver its electric energy anywhere, to anyone, at any one time, at one common rate...All this accounting switchover must also be accomplished before 2000 A.D* (Critical Path xxxi).

What insight! This self-taught technologist refused to be influenced by contemporary scientists who saw him as a threat. He saw them as too immersed in the past to have any insight into the future. For him most scientists were driving forward by using a system akin to looking into a rear view mirror. The past was dictating the future an asinine approach to science. Fuller was a Renaissance man enamored with philosophy, poetry, math, engineering, cosmology, invention, and architecture. He would ultimately hold more than 2000 patents and author 25 books including his famous *Operating Manual for Spaceship Earth* (1969). He became a popular college lecturer and research professor at Southern Illinois University despite no college education. Fuller had been thrown out of Harvard, not once, but twice. Intuition was his god. His boat was named *Intuition*.

Bucky Fuller had a penchant for detail that belied his predilection for intuitive insight. He obsessively documented everything in a file labeled Chronofile. At his death this file was brimming with innovative ideas and even two unpublished books. Testimony to his prodigious output was a comment in *Critical Path*, "I have owned 43 automobiles, three of which I invented and built and have personally driven a total of one-quarter million miles, lived in ten states, flown over 1.5 million miles, rented over 100 cars and voted in eight states." He went on to list 37,000 media articles and interviews, 100 TV and radio appearances, mainly on Dymaxion utilized in modular homes, cars, maps, and other innovations like sleep deprivation.

SYBARITIC GENIUS

DYMAXION: DYNAMIC + MAXIMUM

Bucky wrote, "Innovation is the manifestation of the invisible" (Hatch p. 186). What did he mean? That losses are never quantifiable, only productive outputs are ever accounted for in our creative productions. The majority of what we do is lost and quantifying it is just a waste of time and energy. For him the two majestic forces in all creativity are inextricably involved in how *dynamic* we are and how much we are able to *maximize* our outputs.

Bucky was one of the first Futurists. He saw things in their totality and worked meticulously to see if they made sense. He wrote, "The physical and metaphysical are altogether one reality." For him one had to have a dream and see it through to success or failure. It wasn't important which happened as long as you pursued a dream. Fuller was a visionary who was capable of quantifying it. He was driven to pursue life's mysteries but found it fun to search for the synergy between diverse concepts. His life was dedicated to finding the pathway between those links. Speed was godly to Fuller. He wanted to speed up the world's engines, especially bureaucracies. Beginning in 1927 he began to preach about the inefficiencies of our machinery. He proved rotating machinery was only 5% efficient with automobiles only 6% efficient, concluding that for every $100 spent on food 94% was wasted.

DYMAXION SLEEP. *Ephemeralization* was coined to lead the world out of a morass and into optimum productivity. It was his belief that "more and more must be produced in less and less time." Was he in a hurry? Big time! Fuller believed sleeping was a waste and must be automated. To this end he used himself as a guinea pig to see if he could sleep less and less in order to produce more and more. He labeled this *Dymaxion Sleep*, aimed at reducing man's need for sleep. Fuller conditioned himself to fall asleep for 30 minutes after which he would awake and work for another six hours. Then he would put himself back into a trancelike state in about 30 seconds and after another 30-minute "power nap" would awake for another six hours of vigorous work. He was able to do this successfully for many years and according to associates could "outwork many of his younger colleagues."

Fuller was often denigrated for his disdain for profits. Profit at the expense of quality or productivity was one of his pet peeves. Those executives who sacrificed long-term creative opportunities for short-term profits were the reason for America's failure to move forward. He preached, "You must decide whether you want to make profits or make sense, because the two are mutually exclusive" (Fuller p. 225). Most of the world's creative geniuses would have agreed. Edison, Einstein, Frank Lloyd Wright or Bill Gates never once did anything exclusively for money. Do you think Picasso ever considered the worth of *Guernica* prior to working on it?

RISK-TAKING & SUCCESS

Bucky admitted to making far more mistakes than other men. For him errors were part of the learning process and the price paid for innovation or pushing the envelope of creativity. In *Critical Path* (1981 p. 151) he said, "I seem to have made more mistakes than any others I know." Fuller lived on the edge from an early age. He drove his first car at twelve. During that era it was not illegal, but it was still dangerous. He flew his first airplane 1917 when just 21. The intrepid inventor owned three airplanes and a sailboat. He liked to say, "Life itself is entirely metaphysical – a pattern integrity" (Fuller 1981 p. 342). He referred to himself as "rash" and lived way outside convention in his work. His only rule was to not give up until he had exhausted all possibilities, and to rely on his gut. "I intuited to articulate my own innate motivational integrity instead of trying to accommodate everyone else's opinions, credos, educational theories, romances and mores" (Fuller p. 125). He admitted to a renegade style saying, "I am a design science revolutionary."

He hated designers who created for their personal aggrandizement or money. To prove his thesis he created a mythical firm Obnoxico and used it to show what stupidity exists in such short-term attitudes. His model showed the fantasy firm would make millions in the early days and then cease to exist. He wrote, "You can either make money or do what is right but when money enters the equation the greed interferes with optimal success in any venture. I didn't take out patents to make money and I can prove that an individual can be world-effective while eschewing money" (1981 p. 149). His metaphor for business was based on his early hero Robin Hood. He wrote, "I took away Robin Hood's longbow, staff and checkbook and gave him only scientific textbooks, microscopes, calculating machines" (Critical Path p. 134).

A PASSIONATE PERSONA

The young Bucky Fuller was a party animal whom used his college funds to throw a wild party in Manhattan. He was infamous for drinking all night and sleeping wherever he happened to end up. Life for Bucky was to live on the edge without leaving any experience untapped. He was an insatiable workaholic, but played equally as hard, leaving his wife and baby in Long Island while living a Bohemian life in Greenwich Village. He wrote, "Love is the most important principle in the universe," but as a young man love and lust were the same. He admitted to sleeping with 1000 prostitutes before 30.

SYBARITIC GENIUS

EARLY LIFE

The man often compared to Leonardo da Vinci was born on July 12, 1895 in Milton, Massachusetts. He was the second of four children. His father was a successful merchant but who died from a stroke when Bucky was ten. The boy had been highly influenced by his father's reading of Robin Hood just prior to his death. Later in life Fuller spoke of Robin Hood as a mythical-like mentor who armed him with spirit and defiance. He wrote, "Robin Hood was my most influential mythical hero," as like many other great men tapped into a larger-than-life hero to remove self-imposed limitations. Bucky lived outside the bounds of mere mortals and saw himself as a mythical Robin Hood in his trek to the top that had no limits.

Buckminster was a poor student early due to impaired vision. By four he was wearing eyeglasses,, but by six he had built his first tetrahedronal octet truss out of toothpicks and dried peas. This kindergarten creation was a simplistic model for the geodesic dome. He attended Milton Academy and Harvard, schools where his ancestors had matriculated. But tradition was never too important for Bucky and he seldom abided by rules and was intolerant of useless conformity. After he took his college funds and threw a lavish party for the cast of the Ziegfield Follies he was expelled from Harvard. But seeing his potential the school invited him back the next year only to expel him once more for frivolous behavior unbefitting a Harvard student.

Fuller learned to love boating in the family's compound in Maine. He joined the Navy in 1917 and graduated from an officer-training course in Annapolis. He credits the Navy training for much of his engineering knowledge. During his tenure at the Naval Academy, he invented two new products, both aimed at preventing drownings after carrier crashes. On July 12, 1917, his birthday, and while serving in the Navy, he married Anne Hewlett, the daughter of a renowned architect. They had a daughter named Alexandria the next year. Alexandria contracted polio and died in 1922 casting Fuller into a deep depression. He blamed himself for not having given her the best medical care due to his travel and frenetic business activity and called such a situation a "critical detonation point."

CRISES & AN EPIPHANY

Fuller decided to commercialize one of his father-in-law's new building block products and launched a Chicago firm named Stockade Building Systems. Bucky was the founder and president. He began a life-long habit of working day and night. He was off in the stratosphere creating new markets and built

234 homes featuring the innovative fibrous building blocks. Fuller was always more interested in long-term potential, and making a difference in the world than near-term returns, a concept that would prove his downfall more than once. The first got him fired from his own company. The Board of Directors was controlled by key investors with Bucky having but one vote. They were only interested in near-terms returns while Bucky was intent on dominating the world of innovative building materials. The Board fired him for what they described as unorthodox business practices. He described the firing due to his being too innovative for the tradition-steeped businessmen.

Bucky was so devastated he went into a deep depression and finally decided to commit suicide. His wife Anne was newly pregnant after the untimely death of their daughter Alexandria. Bucky was suddenly unemployed, unable to pay his bills, with Allegra just born. Even his family started calling him a loser driving him further into depression. He decided life in a world without vision was worthless. "I really thought I was some kind of freak," he wrote that night in 1927 when he decided life was not worth the struggle. The 32 year-old told friend and biographer Alden Hatch, "I've done the best I know how and it hasn't worked. I guess I'm just no good, even my mother said I was worthless. I guess she was right."

Bucky walked down to the edge of the cold blustery Lake Michigan in a state of despair one night, intent on ending it all. He stood looking into the water preparing to jump into the frigid waters when he says he experienced an epiphany. It occurred to him that the world just might be more deranged than he, and he was here for a reason and that wasn't to adhere to others. He decided to "unlearn" and "dropout" concluding: (Hatch p. 88)

> *You do not have the right to eliminate yourself; you do not belong to you. You belong to the universe, perhaps I am part of the great design. If I am to believe in myself and the validity of my own ideas I must stop thinking as other people told me to and rely on my own experience.*

He went home and told Anne, "I am going to embark on a new life mission," that entailed going within and ignoring mankind for a sustained period. He vowed not to speak to another human being for two years. He kept his promise. The only human he spoke with was his baby daughter Allegra who was unable to speak back. It was an inner search for truth where he came upon the *will-power* that empowered him. External reality was out of synch with life. He would go internal to where the essence of man's ability to function at an optimum level could be found. He was transformed into a man who would never again allow others to interfere with his trek through life. Never again would he allow another human being to control any facet of his life. Only Bucky Fuller would be the master of his destiny. He moved the family to a Southside ghetto where he could afford to pay the rent without working, and embarked on becoming "the most unlearned man in the world."

Bucky had unknowingly put himself into a sensory deprivation state that contemporary psychologists now know can be the genesis for "superlearning." Fuller wrote, "I became very suspicious of words." He regressed back into a childlike state of consciousness explaining, "I gradually regained those precious childish sensitivities to such an extent that I really see and feel very much like a little kid." Bucky had dropped out but tuned in to what he would call the "metaphysical aspects of the universe" (Hatch p. 92). His description is strangely like self-hypnosis or brainwashing techniques as practiced in POW camps. Hatch described his transformation:

> *Out of this intense period of silent thought emerged in embryo most of the great philosophical and mathematical innovations that have made his fame and moved the world. He decided that experiences are finite and tried to catch himself thinking in terms that did not have to do with experience.* (Hatch p. 94)

PSYCHOSEXUAL ENERGY (PASSION)

The inner drive and passion of Fuller was legend. He was a man on a mission and the mission was self-ordained. Life was to be lived in double-time. Sleeping was a waste. Once in his seventies he was on a Greek cruise when asked to give a short lecture. He went to the lectern, began speaking, and didn't stop for nine hours. Such was the power of the introverted Fuller.

While working in Greewich Village Bucky would visit his wife and daughter on weekends, but he was willing to go anywhere to pursue his dreams. During this period he lived a Bohemian lifestyle, slept and ate sparingly, and became a kind of cult figure among wannabe entrepreneurs. "I found myself being followed by an increasing number of human beings, particularly women, who were beginning to make me into some kind of messiah. I became a cult figure, and that was not exactly what I wanted to be."

Speed was godly to Bucky. He believed it was possible to outlast and to outwork major problems if you would look on it passionately. To him "Progress meant mobility." His brother-in-law Roger Hewlett said, "Bucky will do anything, including inventing geodesic domes, to make you love him. I think that is why he charms the great and the famous and the powerful like Indira Ghandi" (Hatch p. 268).

An example of his frenetic drive was the time he agreed to design a new car for Henry J. Kaiser. It was during WW-II when he took on a project to design a car that was "everyman." He had already designed a number of Dymaxion cars in the 1930's, cars so radically innovative, they brought fear to Detroit. His innovativeness interested Kaiser who contracted with him to build a revolutionary automobile. Bucky had already found that banks would sabotage any radical new design that would seriously lower the market value of cars for which they held the lien but this time that would be Kaiser's problem. But it was Bucky's since engineers will also demean anything they don't understand and will be reticent to alter standard manufacturing processes. Bucky's Henry J was once again way ahead of its time and Kaiser didn't dare raise the ire of those needed to put the car into production. .

At the time, Bucky was working full-time as Director of Mechanical Engineering for the Board of Economic Warfare in Washington, DC. Kaiser's design group was located in upper Manhattan. But such matters were of little concern for the hyper-manic Fuller. He took on the project, and would work all day in Washington, catch a 5 o'clock train for New York, and then work all night in Manhattan. The next morning he would catch an early train back to DC in time to get to his office. He napped on the train since on the way he was too excited about new ideas to sleep. "The only sleep I got was on the train." He maintained this tortuous schedule for many months only to get stiffed by Kaiser when he decided to alter Bucky's innovative designs. Consequently, the Henry J was short-lived since it wasn't unique enough to persuade buyers to invest in something different.

DIVERGENT THINKING - ANTIESTABLISHMENTARIANISM

Eccentricity was Bucky's trademark. He went so far as to label a term for his methods – "Antiestablishmentarianism," Always an out of the box thinker, he refused to comply with any corporate, scientific, political or religious dogma. Fuller admitted to being a "design science revolutionary" who "made more mistakes than any other I know" (Hatch p. 151). In the 60's and 70's he became a cult figure with the university set, but was never accepted by the scientific community. Friend J. Baldwin says they saw him as an upstart without the correct pedigree and they "have a way of savaging upstarts." No ideology was safe. He infuriated the Religious Right saying, "The next most dangerous thing to the atom bomb is organized religion" (Baldwin p. 82).

Darwin was also fair game as were all politicians and lawyers. He said, "Politicians don't like me because I am transpolitics." He blamed what he called "self-serving politicians and lawyers" for the Los Angeles smog. The maverick openly celebrated metaphysical groups and numerology. He was a lecturer at Werner Erhard's EST sessions in the hippie era in San Francisco. Feminists disliked him for saying the genders were different.

Dymaxion sleep kept him ahead of his younger associates. Longtime associate and confidante, J. Baldwin wrote in *Bucky Works* (1998), "He never seemed to tire. His lectures could go on for ten hours or more. He seemed to be always scribbling notes, reading, making models, or just prowling around. The ability to keep going in that manner continued undiminished well into his 70's." One of his quirks was a bizarre diet consisting of steak, prunes, Jell-o, and strong tea consumed three times a day. A high protein diet and little sleep allowed him to be far more productive than much younger colleagues.

Fuller was pathologically shy yet would talk non-stop for hours. When invited to a private audience with Indian Prime Minister Ghandi he started talking and didn't stop for an hour and a half. Ghandi got up and left without saying a word. Such excess was standard fare for this Renaissance man who admitted in his youth of a passion for prostitutes. "I visited a thousand of them. They seemed the only place where people really talked straight to me; those girls, many of them had babies. I wanted to see them as human beings, to know how they got there" (Hatch p. 84). Another example of his eccentric behavior was the time during the depression when he acquired an architectural magazine. He believed promotional ads were a conflict with editorial credibility and cancelled all advertising, the lifeblood of any magazine. It was not surprising that his publishing career was short-lived.

CREATIVITY – DYMAXION & GEODESIC DOME

Bucky was a philosopher with a scientific bent, a talent allowing him to marry function with form for a variety of mechanical systems. He had a prescient insight into a wide range of disciplines including physics, poetry, architecture, inventing, math, geometry and engineering. He wrote, "The physical and metaphysical are altogether one reality" (Hatch p. 186). One of his creations was *Tensegrity* – the conjunction of Tension and Integrity in product design. "I use energetic and synergetic geometry – the basic building block of the universe because it has the greatest strength with the least surface (Hatch p. 97). Underlying it all was his concept Dymaxion - Dynamic & Maximum. Marrying speed with maximization would become a corporate umbrella Dymaxion Corporation founded in 1933 to launch a myriad of products.

Bucky's first three product concepts were the Dymaxion House, Dymaxion Map, and Dymaxion Automobile. Later he would develop the Dymaxion Deployment Unit and even called his power-napping Dymaxion Sleep. The Dymaxion House was a doughnut shaped structure suspended from a central mast aimed at optimal space at low cost. It would evolve into what is today known as the Butler Buildings. The Dymaxion World Map is a flat cartographic projection that eliminates the distortions of other standard maps. It was the first map to show continents on a flat surface with the earth envisioned as one island in one ocean. The Dysmaxion Car was a three-wheel vehicle capable of carrying ten people at 120 mph. It could make 180-degree turns in a distance no greater than its own length and powered by a standard combustion engine. It was scheduled to go into mass production when an accident killed the driver. The investors pulled out and the factaory was cancelled. Fear is rampant with innovative concepts.

GEODESIC DOME. The culmination of Fuller's work was the geodesic dome. Ironically, many of the world's domes such as EPCOT at Disney World do not even mention his name. The dome was perfected in 1947 and first erected as the U. S. Pavilion at the Montreal World's Fair in 1967. His masterpiece can be seen at Ford rotunda Dome in Dearborn, Michigan. It is a marvel of engineering elegance that optimizes material, space, cost, and esthetics. Scientists have called his invention the most significant structural innovation of the 20th century. It is a hemisphere composed of tetrahedrons stacked together to allow the most efficient use of space with the least surface while maximizing inner and external strength. The dome is still the most versatile, mobile, elegant and economical building form.

Bucky had passion, verve, and intensity and despite a schedule that would kill an ordinary man seldom got sick. Norman Cousins commented on his unique ability to go beyond the limits without any ill effects. He said, "Bucky's life demonstrates that the key to longevity is creativity; the notion of degeneration of brain cells beyond a certain age is true only in the absence of creativity" (Hatch p. 235). Fuller was not only unusually healthy, but he outlived the life expectancy for his era while working right until his death at 88. The poet of science had a unique perspective saying, "I just invent and then wait until man comes around to needing what I've invented."

6

EGO & PASSION

Carl Jung

Bertrand Russell

"I don't believe, I know"   **"Vanity is closely intertwined with sex"**

"I am the universe" - Mao Zedung

"Optimism leads to higher achievement than pessimism"
Psychologist Martin Seligman

"Self-esteem, high or low, tends to be a generator of self-fulfilling prophecies" Nathaniel Branden

"Study after study has shown that children with superior intelligence but low self-esteem do poorly while children with average intelligence, but high self-esteem, can be unusually successful" Linda Erikson Denning

CARL GUSTAVE JUNG
ANALYTICAL PSYCHOTHERAPIST
b. Kesswill, Switzerland, July 26, 1875
d. Kusnacht, Switzerland, June 6, 1961

NOTABLE TRAIT:	ZEALOT WITH IMMENSE LIBIDINAL DRIVE
PHILOSOPHY:	"MAN IS TEMPTED TO WIN THE WOMAN WHO BEST FITS HIS OWN UNCONSCIOUS FEMININITY"
SELF-ANALYSIS:	"SEXUALITY IS THE *SINE QUO NON* OF SPIRITUALITY"
MOTTO:	"FREE LOVE WILL SAVE THE WORLD"
MARITAL STATUS:	EMMA RAUSCHENBACH AT 28; FIVE CHILDREN
RELIGION:	MYTHICAL AGNOSTIC WITH BUDDHA SLANT
INNOVATIONS:	COLLECTIVE UNCONSCIOUS, ARCHETYPES, SYZYGY (Anima & Animus), SYNCHRONICITIES, ACTIVE IMAGINATION, PERSONALITY TYPES
PASSIONS:	"SEXUAL ENERGY SURGED THROUGH HIM WITH A POWER THAT FRIGHTENED HIM"
AGGRESSIVENESS:	ARYAN CHRIST WHO DEMANDED RESPECT
THRILL-SEEKING:	FEARLESS BUILDING CULT FOLLOWING
CHARM:	"JUNG WAS THE CHARISMATIC LEADER OF HIS OWN MYSTERY CULT, AN ARYAN CHRIST"
EGOISM:	"HE HAD COLOSSAL NARCISSISM & GOD COMPLEX" (ERNEST JONES) - MESSIANIC
ECCENTRICITIES:	FREE LOVE, POLYGAMY, ALCHEMY, MYSTICISM
MANIAS:	NICKNAME = STEAMROLLER

BERTRAND RUSSELL
PHILOSOPHER & MATHEMATICIAN
b. Ravenscroft, Wales May 18, 1872
d. Penrhyndeudreaeth, Wales February 2, 1970

NOTABLE TRAIT:	LIBIDINALLY DRIVEN RENEGADE GENIUS
PHILOSOPHY:	"EMOTION VARIES INVERSELY WITH ONE'S KNOWLEDGE – THE LESS YOU KNOW THE HOTTER YOU GET"
SELF-ANALYSIS:	"I CANNOT KNOW A WOMAN UNTIL I SLEEP WITH HER"
MOTTO:	"SEX, PARENTHOOD AND POWER ARE THE CHIEF INSTINCTUAL PASSIONS"
MARITAL STATUS:	ALYS SMITH AT 22; DORA BLACK AT 49; PATRICIA SPENCE AT 66; EDITH FRENCH AT 80; FOUR CHILDREN – LAST AT 66
RELIGION:	ATHEIST = "NOTHING CAN BE KNOWN"
INNOVATIONS:	ANAYLYTICAL PHILOSOPHY & MATHEMATICAL LOGIC – "RUSSELL'S PARADOX"
PASSIONS:	"I HAD ABNORMALLY STRONG SEXUAL URGES"
AGGRESSIVENESS:	FIERY OPINIONS, RADICAL CAUSES IMPRISONED
THRILL-SEEKING:	"FEAR IS AT THE BOTTOM OF ALL THAT IS BAD IN THE WORLD, ONCE YOU ARE FREE OF IT, YOU HAVE FREEDOM OF THE UNIVERSE"
CHARM:	MAGNETISM ATTRACTED LEGIONS OF DISCIPLES
EGOISM:	AWESOME SENSE OF SELF
ECCENTRICITIES:	PACIFIST, ANTI-RELGION, FREE LOVE, SKEPTIC
MANIAS:	"GALLOPING SATYRIASIS" (WALLACE 1981)

BELIEVE & THE WORLD WILL FOLLOW

Self-esteem and success are intertwined. What the mind can conceive and believe it can achieve. This is the case even if the belief is deluded. Were Napoleon and Hitler messiahs? No, but they thought they were and consequently achieved far beyond their natural ability. A real estate salesperson cannot sell a house if they don't think it is a good buy just as an individual never gets a job they do not think they are suited for. The lack of belief comes through in body language, voice inflection, and an unspoken aura. Optimism is contagious in the same way as enthusiasm.

Life is but a subconscious script being played out in our conscious. We become that internal image whether we like it or not. If we believe we are worthy of becoming a president, we may or may not become one. But if we don't believe we can, we are certain to never become one. If we believe we are victims to be kicked around, we will be kicked around. Early conditioning - *success imprints* and *failure imprints* – insure eminence or collapse. Each is a self-fulfilling prophecy. The only difference between a prostitute and a Prime Minister is perception just as it is between a middle manager and the CEO. Each envision themselves in a given role, and live to fulfill that level of expectation. Winners and losers are but different extensions of a frame of mind. One accepts setbacks and moves on while others see them as part of their victimization. The eminent use life's reversals to catapult them to the exulted state they deign as their right. The bottom line is that perception often becomes reality. We are what we are only because of our inner self-image.

IMAGE IS EVERYTHING. It is not trite to say that those who dress for success are successful in getting the job, just like the politician who looks the part gets elected. This is true of finding a mate, hitting a golf ball, writing a play, painting a picture, or becoming president. Omnipotent belief separates the winners from the also-rans. Those who try to win don't always win, but have a chance to win. Those trying not to lose, may not lose, but are sure never to win. It is a fine line between the two that is only psychological.

Winners never consider the possibility of failure. When asked about the chances of not succeeding in business, Mary Kay responded, "I never considered it." When Babe Ruth was asked about striking out when he pointed to centerfield in the "called-shot" homer in the 1932 World Series he said, "I never thought about that" (Creamer p. 365). While at Oxford Oscar Wilde said, "Somehow or other I'll be famous; if not I'll be notorious." Alfred Adler described this as "ego instinct" or "striving for power."

FEAR & SUCCESS. Eminent overachievers are motivated by opportunity never fear. Conversely, the mediocre opt for security in lieu of striking out in some new venture. Fear is the biggest difference between winners and losers. One thrives on embarking on a new road without any knowledge of where it may lead. The other must know in advance what lies at the end of that road before embarking on a trip. Visionaries love unknown destinations. Bureaucrats fear them. The only difference between the two is mental. Some people are titillated by the unknown, others are debilitated by it.

Any person who allows fear to dominate their decisions or life is destined to failure or compromised success. Eminent psychotherapist Alfred Adler wrote, "Behind every neuroses is a weakling incapable of adapting." Tennis players are typically afraid of hitting a running backhand down the line – an extremely difficult shot to master, and will not attempt it due to the fear of failure. An inner *failure imprint* dominates their bodily functions. Only by modifying that imprint with a positive one can a player ever execute the shot successfully. The mind interferes with successful execution in all disciplines. This is true of all things including romance (impotence occurs because of a fear of failing), sports (inhibited or tentative swings), in business (analysis-paralysis leading to non-action), and learning (rationalization).

FEAR – MAN'S INNER ENEMY. FDR was correct, fear is our only viable enemy. Fear inhibits achievement, warps thinking, diffuses talent, and stifles growth in business or personal pursuits. Winning the hand of a beautiful damsel depends on a positive demeanor that assumes success. Frederick Nietzsche wrote, "Power accedes to he who takes it." And power assumes success. The invention of a new product, designing a new software program, or creating a new paradigm depends on an omnipotent belief system even when your family and friends say you are nuts. Walt Disney's brother called him crazy for daring to think anyone would ever walk into his stupid park Disneyland. Walt ignored his brother and the Board of Directors, hocked his insurance policy, sold his house in Palm Springs, and bought the land in Anaheim. What if he had allowed his brother's negativity to affect his decisions? Or had questioned his own creativity? Disneyland would never have been built. Such belief systems demand an indomitable self-image and self-esteem. Winners believe and losers question, such is the nature of the world and that is why the winners become rich and famous. One approach is steeped in positive energy, the other with negative energy.

EGO & PASSION. Carl Jung and Bertrand Russell were not only self-confident they were raving egomaniacs. Charlie Chaplin, Howard Hughes, Madonna, and Picasso were overly optimistic. Larry Ellison of Oracle has been called a narcissist. The founder of Oracle, didn't go to college, that anyone can find out, had no training in software development, and is a horrible manager. But his success has been awesome due to an unrequited passion, an ego without limits, and the ability to risk it all to win. He had no reason to believe he could compete with giants like IBM and Microsoft but he never saw it that way. One Silicon Valley reporter suggested he believed he was God. Another said, "He needs a wheelbarrow to carry around his ego." But this man without much else is now the second richest man in the world.

Bertrand Russell and Carl Jung were contemporaries and ironically raised in highly devout households yet became free love advocates and so passionately confident nothing could stop them from their march to the top of their professions. They were born just three years apart, Russell in Wales, Jung in Switzerland. Jung's associates, Sigmund Freud and Ernest Jones, called him "An Aryan Christ with colossal narcissism and a god complex." But could a man concoct a whole new system of psychological thought without such arrogance? I think not! Russell had a similar esteem that refused to bow to popular beliefs in anything. He exuded an almost ethereal countenance that catapulted him into a philosopher sage. His work pervaded wide areas of knowledge including such diverse fields as mathematics, philosophy, economics, politics, literature, political decorum and sexual behavior.

Jung's huge following spoke of him in reverence as a kind of deity. Many considered him a messiah sent to deliver the word on how to function effectively in modern society. He didn't dissuade such allegiance. Jung used his omniscience to develop a whole system of thought known as Analytical Psychology. His disciples spread his gospel in a cult-like web of international intrigue. Many women worshipped him. Edith Rockefeller, the daughter of John D., left her husband and children and moved to Switzerland to be near the master. She didn't return for over ten years. Edith donated $2 million to finance Jung's works in the West.

Russell's mystical brilliance became a magical force and appealed to young women even after he was quite old. He had his last child at age 68, had a blatant affair with the young wife of a fellow educator at 77, and married his fourth wife at age 80. In contrast, Jung married once but probably had a more active sex life than Russell. Lust pervaded the life of both men who were enabled by a self-esteem that was without peer. Both preached free love and polygamy, and Jung even dared sleep with patients and moved one long-time mistress, Toni Woolf into his house with his wife and children.

SYBARITIC GENIUS

HISTORY OF PASSIONATE EGOISM. Existentialist writer Fyodor Dostoevsky wrote, "I'm a braggart." The Father of the Psychological Novel admitted "Passion alone ruled my life." Frank Lloyd Wright was obnoxiously overconfident. He liked to say, "Early on I had to decide between honest arrogance and hypocritical humility. I chose arrogance." Once while being interrogated on the stand in court he referred to himself as a "genius." As he exited the courtroom a reporter stopped him and asked, "Mr. Wright how could you have the audacity to refer to yourself as a genius?" Without hesitating, Wright responded, "I was under oath, wasn't I." The reporter walked away shaking his head.

Margaret Mead once arrived at the airport and when told there were no seats left on the flight told the attendant, "But I'm Margaret Mead," fully expecting the airline to make special accommodations for her. The Irish dramatist George Bernard Shaw wrote, "The critic who is modest is lost. My prodigious conceit towers over all ordinary notions of success" (Holroyd p. 246). When Elliot Roosevelt met Jack Kennedy when he was running for the Oval Office he told a reporter, "I never met anyone so completely obsessed with himself" Reeves p. 151).

Picasso's self-portrait was titled, "I, the King." Jean Cocteau said, "He radiated an almost cosmic and irresistible self-confidence. Nothing seemed beyond him." When the media questioned Isadora Duncan on her training in dance, she responded, "Terpsichore taught me to dance." Charlie Chaplin once told the media, "I'm more famous than Jesus Christ." Successful people believe they are special and their resulting self-esteem allows them to go where few others dare. Leonardo da Vinci and Michelangelo went through life with a superiority complex and even refused to listen to the Pope. Both Sigmund Freud and Albert Einstein had "sublime confidence." One biographer described Mark Twain as an "arrogant cynic."

One of the world's most haughty women was Ayn Rand. Talk show hosts feared her for her acidic tongue. She assumed she was right and the rest of the world wrong. High self-esteem was at the root of her epistemology that proclaimed, "I am, I think, I will. Egoism is rational selfishness." Ego was manifest in her Objectivism philosophy:

> *The man who accepts the role of sacrificial animal will not achieve the self-confidence necessary to uphold the validity of his mind and the man who doubts the validity of his mind, will not achieve the self-confidence necessary to uphold the value of his person* (Sciabarra p. 305).

EGO & PASSION

CARL JUNG – PASSIONATE PSYCHOLOGIST

The Swiss psychoanalyst is universally acclaimed as the Father of Analytical Psychology. He was also the leader of a mystical cult of bright women who saw him as a prophet, a man who told them, "Sexuality is the *sine quo non* of spirituality." While being interviewed by the BBC he was questioned on how religion fit into his system of thought and what made him so sure he knew. He told the BBC interviewer, "I don't think. I know." One biographer wrote, "He was overly self-confident." Ardent follower Jolande Jacobi said, "He behaved as if his psychology was another religion" (Noll p. 251).

Carl Jung was a disciple of Freud despite espousing statements like, "Free love wills save the world," a concept totally foreign to Freud. The two broke over the role of sex in human psychology. It is interesting that Freud saw sex as pervasive in all things but was quite ascetic while Jung disagreed with the role played by sex in human dynamics but believed it should be practiced freely by rational adults. Freud was preoccupied with sex professionally yet disdained it personally and did not sleep with his wife after age forty. In contrast, Jung relegated sex to an emotional release necessary for optimum health but not the only motivator of man. However, Jung elevated sex to a godly state in his personal life.

Jung promoted free love and polygamy, slept with patients, wives of friends, and employees. His devoted wife Emma tolerated his philandering as long as he didn't embarrass her or the children. Ironically, Freud was derided and despised for placing sex at the pinnacle of the human dilemma, and Jung has not been demeaned for his womanizing since he didn't infuse it into his psychological hypotheses. Sex for Jung was passion and the energy behind drive and motivation. Jung's "creative life energy of the libido" took a number of directions including Personality Types (bipolar preferences like extroversion & introversion), Syzygy (conjunction of male & female in unconscious), Collective Unconscious (Archetypes), Synchronicities (there are no accidents), Individuation (epiphanies), and Active Imagination (tapping into the subconscious).

MYSTICAL ARCHETYPE. Jung had a mystical view of the world derived from his own interpretations of symbols. These had a genesis in religious icons, visions from dreams, and his work in African and Eastern mysticism. He spent a good deal of his life looking for the mythological meaning of religious symbols in a manner not unlike American Joseph Campbell. To say he was a metaphysical scientist would be a gross understatement.

In December of 1913, Jung experienced what he called a "visionary ecstasy." He admitted to having experienced a "psychotic experience" that would last four years. He would later refer to it as his "epiphany." It transformed him from a medical doctor into a visionary psychoanalyst. During that era the Mithraic mysteries were considered the most ancient form of Aryan spirituality. According to biographer Richard Noll (1997), Jung went through his epiphany while in a psychotic state that transformed himself into the lion-headed god Aion. Noll wrote, "Jung became the charismatic leader of his own mystery cult... Sexual energy surged through him with a power that frightened him" (Noll pgs. 98 & 251). It was during this period that he resigned as president of the psychological movement in Vienna, which Freud had founded. His break with Freud coincided with the beginning of his lifelong affair with former patient and associate Toni Wolff. His creative innovations in the discipline followed close behind.

Symbols were important to Jung. He pioneered the concept of the Archetype in personality development. Jung's own Archetype was that of a zealot, described by Ernest Jones as a "God Complex." Jung's awesome sense of self began attracting legions of women to his couch and beyond. He molded himself into a kind of magic man for intelligent, powerful, but often needy women, who left their homes to worship at the altar of the master.

CHARISMATIC CULT LEADER. Jung attracted many erudite women to his side. His magnetic attraction proved irresistible to strong female personalities like Fanny Bowdithc, Edith Rockefeller McCormick, Dr. Constance Long, and Harvard Professor Christina Morgan (creator of TAT tests). To them he was a spiritual prophet. His power was based on his consummate certainty and majestic belief in his theories. The most amazing story of Jung's seductive powers was Edith Rockefeller McCormick. John D. Rockefeller's daughter had married Harold McCormick, heir to the International Harvester fortune. Edith took a trip to Zurich in 1913 and met Jung. She refused to return home until 1921. Jung influenced her to such an extent she wrote to her father for monies to finance his work.

Mythological hope around a state of emotional adjustment was his promise to faithful followers. He was the spiritual prophet leading the emotionally wounded to the Promised Land. What land was that? It was the land of the Collective Unconscious where the Archetypes reigned supreme. Archetypes for Jung were primordial images or what he called "typical forms of behavior" lying in the unconscious that once "they become conscious present themselves as ideas and images" (Storr 1983 p. 16). Jung wrote, "Archetypes are not themselves conscious but seem to be like underlying ground themes. All the most powerful ideas in history go back to archetypes."

Jung came up with the word Syzygy to define that place within where maleness for females and femaleness for males are found. He picked the word Anima - the unconscious femaleness in men - with the root word animosity and the word Animus as the place where women went to find their male side. By 1920 he had developed a whole comprehensive system of personality he labeled *Psychological Types*. In this he found temperaments differing with *extraverts* energized externally, *introverts* energized internally, *feelers* making decisions emotionally, *thinkers* deciding rationally, *intuitors* seeing the world holistically, with *sensors* seeing the world as a bunch of details. Jung dedicated his whole life to finding what makes people tick:

> *My life has been permeated and held together by one idea and one goal; namely, to penetrate into the secret of the personality. Everything can be explained from this central point and all my works relate to this one theme*. (Storr 1983 p. 253)

But it was his *Individuation*, or transformation via an epiphany that he saw as "visionary insight" (Noll p. 141). Jung used his own brush with insanity and emotional survival as the basis of this concept. He spoke of his 1913 debacle as being "seized by an overpowering vision" (Storr 1996 p. 90). Jung wrote, "The years when I was pursuing my inner images were the most important in my life, in them everything essential was decided" (Storr 1996 p. 92).

PASSIONATE PERSONA

Libido gone amok describes much of the life and work of Carl Jung. Constance Long was one of his female disciples and one of England's most prominent physicians. She was his emissary in Britain and when she decided to defect from his cult he wrote her a vicious letter. According to biographer Noll, Jung had seduced Long, "physically, spiritually and emotionally." Jung promised "spiritual insemination" allowing her to "become pregnant with the spirit" and "give birth to the divine child-god who would save humanity" (Noll p. 337). Jung's diatribe demonstrates his fervor and offers insight into how he saw the functioning of the collective unconscious:

> *The blind creative libido, becomes transformed in man through individuation and out of this process, which is like pregnancy, arises the divine child, a reborn god, no longer more dispersed into the millions of creatures, but being one and this*

144

individual, and at the same time all individuals, the same in you and in me. (Noll p. 251)

Noll wrote, "His female patients fell in love with him, not for who he was as a man, but for his underlying godliness." British author and psychiatrist Anthony Storr found at least two patients who slept with him - Sabrina Spielrein and Toni Wolff. But outside liaisons were extensive. Among his conquests was, Olga Frobe-Kepteyn, an ex-circus rider who worked with him on establishing a group known as Eranos, an intellectual discussion group that met monthly. One meeting degenerated into an orgy. Another friend and lover was Ruth Bailey. He met her as a young man while traveling in Africa. Bailey was an Englishwoman who kept in touch with her guru lover for thirty-five years, and when his wife Emma died, she moved in with him as housekeeper. Americans Fanny Bowditch, Edith Rockefeller, Mary Mellon and Christina Morgan were faithful admirer. Office manager psychiatrist Maria Moltzer was purportedly another of his many lovers.

Jung wrote, "Man in his love choice is strongly tempted to win the woman who best corresponds to his own unconscious femininity" (Hull 1989 p 78). This appears to the attraction of bright, strong-willed, and spiritual women to his side and bed. He said, "The Animus draws his sword of power and the Anima ejects her poison of illusion and seduction" (Hull 1989 p. 172).

EARLY LIFE EXPERIENCES

Jung was born into a highly spiritual environment. His father Paul was a Bishop in the Swiss Reform Church. His mother Emilie Preiswerk was a wealthy daughter of a theologian, but he found the dogmatic religious life stifling and broke with the church as a young man. Jung was the first-born child with a sister born when he was nine. By this time he had been indulged and was both conceited and arrogant. As an only child he escaped into books and was highly influenced by Nietzsche's *Zarathustra*, Goethe's *Faust,* and the philosophy of Schopenhauer. Wagner's *Parcifal* imbued the Germanic power of will along with Nietzsche. Goethe would become his role model and early hero. He actually began to believe he was the reincarnation of Goethe. After reading *Faust* he said, "Faust poured into my soul like a miraculous balm...*Faust* is the most recent pillar in that bridge of the spirit which spans the morass of world history" (Noll p. 20). One of his great insights into man's power and inspiration came out of this early adulation of books. He would write, "It is not Goethe who creates Faust, but Faust who creates Goethe."

Jung, like his hero Nietzsche before him, found it difficult to live without faith. He was forced to create a *superman* persona to survive in a desolate world. He adopted a *will-to-power* as had his philosopher-hero, but in his case, Superman was himself reincarnated as a mythical leader. Jung offers great insight into his childhood from his autobiography:

> ***As a child I felt myself to be alone, and I am still, because I know things and must hint at things, which others apparently know nothing of, and for the most part do not want to know.*** (Storr 1996 p. 87)

These are the words of an introverted renegade who went within to find power and energy. Jung remained a solitary person his whole adult life despite being surrounded by disciples. Like Napoleon, Hitler, Jim Jones, and David Koresh, Jung was a loner, who listened to no one on the important matters in his life. He was always more comfortable around women than men. Women would be the dominant force in his life from age twenty.

Jung was reared in Lake Constance but relocated to a city near Basel at age four. He never left Switzerland despite travelling extensively to the Far East, Middle East and America. Jung graduated from the University of Basel Medical School in 1895 and began his internship at the Bughalyi Mental Hospital in Zurich where he continued to work for nine years. His medical practice was established near Zurich. His father died of cancer when he was twenty and the older Freud became an early mentor. Freud saw the genius in Jung and selected him as heir apparent to psychoanalysis, making him President at the First International Association in Vienna held in 1910. It would take three years for the break with Freud but Jung sensed it as soon as he began work on his classic *Symbols of Transformation*.

CRISES & AN EPIPHANY

Jung wrote, "There is no coming to consciousness without pain." He was relating to his own transformation in the abyss when he came close to dementia. During the time he drew strength from Nietzsche who had said, "I tell you, one must have chaos in one, to give birth to a dancing star" (Storr p. 92). He told protégé and biographer Barbara Hannah, "when you touch rock bottom and nothing can be worse, that is when you discover inner peace" (Hannah p. 127).

At age twelve Jung first encountered what he called the duality of his personality. He labeled them #1 personality - his cognitive self, and the #2 personality – those buried demons within his unconscious that drove him in mysterious ways. While writing his classic *Symbols of Transformation* (1912) he was in a severe state of depression. He had just broken off with Freud and was now on his own and fighting off insanity. Sex was the end all and be all for Freud and Jung could not come to accept the masters thesis. Jung wrote, "Fantasies can unite the conscious and unconscious. Take part in plays, don't just sit in the theater, it is the only way to gain insight into the complex nature of one's own personality." (Hannah p. 320).

During this traumatic period he produced his most outstanding work. He actually fashioned all the concepts for which he is famous during these four years. He then spent the rest of his long life refining them. During his "psychotic state" he was able to go into a transcendent hypnotic like state in which he would find himself in a reverie where lucidity was profound. Later this altered state of consciousness would be commercialized in the Far East as "transcendental meditation." Jung wrote of being able to take himself into these states at will. He described these "intense visionary experiences" as more spiritual than empirical, leading to "an extraordinary epiphany." While in them "his head changed into that of a lion and he became a god." Noll said this was "The defining moment in the secret story of Jung's life. It happened the day he was deified" (Noll p. 121). Jung lived and wrote way outside the normal bounds of scientific inquiry. He flirted with alchemy, sorcery, witchcraft and mystical spiritualism. All were by-products of his traumatic period when lucidity was incredible but normality was non-existent. Jung saw Buddhism, with god within, something he could totally identify with, as the only religious system that was viable. His spiritual and metaphysical leanings appealed to female patients and disciples.

PSYCHOSEXUAL ENERGY

Passion and intensity were pervasive in Jung's long life. His passions were so intense he found logic in their existence and justified many illicit liaisons on the premise they calmed him and made him more productive. Emma went along with many of his bizarre schemes including allowing him to bring his mistress Toni Wolff into their home as an associate. Wolff had begun as a teenage patient, became a valued disciple, assistant, and then matriculated to protégé and finally lover. She would remain his mistress for thirty years. His most famous rationalization on his behavior was, "The prerequisite of a good marriage is the license to be unfaithful" (Wallace p. 247).

Jung's tower in Zurich became a sexual refuge. Around 1908 when he was in his early thirties he became convinced that "not giving into your sexual impulses could lead to illness or even death" (Noll p. 87). Therefore in pursuit of pure adjustment and health he allowed free reign to his passions and began attracting many young attractive disciples to his cult. His overwhelming zeal was so captivating for Toni Wolff she never had a life outside her master. She never married and was there for him for 40 years.

DIVERGENT THINKING

Renegades see the world through a different filter. Here was a respected medical doctor who was head of the International Psychological Association who said, "free love will save the world." Jung held séances for many years and used such data as scientific evidence for his doctoral thesis. Earnest Jones, the British head of the Freudian school said, "Jung is a heretic by nature," strange comments on the son of a Bishop. Jung preached the virtues of the occult, free love, polygamy, astrology, and regularly participated in séances. In perpetual fear of going insane he kept a loaded pistol near his bed just in case he felt himself slipping into that dreadful abyss he flirted with between 1912 and 1916. Psychiatrist Anthony Storr says Jung, "thought of himself as a spiritual leader rather than as a psychiatrist treating neurotics" (Storr 1996 p. 96). Jung's eccentricities were widespread, ranging from the spiritual to pure mysticism. Horoscopes were a key to his psychology.

One of Jung's major contributions was the repression of male and female qualities that he labeled Syzygy. He wrote, "In the unconscious of every woman there is a hidden male personality. The more feminine the woman, the more her masculine will be repressed." In Jung's system men tap into what he called an *Anima* – the soul, eros and emotional side. Anima means mood and is the root of animosity. In each woman he defined a repressed *Animus* – the spirit, logos, and rationality. He called the conjunction of these the Syzygy, where optimization of the personality could occur. He wrote:

> *A woman who is a woman from the crown of her head to the tip of her toe can afford to be masculine, just as a man who is sure of his masculinity can afford to be tender and patient like a woman* (Hull 1989 p 112).

CREATIVE INSPIRATIONS

Carl Jung is arguably the most influential psychologist of modern times. His contributions, even though not as well known as Freud's, are more used in ordinary business dealings. We speak of being *introverted* or *extroverted*, making decisions based on how we *feel* versus how we *think*, all concepts originating with Jung's *Personality Types*. He conceived many innovative concepts to define the human condition, namely, the *Collective Unconscious* (certain innate instincts are in-born); *Archetypes* (preordained personality preferences); *Synchronicities* (there are no accidents); *Syzygy* (conjunction of femaleness and maleness); *Psychological Types; Active Imagination, Individuation*, and *Cryptomania* (false memory syndrome).

The Myers-Briggs (personality) Type Indicator was derived from the Jungian Personality Types. This is by far the most used personality test in the Western World. It is the definitive test on differing temperaments such as Introvert vs Extrovert, Feeler vs Thinker, Intuitor vs Sensor, and Perceiver vs Judger.

Jung was obsessed with personality. He once said, "My life has been permeated by one idea, the secret of personality." He was also obsessed with seduction of both women and the meaning of life. In the words of biographer Noll (p. 87), "Jung founded a spiritual mystery cult of renewal and rebirth as the catalyst for a well-adjusted life." His statement "Sexuality is the *sine quo non* of spirituality – one only exists through the other" gives testimony to his belief in the freedom of all aspects of sexual expression. His living on the edge based on his own perception of reality caused his one-time mentor Freud to comment, "he seems to be Christ himself." Jung lived by passion as seen in his words, "If one honors God, the sun or the fire, then one honors one's own vital force, the libido" (Noll p. 99).

EGO & PASSION

BERTRAND RUSSELL – PHILANDERING PHILOSPHER

Bertrand Russell had a majestic persona, superior intellect, awesome self-esteem, and a compulsion to stand up and be heard even when his message was contra to his audience. Like many bright and articulate people he was empowering to be around and had an irresistible charm. Bright women were attracted to him as they were to Carl Jung.

Bertrand Russell had a penchant for living life on the edge, but it was passion that defined him. He wrote, "I have sought love, because it brings ecstasy – ecstasy so great that I would often have sacrificed all the rest of life for a few hours of this joy." He began:

> *Three passions have governed my life: the longing for love, the search for knowledge, and unbearable pity for the suffering of mankind. These passions, like great winds, have blown me hither and thither, in a wayward course, over a deep ocean of anguish, reaching to the very pinnacle of despair.* (Russell 1967 p. 3).

Russell had a mythical aura and rebellious spirit. He dared violate the puritanical traditions of Victorian England. Such flare was exciting to young women. Many were willing to leave their mates to be with the man who was famous for *Russell's Paradox*. Russell came armed with intellectual precocity and an indomitable ego. He was brilliant, radical and analytical to a fault. He is generally recognized as the founder of analytic philosophy - based on his rational and logical approach to life's mysteries.

Russell first married at age 22 in 1894. Six years later, while working with Alfred North Whitehead on their mathematical masterpiece *Mathematica Principia,* he fell madly in love with Evelyn Whitehead. Evelyn was the wife of his collaborator. This experience led to his purely rational view of the marital pact. He believed men and women should pursue their passions rationally regardless of marital or other societal rules of decorum. He would write, "Where sex is repressed only work remains, and a gospel of work for work's sake, never produced any work worth doing. A sense of duty is useful in work but offensive in personal relations." This philosophy evolved out of his frustration of not being able to sleep with the women he loved just because she was already married. In *Ethics, Sex & Marriage* (Russell p. 223) he argued, "If marriage and paternity are to survive as social institutions, some compromise is necessary between complete promiscuity and lifelong monogamy."

SYBARITIC GENIUS

PASSION - THE HEART OR THE HEAD

Russell was a logician. All things were analyzed in a very rigorous and logical framework – both personally and professionally. In his memoirs, he wrote of taking a bicycle ride after a few years of marriage and concluding his life with American Alys Pearsall Smith was not working. Alys was five years older, but unable to bear children. On this bike ride he experienced a "personal epiphany," and concluded that his "love was dead" and "I no longer loved Alys." In his inimitable style, he used a scientific methodology beginning with a hypothesis and ending with a rational conclusion. When he had it clearly worked out in his head, he called a meeting with her and dispassionately gave her the harsh reality. It was a good approach for a Calculus class, but not the most sensitive approach to breaking up a marriage. She left for a rest cure, and when she returned they never slept together again despite remaining together for another nine years. The marriage would last another twenty but Russell moved out in 1910 when he met Lady Ottoline.

Russell had married Alys at twenty-two. In his memoirs he wrote, "I had no wish to be unkind, but I believed that in intimate relations one must speak the truth." From this point forward Russell began a long series of adulterous affairs with secretaries, socialites, and other teachers. When his love affair with Lady Ottoline Morell, the wife of a liberal member of parliament, became heated she threatened a scandalous lawsuit, only diverted when Russell threatened to kill himself.

PARADOXICAL GENIUS

Russell gained world renown for his mathematical principle *Russell's Paradox*. He first concocted the theory in 1901, ironically in concert with his love interest in Whitehead's wife. It would not be refined into a formal principle for another ten years. It first appeared in his magnum opus - *Principia Mathematica* (1910-1913) written in concert with Lord Whitehead.

Many of Russell's mathematical theories are lost on the average person. His two most popular books were *The Problems of Philosophy* (1912) and *The History of Western Philosophy* (1945). He won the Nobel Prize for Literature for the latter in 1950. One of his most controversial books was *Marriage and Morals* (1929). In this book he dared speak to his radical ideas on adultery, pre-marital sex, polygamy, sex education, women's rights, and social morality. It is important to remember that he was writing at the end of the Victorian era. While his theories set him free sexually, they were instrumental in destroying his professional career. His blatant pacifism,

151

sexual philandering, and rabid atheism ultimately made him *persona non grata* at Cambridge. It also would cost him valuable lecturing and teaching contracts at Harvard, UCLA, and City College of New York. Fortunately, an inheritance allowed him to live, lust, and write without constraint.

PHILOSOPHY OF PASSION

Russell wrote, "Very few adults, men or women, can preserve instinctive happiness in a state of celibacy." Libidinal drive characterized his long and seductive life. Irving Wallace described him as having a "galloping satyriasis." Russell wrote in his memoirs of a teenage obsession with masturbation. He wrote, "I was distracted by erections." Once he had dissolved his marital romance he began a long torrid series of affairs. The first was with a secretary with the unlikely name, Miss Ivy Pretious. His most notorious liaison involved the wife of a member of British parliament Philip Morrell, Lady Ottoline Morrell. He said, "Lady Ottoline made me much less of a Puritan." The two remained lovers for many years.

Love and lust were part of the Russell mystique and his weapon was logic. An example was his aphorism, "Emotion varies inversely with one's knowledge and the less you know the hotter you get." He adamantly believed, "there is no reason to condemn sex if you are doing no wrong, especially because some ancient taboo has said it is wrong." He wrote, "The doctrine that says there is something sinful about sex is on in which has done untold harm."

Russell was convinced, "I cannot know a woman until I sleep with her." That left him with no other rationale than deciding to *know* any woman with sexual appeal. Quite the system of logical seduction! He wrote essays and lectured extensively on the right of all men and women to engage in free love, trial and open marriages, and uncontested divorces. After years of lechering, he finally concluded he was unable to remain faithful to any woman for longer than seven or eight years.

MARITAL BLISS. Russell's life was one long series of near-scandalous trysts, affairs, and promiscuous wanderings. He was married four times. The first to American Alys Pearson lasted but a few years in fact, but legally went on for 27 years. With his second marriage he entered into the relationship with a pact that "the marriage would be compatible with minor affairs" (Wallace p. 386). Second wife Dora Black was a bright and ultra-liberal fellow-teacher who bore him two children. They collaborated on the experimental Beacon Hill School in London. It's liberal policies included advocacy of free love for teachers and staff. Russell partook of his policy and ended up marrying two of his teachers after long affairs. Dora bought into Russell's open marriage far more than he anticipated. She had an affair with an American journalist Griffin Barry and bore him two children. That irritated Russell who ended the marriage in 1935 with the proclamation, "We had agreed that if she should have a child that was not mine there would be a divorce." That marriage ended in 1935 when he was 63.

In 1930 Russell began a long affair with teacher Patricia `Peter' Spence. She worked for him at the experimental school and was also governess of his two children. After his divorce from Dora, they married in 1936. A son was born the next year when he was 65. He continued philandering well into his 70's when he took up with the young wife of a Cambridge lecturer named appropriately Colette. He was eighty in 1952 when he married a American author Edith Finch. It was his fourth and last marriage. Testimony to his magnetic appeal was an old mistress Colette sending him red roses on his last birthday at age 97.

EARLY LIFE EXPERIENCES

Bertrand was the second born child of a distinguished, but Puritan Welsh family. His father, Viscount John Amberley was a "free-thinker." His mother Kate was known for having "radical opinions." He had a seven year older brother Frank who was more mentor than brother due to their age difference. He had a younger sister but she died along with his mother with diphtheria when Bertrand was just two. A year later his father died and his grandfather, Lord John Russell, former Prime Minister had his father's will overturned to win custody of Bertrand and Frank. It proved short lived as his grandfather died two years later. His paternal grandmother, Lady Frances Russell, was a devout Unitarian. She would be the most dominant influence his life. She spoke fluent German, French, and Italian and groomed him on Shakespeare, Milton and Goethe. He said, "She molded my outlook on life," but it was both intellectual and divergent, since she was a Puritan and forced him to spend hours praying. He began to detest all things dogmatic.

Even so Russell said, "My grandmother was the most important person to me throughout my childhood" (Russell 1967 p. 15). She tutored teach him colors and structure via Froebel blocks and had a German nanny who taught him German as a child. He speaks of being "very lonely" as a child and escaped into books, saying, "Nature, books, and mathematics saved me from complete despondency" (p. 39).

Russell claims that his grandmother's Scottish Episcopal leanings were all-consuming and were responsible for his early religious rebellion. He wrote in his memoirs, "There were family prayers at eight o'clock every morning. Alcohol and tobacco were viewed with disfavor. Only virtue was prized; virtue at the expense of intellect, health, happiness, and every mundane good" (Russell, *Portraits from Memory* p. 9). One agnostic tutor influenced him as did is discovery of Mill, Comte, and Carlyle. He read voraciously and wanted to know the derivation of man and the universe. Mill's autobiography with the section "Who Made Me" began his doubts about a prime mover. He says *"Gulliver's Travels*, especially the account of the Yahoos, had a profound effect upon me, and I began to see humans in that light... by age eighteen I had abandoned all belief and became an atheist" (Russell 1967 p. 48).

After graduating from Trinity College with a Bachelors Degree in mathematics in 1893 he toured France, Germany and America. He became taken with Alys Pearsall Smith, an American Quaker, and married her despite the objections of his family. Already a rabid renegade, he ignored all outside advice, and proceeded to marry her at twenty-two.

Russell believed mathematics saved him from a boring life of Unitarian fanaticism. He said "At age eleven, I began Euclid, with my brother as my tutor. This was one of the great events of my life, as dazzling as first love. I had not imagined there was anything so delicious in the world. From that moment until I was thirty-eight, mathematics was my chief interest and my chief source of happiness." At age 38 he began his interest in philosophy and wrote *the Problems of Philosophy* in 1912. A short time later he became an avid pacifist due to the conflict in Europe and took up the cause of the Russian Revolution and anti-war demonstrations. This was done in the midst of a massive pro-war effort to support the allies against Germany that cost him his teaching assignment at Cambridge and other valued relationships.

CRISES & AN EPIPHANY

Russell's youth was one continual crisis. He lost his mother, sister, father and grandfather by age six. He wrote, "In adolescence, I hated life and was continually on the verge of suicide" (Russell 1987 p. 317), and admitted that a passion for mathematics saved him. Despite many misgivings he attempted to conform to social mores and was monogamous during his first marriage. But the epiphany he wrote of on his bicycle occurred coincidentally with the Boer War in South Africa. It would become a rallying call for the one time Imperialist and his latent pacifism came to the fore. His marriage was over, at least in his mind, and he began thinking about the ethical and moral aspects of the marital contract and love, lust, and romance. It was at this time that he concocted his most famous hypothesis – Russell's Paradox, although it would not be officially published until 1910. In this same year of 1901 he fell madly in love with Evelyn Whitehead.

Russell's next bout with trauma was self-imposed due to his anti-war and free love theses. He was fired by Cambridge for his anti-war demonstrations. Then he was offered a position at Harvard that was cancelled when the British government exacted punishment for his anti-war stance by revoking his passport. In 1918 he was sentenced to six months in prison, but used the time to write two books, *An Introduction to Mathematical Philosophy* and *An Analysis of Mind.* Due to the derision from long time friends and teachers he vowed to refute any and all faith in puritanical ethics - professionally and personally. He took up a number of radical causes and opened a revolutionary experimental school in London. It set him free to write and explore philosophical treatises on the nature of love and ethics. His cynicism rose with comments like, "Chastity, I gave it a good try once, but never again." He divorced his estranged wife, accepted a teaching engagement in Peking, China, took his pregnant mistress Dora Black with him, and embarked on a life of radical intellectualism that defied the establishment.

PSYCHOSEXUAL ENERGY

"I had abnormally strong sexual urges," he wrote in his memoirs of his early life that were repressed until he decided to live life outside convention. He began to lecture on the ludicrous system of marital monogamy as stupid and ill-logical. In his infamous book, *Marriage and Morals* 1929), he wrote, "The idea that there is something sinful about sex is one which has done untold harm to individual character" (Russell 1987 p. 264). He went on to say, "It is fairly clear that the impulse to every kind of aesthetic creation is psychologically connected with courtship" (p. 216). He ranted against religious taboos as rank superstition.

Free love, uncontested divorce, and adultery within bounds became his cause. This infuriated the religious right and caused him loss of work, dignity, and income. He fled to America, becoming a teacher at UCLA and the City College of New York in 1940. His teaching assignments were mathematics and logic. Keep in mind Russell was now 68 years old and hardly someone who was going to seduce America's young. But New York City Anglican Church Bishop Manning began a crusade to have Russell banned from all educational institutions. The good bishop called him a "propagandist against both religion and morality, a man who defends adultery." A lawsuit was filed calling his books, "Lecherous, salacious, libidinous, lustful, venerous, erotomanic, aphrodisiac, atheistic, irreverent, narrow-minded, bigoted and untruthful." The campaign prevailed and Russell was banned from teaching at CCNY. The New York judge ruled against Russell since he was "not American, had not been given a competitive exam, and his books were immoral and full of filth." What a travesty of justice! The land of free speech had spoken, and free speech marched backwards into the dark ages.

After much frustration in trying to appeal to logic and use rational arguments to win the day he finally wrote, "The people who are regarded as moral luminaries (Bishop Manning) are those who forego ordinary pleasures themselves and find compensation in interfering with the pleasures of others."

DIVERGENT THINKING

Russell's progressive views on war, sex, education, marriage, and divorce shocked early century traditionalists. His anti-war, anti-religion, and open-marriage stances made him appear as a licentious sex offender. He was a philanderer but was strongly against sexual abuse and any other forced attentions. Consenting adults should have the right to live without governmental interference. What is now called victimless crimes were how he viewed such legislation that had been born of religion not logic.

Russell's books *Why I am not a Christian* (1927) and *Marriage and Morals* (1929) were the two most controversial of his erudite writings. But he tended to push the envelope when he opened his experimental Beacon Hill School and established an open policy of romance between teachers and staff. The school was a pioneer in progressive education despite its liberal reputation.

Russell had moxie. He seldom minced words. The media always got a candid answer to any inflammable question. Logic and passion were his only masters and he devised a comprehensive system of ethics with which he lived his life. But when his pacifism became a threat to the establishment they put him in jail, once when he took strong anti-war, anti-arms, and anti-nuclear stances. He was put in jail at 46 and 89, but neither curtailed his vocal tirades against the continuation of the Cold War. He and another brilliant curmudgeon, Albert Einstein, jointly signed the Russell-Einstein Manifesto against Nuclear proliferation in 1953. He was 81 at the time and at the height of his rebellion.

SYBARITIC GENIUS

Russell's sexual philosophy was delineated in his book *Marriage & Morals* written in 1929 that are now not so radical but in that era were considered a major departure from the Christian ethic.

- Women should not have children if they are under the age of twenty

- Men should sleep only with girls of their own class

- Young unmarrieds should have considerable freedom as long as children are not involved

- Divorce should be possible without blame

- A childless marriage should be terminable at the wish of one of the partners

- Any marriage should be terminable by mutual consent with one year's notice

- Wives, like prostitutes, live by the sake of their sexual charms. This is a sordid triangle of money, people and sex and is not right.

- Lifelong alimony should be outlawed

- Sex education for children should be mandatory

- Trial marriage should be allowed

- Men and women should have premarital sex to insure compatibility

- Occasional affairs should be permissible in marriage

CREATIVE CONTRIBUTIONS

Few serious thinkers have had such a profound influence in so many diverse disciplines. Russell's "logical paradox" was part of his magnum opus in *Principia Mathematica* (1910 – 1913). He followed this masterful work in higher mathematics with two magnificent works, *The Problems with Philosophy* (1912) and *The History of Philosophy* (1945) for which he would receive the Nobel Prize for Philosophy. He wrote extensively on the reform of education, ethics, morals, and social mores. His anti-war and anti-nuclear stances were documented in *Man's Peril* broadcast on the BBC in 1954. This documentary condemned the Bikini H-bomb. *The Principles of Social*

Reconstruction (1916) was the beginning of his life-long pacifism that culminated in the Russell-Einstein Manifesto in 1955.

Russell launched a myriad of progressive educational programs in his non-traditional school known as The Beacon Hill School. He was most hated for his repeated attacks on organized religion expounded in *What I Believe* (1925) and *Why I Am Not a Christian* (1927). His impact on ethics and marriage were devised in *Marriage & Morals* (1929) and *The Conquest of Happiness* (1930). His influence even reached into grammatical elocution when he attempted to show the illogic in the meaning and use of words. He insisted that logical meaning should always take precedence over the rhetorical.

Bertrand Russell will be long remembered as the first man of renown to object to the Viet Nam War. He was in a rare minority at the time when Imperialism was at a peak. He went to jail at age 89 for his efforts. Passion was omni-present in his life and he dedicated his later years to overcoming the puritanical attitudes pervasive in society. One of his infamous metaphors that infuriated his adversaries was as follows: (Russell 1987 p. 154)

> *A businessman who is generous to all his employees but falls in love with his stenographer is wicked; another who bullies his employee, but is faithful to his wife is virtuous. This attitude is rank superstition*

This visionary genius saw the big picture in most things and allowed passion to fuel the trip to reach his goals. One of his adages offers testimony to his intuitive view of the world – "The sense of certainty and revelation comes before any definite belief."

MAGNETISM & PASSION

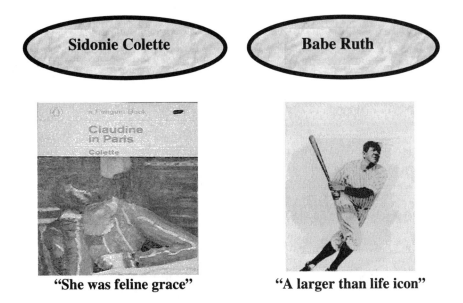

| Sidonie Colette | Babe Ruth |

"She was feline grace" "A larger than life icon"

"Eloquent statement of ideas is my greatest talent"
Martin Luther King, Jr.

"The charismatic leader is able to forge a bond with followers, have a talent for persuasion, and the ability to motivate and inspire"
Jay Conger (1989)

"Passions are the mistresses of the world"
Charles Fourier (*Oevres Completes* 1966)

"The success of psychoanalysis is as much a tribute to Freud's communication genius as to the power of ideas"
Howard Gardner, Harvard

"Tesla was a God whose ethereal brilliance created the modern era"
Pulitzer Prize winning *New York Times* writer John O'Neill

SIDONIE GABRIELLE COLETTE
AUTHOR, ACTRESS, JOURNALIST & DRAMA CRITIC
b.   Saint-Saveur en Puisaye, France, Jan. 28, 1873
d. Paris, France Aug. 3, 1954

NOTABLE TRAIT:	HEDONISTIC NEED TO SEDUCE ALL THINGS
PHILOSOPHY:	"I AM A CHILD OF NATURE AND PREFER PASSION TO GOODNESS AND COMBAT TO DISCUSSION"
SELF-ANALYSIS:	"IF I WERE A MAN AND KNEW MYSELF PROFOUNDLY, I WOULDN'T LIKE MYSELF"
MOTTO:	"LOVE IS ALL OR NOTHING"
MARITAL STATUS:	HENRY GAUTHIER AT 19 BARON DE JOUVENEL AT 40, DAUGHTER MARUICE GOUDEKET AT 62
RELIGION:	"THERE IS NO SOCIETY & THERE IS NO GOD"
INNOVATIONS:	CAPTURED ESSENCE OF MALE/FEMALE REALTIONSHIPS IN *CHERI* (1920); *GIGI* (1945)
PASSIONS:	"THE SEDUCTION EMANATING FROM A PERSON OF UNCERTAIN AND DISSIMILATED SEX IS POWERFUL"
AGGRESSIVENESS:	A DOMINATING PERSONA & CONTROL FREAK
THRILL-SEEKING:	LEARNED TO SKI AT 50; ONE OF FIRST FEMALE REPORTERS ON FRONT LINES IN WW-I
CHARM:	"SHE IS HYPNOTIZING" – FEMALE ADVERSARY
EGOISM:	CERTAINTY DEFINED HER
ECCENTRICITIES:	OPEN LESBIAN AFFAIRS, SCANDALIZED MOULIN ROUGE IN PARIS, SEDUCED 16 YEAR OLD STEPSON – A NOTORIOUS PARIAH
MANIAS:	EXCESS & VITALITY DEFINED HER LIFE & LUSTS

GEORGE HERMAN `BABE' RUTH
BASEBALL'S ARDENT ICON
b. Baltimore, Maryland February 6, 1895
d. New York City, August 16, 1948

NOTABLE TRAIT: BOYISH HEDONIST; AN INSATIABLE LIBIDO

PHILOSOPHY: NICKNAMED `BABE' FOR CHILDLIKE NATURE

SELF-ANALYSIS: "I COULD HAVE BATTED 600 IF I HIT SINGLES, PEOPLE PAID TO SEE ME HIT HOMERS"

MOTTO: "I HIT BIG OR I MISS BIG, I LIKE TO LIVE AS BIG AS I CAN"

MARITAL STATUS: HELEN WOODFORD AT 19
MODEL CLAIRE HODGSON AT 35

RELIGION: ROMAN CATHOLIC

INNOVATIONS: CHANGED BASEBALL FROM A GAME OF DEFENSE, STEALS, AND SINGLES TO DRAMATIC POWER AND THE HOMER

PASSIONS: YANKEES ROOMMATE - "I DON'T ROOM WITH HIM, I ROOM WITH HIS SUITCASE"

AGGRESSIVENESS: "I DON'T KNOW HOW HE KEPT GOING" SUSPENDED FIVE TIMES DURING 1922 SEASON

THRILL-SEEKING: RECKLESS DRIVER, LOVER, GAMBLER

CHARM: "BABE RUTH IS AMERICA" JAPANESE WW-II

EGOISM: CALLED HOME RUN SHOT IN 1932 WORLD SERIES

ECCENTRICITIES: IGNORED CONVENTION IN LIFE AND LOVE

MANIAS: AFTER ST. LOUIS VICTORY TOOK OVER BROTHEL AND MADE LOVE TO EVERY PROSTITUTE

CHARM & THE PASSIONATE PROCESS

Few people ever hope to become an icon. And virtually none ever achieve such status while still alive. Elvis had to die to become an icon, as did Napoleon. Babe Ruth is an exception. He is in rare company like Mother Teresa, Michael Jordan and Tiger Woods. And a woman writer known just as Colette came close in the early days of the 20th century. Colette wrote her way into fame and then capped it off with a provocative stage career.

What elevates such individuals to Colossus status? It differs, but they are typically larger-than-life and have left a huge gap between their skills and their adversaries. Tiger Woods was so acclaimed in the year 2000 when he won more golf matches by a larger number of strokes than anyone in history and he did it by the unbelievable age of 24. A few years earlier His Airness, Michael Jordan was unstoppable on the basketball court. Others like Napoleon won battles that he was supposed to lose and did it repeatedly. His very presence was mesmerizing. When he was captured at Waterloo the British Admiral Lord Keith was charged with taking him to St. Helens and commented, "If he had obtained an interview with his Royal Highness in half an hour they would have been the best of friends."

During his heyday Babe Ruth was baseball and to the Japanese was everything Americana. During World War II, when the Japanese charged American troops they screamed the worst epithet they could think of, "To hell with Babe Ruth." To the Japanese, the Bambino was the consummate American hero. During his career he was looked on as mythical. By the end of his career his image had transcended baseball. Millions of school kids and their parents had elevated him to sainthood. The Babe was a New York Yankee but the stadium was known around the world as the "House that Ruth Built." He was the symbol of the flamboyant and brash American. And for many years he symbolized the national pastime, and was a hero to every kid who ever owned a baseball glove. How did he become such a titan? By daring to do what others only imagined. By telling sick kids he would hit a homer for them and doing it. By pointing to the center field stands in a kind of defiance to his opposition and hitting the ball where he pointed. Such feats are beyond the pale of ordinary mortals. His charm was acting as if his Herculean feats were of little import. The Babe was incorrigible but impossible to hate. Even his worst detractors admitted they couldn't dislike the Babe. His persona is best defined by his adage, "I swing big with everything I got. I hit big or I miss big. I like to live as big as I can."

SYBARITIC GENIUS

Few men in history are willing to risk total ridicule to perform the impossible. Ruth did so on many occasions but never so blatantly as in the 1932 World Series when he called two strikes on himself and then hit the next pitch over the centerfield wall. This was a brazen act that, had it failed, would have made him a goat and fool. But such is the temerity demanded of sainthood. The Sultan of Swat didn't even think of the consequences. His charm was his arrogance. Such fulfillment of wild fantasies is the fuel of the world's titans. It is the stuff of legends and why the Babe was the sports writer's dream. Nothing seemed beyond him and he saw no limitations to his own success.

A provocative French writer went by one name on the covers of her books and on the marquees that blazed her act. Colette was an ingénue turned libertine. She had a similar magical effect on the French nation as the Babe did on American baseball. Colette was of the people and wrote of the people, but had risen above that station in her turbulent life. She was touchable but untouchable, one of the defining qualities of fame. Colette socialized, and slept with, the washed and unwashed, the literary elite and the illiterate, royalty and peasants, heterosexuals and homosexuals, the politically correct and the denizens of the night. She left us with a long list of books that were little other than biographical treatises on her life and lusts. Her classics *Cheri* and *Gigi* were a bit more erudite.

Colette was a country girl with no formal education who rose to the top of society and presided over a salon attended by Andre Gide, Cosima Wagner, Georges Clemencou, Maurice Chevalier, Paul Masson, Anatole France, and literary types like Cocteau, Proust, Beardsley, and Montesqiou. Most were famous in their own right but were intrigued by her charms and swept up by her perverse energy. Even her enemies described her as "mesmerizing" and "electrifying," including the mistresses of her ex-husbands. Biographer's Francis and Gontier (1998) described her as, "the first generation of sexual revolutionaries." They also described her appeal as a kind of "divine grace."

Colette had been highly influenced by her iconoclastic mother and the teachings of Charles Fourier. Biographer Thurman (1999 p. 297) said, "Colette had a powerfully seductive aura that's not obvious from her photographs." The young male secretary to Colette's third husband offers insight into her appeal. When asked about the reason her 16 year-old stepson, Bertrand de Jouvenel, left his girlfriend for a matronly woman approaching fifty, he wrote, "Her whole life was a theater piece. She was a *provacatrice*. And Colette was so desirable, oh, extremely" (Thurman p. 297).

MAGNETISM & PASSION

DARING + FLARE = CHARISMA

Colette wrote, "You will do foolish things, but do them with enthusiasm." Such is the essence of the magnetic personality. What is foolish to others is standard fare for them since true eminence emanates from the impossible. Consider the daring of the country girl Colette who blasted her way out of the gutters into the drawing rooms of Paris. She married a man of social standing at age nineteen. Willy, his literary name, was one Henry Gauthier-Villars who opened up the doors but once through she went on to further her career and when she found a door closed she knocked it down.

When Willy stole her only source of income by selling off the royalties to her books she made a deal with a notorious but wealthy lesbian Missy and then dared appear on stage at the Moulin Rouge with her. She gained a reputation as a woman who would dare anything to achieve her goals. Her lesbian lover Missy was a descendent of Napoleon III, and the love scene enacted with her estranged husband Willy in the audience was too much even for a liberated Paris. Her act was as profound as Ruth's called shot in the World Series, Kennedy's standoff with Khrushchev, and Martin Luther King's *I have a Dream* speech. All were huge risks that left their owner with a legacy.

SELF-PROMOTION. Colette was a genius at self-promotion. She lived by the maxim, "First become famous and then do whatever you please." She had already sold close to 500,000 thinly disguised autobiographies on the love life of a country girl named Claudine. Claudine was Colette in all her glory and ignominy. She married Willy to live in the bright lights of Paris. Each move was calculated to take her to another level of achievement, none of which were grounded in money, but all were based on possible glory. Colette's acts were identical to the others in this work. They were right on the edge and had they missed by only a little the glory would have led to debacle. Brazen acts of pure magnetism led her to the top as surely as they did Babe Ruth. Her playground was Paris, the Bambino's was Yankee Stadium. Both transcended their professions, and both led flamboyant and lustful lives.

A wide range of men and women were seduced by the charms of Colette. They included a long line of sophisticated female lovers including actress Polaire who played Claudine on stage as well as in her chambers. Heiresses Georgie Raoul Duval, Lily De Reme, and Marquisee de Belboeuf were long-term lovers as were Americans Natalie Berney and Renee Vivien. She even devoured her first husband Willy's mistress Meg Villars, a woman unable to resist her adversary's charms.

Colette and Ruth had devoted follower many of whom would have paid to be near their messiah. Many did pay, but in ways they didn't expect. Both transformed their respective domains. After the White Sox scandal baseball was in dire need of a hero and most historians say that Babe Ruth saved baseball. His mammoth homeruns made kids gasp, pitchers fear taking the mound against him, and reporters enjoy featuring him in headlines. Colette's contribution to her genre was a simplistic but cathartic release of her passions. Both were notorious for their uninhibited flight through life and rode their way to fame and fortune. Colette has been called the "greatest French writer." (Thurman 1999), and Ruth was named the "greatest athlete in history" by USA Today (12-99), and the greatest baseball player of the 20th century by an ESPN poll in December 1999.

Colette was one of the highest paid performers in France during a period when she was also a best-selling author. She also was the first female reporter for a French newspaper and went on to a career as literary and art critic. Biographers, Francis and Gontier (1998) described her as a "libertine with feline grace who oozed sex appeal." Colette wantonly flaunted her provocative lifestyle, one that included bisexuality, homosexuality, *ménage a trois*, incest, and affairs with married men. She flaunted her seductions and dared anyone to stop her and did so well into old age. In mid-life she seduced two young college students Lucine Fouchon and Auguste Heriot. Second husband Henry de Jouvenel was three years her junior and husband #3, Maurice Goudenket, was sixteen years younger when she married him at age sixty-two. But the *coup de etat* of seduction was her lustful intrigue with her sixteen-year old stepson when she was "fat and fifty."

CHARISMATIC POWER & SUCCESS

Magnetism is a personality trait with a long lineage from Alexander the Great to Oprah. Charismatics have enormous frenetic energy emanating from within a driven person. Such people are highly persuasive and attract legions of followers. They have enthusiasm and use it to captivate and motivate. Unfortunately, many cult leaders have this awesome power and the likes of Hitler, Jim Jones, and David Koresh have used it for their own self-serving agendas. Others like Georgie Gurdjieff, Bhagwan Rajneesh, and Charles Manson used their persuasive power to seduce the weak and disenfranchised. Those using their charms for more positive means are Catherine the Great, Golda Meir, Martin Luther King, Maria Montessori, and Mother Teresa. Without charisma these individuals would have been far less successful in life and the cult leaders would have not been nearly so destructive.

COMMUNICATION SKILLS. The spoken word is critical to success since one must be able to communicate their dreams to bankers, investors, followers, and even to potential mates. Charisma is a first cousin of communication and leaders like Napoleon and Hitler would never have been able to seduce sophisticated nations without it. They talked millions into adopting their dreams and following them to the Promised Land. John F. Kennedy used passionate words to get elected President of the United States while Howard Hughes was able to mesmerize congress when questioned about his $25 million Spruce Goose debacle. In the same way Wilde charmed his way into and out of trouble while Camus won the Nobel Prize for his positive existentialism. Few people who make it to the very top do so with an uncanny ability to persuade others to follow them to their goals.

SMARTS & ATTRACTION. Smart people have a certain appeal as can be seen in the lives of Wilde, Duncan, Russell, Jung, Fuller, and Madonna. They get the message from people and concepts and that is both exciting and makes them eminently more interesting. Bright people are just more interesting and they tend to march to their own tunes making their music more titillating. Oscar Wilde was not only bright but dressed in such sartorial splendor no one ever forgot him. He had style, grace, and unparalleled wit. George Bernard Shaw wrote, "He was without question the most brilliant talker I have ever come across," quite the compliment from a man of imaginative wit himself.

DOUBLE-EDGED SWORD – PASSION & PERVERSITY. Babe Ruth and Colette could charm the flowers into bloom. Both were brilliant at their craft but so far out of context with convention they were seen as eccentric. The masses love to connect with anyone so successful and are willing to leave their own prejudices at the door when visiting the provocative. History is strewn with the bodies of those who followed the passionate to their Utopian village. Rockstar groupies are but one instance of this phenomenon but the cultists offer the most bizarre instances of betting it all on a dream. Charisma is power over people and what incites can defuse. This double-edged sword is one that can energize and make one feel whole but can also strip one of their reason. Charm and passion are inextricably tied together in a way that makes and breaks. In other words, charisma is not without a downside. It caused Chaplin to be deported, led to Hughes becoming a druggie, Bucky Fullers's horrid career as businessman, and it had a great deal to do with President Kennedy's assassination. Success and failure are but a flipside of the same weapon, as is charisma and chaos. One cannot just have the good without the bad, just as you can't win big without betting it all. Passion and charm fuel the trip to the top, as well as forays into the bedroom and anyone who thinks it can be otherwise doesn't get the concept.

COLETTE – LURID ROMANCE WRITER

The pen name Colette was used by Sidonie Gabrielle Claudine Colette to write very thinly disguised perverse autobiographies in the first half of the 20th century. At first she signed her works Colette Willy, her married name. Her husband was a lecherous French publisher Henry (Willy) Gauthier-Villars. He conned his young wife into writing lurid stories about her life in school and then took credit for writing them. Willy was a published writer at the time and had the ability to open important doors for the Claudine series. Without his influence, she may never have become a writer regardless of her obvious talent. Did Willy use Colette sexually and professionally? Yes he did! But she also used him to get started as a writer and to learn her way around the world of publishing. In retrospect, theirs was a mutually beneficial relationship that has been taken out of context by some biographers who have seen the relationship as a one-way affair.

In many ways Willy created a Frankenstein in Colette. She was a bright, nubile, liberal, but naïve young woman when he married her and brought her into the dens of inequity of Paris just prior to the turn of the century. She absorbed the lights and letters like a sponge and loved the good life. In fact, Colette became more inclined to live life at the extreme than Willy and actually would come to embarrass him with her decadent lifestyle. Willy had introduced his young wife to *ménage a trios* relationships for his own titillation, but it wouldn't take long for her to enjoy them more than he. He also introduced her bisexuality, drugs, gambling on horses and cards, bestiality, and life in the fast lane in the salons of Europe. Why then was he shocked when she used the connections to fashion her own life in a lane faster than the one he had proscribed? Men make many of the rules and then are shocked when the women are more adept at playing the game than they. This was what happened in the life of Willy and Colette.

When she found that he was nearly broke and had sold off all her future royalties she made a pact with one of the *ménage a trios* female lovers that he had set up for them and left him. Her new lover was Missy – the Marquise de Belboeuf, a wealthy descendent of Napoleon who bought Colette her freedom from Willy and also introduced her to the Parisian stage of whom she was a benefactor. Colette had already written the first four autobiographical tell-all books that had been so successful they had sold 500,000 copies in less than ten years. The wild couple had become rich and famous through her efforts more than his, although Willy always lived well above his means. The name Colette has since become known outside the Claudine series but for the first

167

twenty years of her writing Claudine was her signature work. Later she would become famous for her two classics *Cheri* (1920) and *Gigi* (1945).

Her first works were intimate secrets of life in school, in Paris, and while married to a man into wild soirees. Colette had written words like, "Passions are the mistresses of the world" and "Pleasure is the only acceptable rule of behavior" (Francis & Gautier 1998 p. 241). In *Claudine at School* (1900) her first book, she had the school principal describe Claudine as "extremely intelligent, imaginative, but with a deliberate will to be different."

RADICAL DISSIDENT

Colette was a revolutionary, a libertine woman with a flare for the erotic and exotic. She taught herself pantomime and then took it to another dimension and in the process scandalized Paris, not an easy undertaking. The theater became a place for Colette to release pent up passions and to allow free reign to her raging libido and physicality. In her inimitable style she would appear on stage with one breast exposed and attired in *avant garde* costumes. She was a fitness fanatic with a lithe body and liked to show it off. She said, "I want to dance naked if I feel like it, a leotard cramps my style" (Thurman p. 144). When not in a revue she wrote for a daily paper and held court in her apartment. In 1907 she had made her deal with Missy to share their life and Missy helped arrange her to appear on stage. They appeared together in drag and succeeded in shocking the *Moulin Rouge* by flaunting their lesbian relationship with her estranged husband in the audience. By this time she was thirty-four but still in superb physical condition.

Her scandalous performance was but one of her daring escapades. She lived life on the edge. One biographer noted, "She belongs to high society without stooping to its rules. She teases, taunts, and defies public morals." The secretary of Bertrand de Jouvenel said, "She belonged to the first generation of 20th century sexual revolutionaries." Colette had longed to gain acceptance in society but she would never bow to any decorum let alone dress codes or social graces. She was a true libertine who believed success was the only price of admission to any kind of behavior. Her motto was, "First become famous and then do whatever you please" (Francis-Gautier p. 243). She had been raised to worship at the altar of freedom and was not about to change. She wrote, "I want to do what I want when I want."

CATHARTIC WRITER. Colette preceded Hemingway in the sense she slept with men and women and then put the whole episode into one of her books without changing anything but the names. For her writing was therapeutic. It was a release of inner turmoil and allowed her to vent her passions and rages against Willy and anyone else who happened to enter her life. To her many of the scenes in her books were merely periods out of her life and she never did quite understand why they were so titillating to her readers. She had lived the whole thing and was merely using the action to fill pages, but to the lonely suburban housewife her books were wild adventures into the fantasy world of passion. One of her early *ménage a trios* relationships with Willy included an American heiress Georgie Raoul-Duval. Georgie was in shock when she found out that Colette had included their affair in vivid detail in her book *Claudine in Love*. Georgie had her legal counsel buy up the first printing and burn them and threatened a lawsuit if they were reprinted. The Machiavellian Willy merely had Colette change a few scenes and published the book under a new title *Claudine Married* (1902). The book gained a scandalous and salacious reputation making it a must read and it went through 100 printings and sold 70,000 copies.

Colette pushed the limits in all things personal and professional. She had been raised to live by the philosophy of Charles Fourier, a 19th century writer that was the French successor to the Marquise de Sade in touting free love for all peoples. Fourier believed "frustrated passion elicits aggression and argued for the relaxation of all rules relative to sex including: *NO PREJUDICE, NO REPRESSION, NO SEXUAL TABOOS.* He wrote, "Passion is the mistress of the world" in *Oevres Completes* (1866). For Colette, life was to live to the limits and passion was her pal. She wrote, "Love: the food of my pen and of my life" in *Claudine in Love*. An example of her free spirit can be seen by her frivolous seductions even with the men of her friends. Her closest female friend was the young actress Polaire who played the part of Claudine on stage. Polaire was both confidante and lover. She didn't think Colette would jump in bed with a new romantic love interest when she left them alone briefly, but when she returned, sure enough she found them in Colette's bed.

In *Claudine at School*, Colette wrote of the lesbian love triangle between the principal of her high school, her teacher and the mayor of Saint-Saveur en Puisaye one Doctor Merlou. At the turn of the century, Paris was noted for widespread bisexuality, estimated at twenty-five percent of the population. But her revelation was too close to home and cost the mayor his job and the teacher to leave the school. The principal stared her down on one visit.

FAME IN THE FAST LANE. By her mid-twenties Colette Willy had become a household name in France. The Claudine Series had been read by millions of adoring fans and she and Willy were living life in the fast lane. Her husband has been demeaned by female biographers who see him as a womanizing chauvinist. There is no question he had few morals and used her in the early years but Colette was not far behind and gained as much as she lost. Henry Gautier-Villars was well educated from the upper middle classes. When he married Colette his family disowned him for marrying a farm girl with no dowry and no formal education. He was fifteen years older than Colette but looked twenty-five. He already had a live-in mistress and an illegitimate son and when the mistress mysteriously fell ill and died Colette's Machiavellian mother moved in and arranged the marriage under suspicious circumstances. After ten years of marital bliss and chaos the marriage had run its course and they decided to divorce. In Roman Catholic France this can take some time. During a protracted separation Colette took to the stage to earn money while living with her lover Missy. During this era actresses were little more than prostitutes and friends were appalled at her daring.

Despite Colette's life on he edge she was awarded the Legion of Honour in 1920. She was the first woman elected to the Academie Goncourt and a century later is still one of France's most read novelists. When she died in 1954 she was the first writer in France to be given a state funeral. Two of her plays are classics - *Cheri* (1920) and *Gigi* (1945), the later written when she was 72. Biographer Thurrman wrote, "The Claudine series, is one of the greatest, if not the greatest, successes in French literary history." John Fletcher, a writer for the *Literary Review*, said, "She lived to become one of the most famous and honoured writers of her generation and did so in a male-dominated society."

PASSIONATE PERSONA

At age fifty Colette was still energy incarnate. She wrote, "I realized that I would not be able to live without great intensity." Excess defined every aspect of her life and it transcended her work. She was aware she had an unusual drive for sex and life and wrote of it, "I am a child of nature and prefer passion to goodness and combat to discussion." In *Break of Day* (1924) she wrote about her need for younger men. "The perversity to satiate an adolescent love doesn't devastate a woman, on the contrary giving becomes a kind of neurosis, a ferocity, an egotistical frenzy." Rene Aujo, her stepson's secretary believed the affair was not only physical, "I believe she really loved him."

Mania was pervasive in her life and the constant need to be on center stage socially, sexually, and professionally drove her to great ends. By age sixty she was still working 16-hour days in a frenetic attempt to experience every little bit that life had to offer. She feared not having it all, but would never give up any lover or contract to another. Passion dominated her life.

For Colette happiness and seductiveness were inseparable. Her mother Sido had instilled in her the importance of freedom and the need for allowing free reign to her inner desires regardless of social taboos. Sido was a fan of Fourier and raised her youngest daughter to believe in free love, and Colette grew up believing that "sexual repression was the root of all evil." This early training led to a libertine philosophy spawning statements like, "So many women want to be corrupted and so few are chosen." Bertrand de Jouvenel's best friend described Colette as a woman with unique powers of persuasion. When biographer Thurman asked, how a 16-year old boy could be seduced by a fat and matronly fifty year-old, Rene Aujo responded:

> *Colette was provocative. She belonged to the first generation of twentieth-century sexual revolutionaries. But one must not underestimate the carnality, the very genuine and passionate physical attraction, between the two of them. Colette was desirable, oh, extremely! She had a powerfully seductive aura. But there was also the thrill of incest – her whole life was theater* (Thurman pg 297).

EARLY LIFE EXPERIENCES

Colette was a love child of Captain Colette and Sido who had been his lover before her older husband passed away. Sido instilled in her the belief that god existed within and not to worship external icons. Sido had a black strain inherited from a Caribbean born grandfather who had immigrated to France. Colette and her mother both had cocoa complexions due to the Caribbean influence. Sido raised her daughter to defy all convention, including organized religion, traditional marriage, and all forms of authority. The renegade Colette would later write, "There is no society and there is on God" (Thurman p. 218).

Sido married twice. Her first marriage was arranged to a wealthy farmer. The marriage produced three older siblings who were on their own by the time Colette was born of the second marriage to Captain Colette. Juliette was 13 years older, Achille ten years older, and Leopold seven years older. When Sido's first husband died, she married the Captain and Sidonie Gabrielle Colette was born in a small village in Saint-Saveur en Puisaye on January 28, 1873. Her mother was central to her thought causing her to write, "Sido was the leading character in my life. The personage of my mother dominates all my work." Captain Colette was an injured war veteran and a true bibliophile. He wrote poetry and proved to be the biggest influence to her writing career.

At age twelve Colette visited Paris and was enchanted by the City of Light. During that first visit she met Willy who to her was a very sophisticated and dashing man of the world. She came home and wrote in her journal, "Willy knows how to speak to a woman." By fifteen Colette had grown emotionally attached to the fantasy that was Willy. By high school she saw little chance with the worldly publisher and went off on a teenage fling with her music teacher. She returned from a lost weekend intact but disenchanted with life in rural France and embarked on a plan to land in Paris. After a trip in which Willy and she became intimate in a taxi her mother used the event to accuse him of seducing an innocent 18-year old on holiday. The impetuous Colette had actually been the aggressor, but mothers have a way of turning the tables on such acts. She had insisted Willy take her to bed and after the sudden death of his mistress he capitulated to the demands of Sido. Willy was 33 when he married the 19 year-old Colette in May 1893. The marriage began well with extensive travel and introducing Colette to the Parisian lifestyle. Wild parties and soirees dominated their early years until they took their toll and Willy's mother's death that led him to try for an inheritance and that did not include having Colette as a wife.

WRITING GENESIS. Willy was already an established writer when they married. He was always on the outlook for new material for his fans, especially tell-all stories by young women. Early in the marriage he urged his young wife to document her wild teenage experiences, the wilder the better. At first he was fueling his own needs for titillation since he never for a minute believed she could write well enough to get published. When she finished the first draft of her life in rural France, he glanced at the work and proclaimed it "unpublishable." He got a second opinion from his publisher who said *Claudine at School* would not sell over a few hundred copies. He put the book in a drawer in 1895 and there it remained for six long years. Colette was 22 at the time and would be approaching 28 by the time it was published. By the end of the century there was a renewed demand for autobiographical novels with an erotic twist. Willy found the manuscript in his drawer, and the rest is history.

Those six years were wild and interesting and would become the scenes of three more books. The itinerant couple lived a wild vagabond life partying with the elite. They lived as if on a continual holiday, entertaining American artists and heiresses, or European poets, and enjoyed music at the Wagner Bayreuth Festival annually. Willy introduced Colette to a swinging lifestyle.

172

Much of their time was spent in Provence, Nice, Monaco, Italy or in Germany. Colette's first attempt at writing was far less provocative than their lifestyle. Her story of a lesbian triangle in a country school was published in 1900. When it became an instant success, Willy pleaded with her to write a sequel. The overnight sensation spawned three sequels each written in three months over the next three years. Within six years the Claudine series was a phenomenon and made its author famous if not rich.

CRISES & EPIPHANY

In 1907 Colette's life fell apart. Captain Colette died, her marriage was at an impasse, they were hopelessly in debt, and she was bored with her life and wanted desperately to be a dancer or actress. When Willy's mother died it caused an irretrievable split. He had been disinherited over his marriage to Colette and the conniving Willy saw an opportunity to get his inheritance by splitting with Colette. But he was too cute for his own good since he told her to move in with Missy as a lark but it became a reality. At the time the couple were dire straits financially due to a lavish lifestyle. They had always lived way beyond their income and Willy had sold off all future royalties to pay off his creditors. The problem is that he failed to tell Colette and that infuriated her. When Colette left him he was still not perturbed since he had a virtual harem of younger mistresses to replace her.

If greatness is born of tragedy the year 1907 was the catalyst for Colette. She was now free to go her own way and to pursue life on her terms, which were always outside convention. When she walked into the waiting arms of her lover Missy she not only thumbed her nose at upper-middle class decorum she embarked on a stage career, and life in the fast lane.

Colette occupied herself with a long series of affairs with wealthy Parisians, American heiresses, and entertainers and artists. Her life was transformed and the Colette we know today was born out of trauma. Change can take the form of evolution or revolution but with Colette it would always take the form of revolution. The submissive wife was suddenly the woman in control and she became independent, insolent, arrogant, and defiant. All things held sacred by Roman Catholic France were fair game for Colette. She would later write of her traumatic transformation, "How young I was, how much I loved that man and how I suffered; he locked me up and forced me to write, I was beaten, exploited, and forced to perform degrading sex acts." It would seem those words were little more than literary propaganda, but they also appear to have been the rationalization for the birth of a licentiously driven woman.

MAGNETISM & PASSION

A BISEXUAL *FEMME FATALE* IS BORN

Claudine in Love (1902) was spawned by Colette's affair with one of Willy's acquaintances. He had brought the American heiress into the marriage for his own amusement in what today would be called a "swinging" liaison. Georgie Raoul-Duval was a beautiful young American with a penchant for bisexual romance. She was a redhead coquette who traveled Europe, and for one year was the constant companion of Willy and Colette. Georgie had enough money to rent her own quarters, but that didn't keep her from spending many nights with her friends. The threesome was on a Bayreuth holiday during this period when Colette decided to document the torrid relationship in a book that would scandalize Paris. It was 1905 and the couple's marriage was on rocky ground and the two were looking for ways to reenergize it. Willy had introduced his young wife to the wild life that included orgy like soirees that included drugs. One of Willy's erotic liaisons included the infamous cross-dresser and socialite Marquise de Belboeuf who went by the nickname Missy. Missy was the most notorious lesbian in Paris and was ten years older than Colette. She had the money and contacts to help Colette make a clean break from a mercenary husband and open important doors to a stage career.

Missy offered her a new apartment below her own in exchange for a conjugal contract. The offer was too good to turn down for Colette who found her new lover compatible sexually and socially. Their common bond was with the arts and theater. What Colette did not know was that Willy had arranged for the tryst in hopes they would hit it off so he could gain his inheritance by a marital split. The intrigue completed her transition out of a marriage of convenience into a provocative lifestyle. The bizarre relationship led to Colette's long and illustrious stage career and a scandalous life on the fringe.

The young author of Claudine would mature into a seductress beyond the pale of even Paris. Her seductions were as notorious as those of Cleopatra and would have made her intellectual mentor Fourier proud. Her most infamous seduction came when she was forty-seven. The ex-wife of second husband Baron de Jouvenel was attempting to improve her station by using his title and felt that Colette had his ear and would assist her. She sent her sixteen year-old son, Bertrand de Jouvenel, to visit the aging actress to exact the favor. The whole thing backfired when Colette decided it was time the boy became a man and seduced him. In her words, "It's time for you to become a man." The liaison turned into more than a sexual tryst for her amusement as she became enthralled that a teenager could find her attractive and she had him move in with her since she and the boy's father were estranged. But the Baron, who was paying for the house in which his son and wayward wife was committing incest was furious. Henry de Jouvenel was a renowned journalist for *Le Matin* and about to run for Parliament and was appalled by his wife's act and his son's defiance.

PSYCHOSEXUAL ENERGY

Passion dominated the life and work of Colette. Her successes can be tied to her libidinal energy that was pure electric. Whether dancing, writing, entertaining, speaking, or making love she was energy incarnate. She was unable to do anything slowly or normally. Such people often seduce to feel whole and Colette was no exception. And they often turn out to be control freaks. It was her way or the highway. She admitted that life without love was not worth living, "The subject of love was the bread of my life and pen." If she found herself in a strange town without companionship she would to to the streets to find a man or woman to share her bed. For her love was akin to lust, and despite a life of wild soirees, she never found the idyllic relationship.

Willy had been tripped and beaten to the ground by the calculating teenager, but after that he would introduce her into the true dens of iniquity of Paris. From that time life was one long bacchanal for Colette who found Paris like a trip to the candy store for a needy child. With her husband's urging she engaged in a long series of lesbian relationships with sophisticated and wealthy women. Her first liaison was with American heiress Natalie Barney. That was soon followed by a love affair with Georgie Raoul-Duval followed by Missy and then a long series of sordid affairs with young attractive bisexuals like the actress Polaire who played her (Claudine) on stage, poet Renee Vivian, and actress Lily de Reme.

YOUNGER MEN. After 35 Colette became enamored of younger men, some who were twenty or more years her junior. They were attracted to her vitality and presence. She was attracted to their virility and interest in her. Twenty year-old Lucien Fouchon pursued her around Europe during her mid-thirties. A young millionaire Auguste Heriot was twelve years her junior and deeply infatuated with the aging star. Each can be found in her book *Vagabond* published in 1911 when she was 38. This work was a travel adventure of life on the road with love gained and love lost. Heriot constantly proposed marriage and life on his yacht if she would give up her lifelong commitment to Missy who by that time had bought her a villa.

Colette's life of debauchery included wild flings of the heart and body. One such encounter took place with Countess de Cummings and her lover the Baron de Jouvenel who would become Colette's second husband. In a typical scene, Colette offered up her young lover Heriot to the Countess in exchange for some romance with her long-term lover the Baron. Henry de Jouvenel, like many before him, became smitten with Colette. At Colette's urging, he informed the Countess that their long-term love affair was over and that he was taking up with Colette. Why the Baron? The Baron was not only sophisticated and attractive, but was a senior editor of *La Matin,* and a man with enormous political connections. Cummings was not amused and threatened to kill Colette. She had been waiting patiently for de Jouvenel's divorce to marry him, and now that it was close Colette had intervened and her life was suddenly turned asunder. It would not be the first time or the last that Colette destroyed a friend for personal gain.

MARRIAGE. During all this Colette's stage career was fading and her love affair with the Baron ended up with her pregnant. She was not into marriage but the child and her fading beauty led her into an impulsive move that she would regret. Her decision was not based on security since her romantic arrangement with Missy allowed her total freedom and security as Missy paid all the bills. When informed of Colette's latest misogyny Missy was furious and young lover Heriot became despondent. Colette was approaching forty when she moved in with Jouvenel and with his divorce imminent they arranged to be married prior to the birth of their daughter. Colette gave birth to her only child and named her Colette Renee. But Colette was not maternal, and the girl was immediately given to an English nanny to be raised.

The marriage to de Jouvenel was doomed from the start. He was an aspiring politician and Colette had a horrid reputation. It would take an imaginative voter to envision Colette as First Lady since lady was not in her vocabulary. Her new husband was also used to maintaining a bevy of mistresses for his pleasure and the control freak Colette was not one to share anything even those things that she wasn't closely attached. And Colette had been down that road once before and wasn't happy unless she was the central figure in a relationship. The French are content with mistresses of their leaders but fully expect the wife to be socially acceptable. Colette didn't fit and the Baron soon saw his lover was more a liability than an asset and they became estranged almost as soon as the ink was dry on the marriage contract. They remained married legally due to his political aspirations and her need to have someone pay the rent. In today's world the marriage would have ended within months. As it was the divorce wasn't filed until she seduced the Baron's teenage son. During this period Colette lived life as a vagabond entertainer. She was seldom in one city for any length of time and she and the Baron maintained separate apartments.

INCEST IN THE NAME OF EDUCATION. Bertrand de Jouvenel was a typical teenager bound for college when his life was altered forever by an uninhibited stepmother. He would later describe his seduction as "Colette's desire to educate me." She was more direct saying, "It's time you became a man." In any case, she carried out the dirty deed as only Colette could. She taught the boy the ways of the world while educating him in the art of love. They were inseparable for three years. He moved out of his mother's house and into her apartment to the shock and dismay of the Baron. She introduced him to the Riviera and Morocco and he introduced her to Alpine skiing. The incestuous relationship found its way into her autobiographical work *Cheri* (1920), with Bertrand the weak younger man being pursued by a strong older woman. Heriot would have his romance immortalized in *The Ripening Seed* (1921) where she explored awakening sexual desire and intrigue. Her stepson would reappear later as the male protagonist in *Gigi*.

ANOTHER YOUNGER HUSBAND. While in the process of breaking up with her stepson Colette met and fell for a bachelor who was sixteen years younger. She was fifty-one when she first became intimate with the thirty-seven year old Jewish pearl merchant Maurice Goudeket. The couple lived together and then opened a beauty business together. They were soul mates more than lovers since she was 62 when she married him and no longer into lust for lust's sake. After ten years of courtship the couple married in 1935 for the most implausible of reasons. Colette had been invited as a guest on the maiden voyage of the new ocean liner Normandie. Part of the itinerary included a tour of New York City. They were informed that provincial hotels in Manhattan would not allow unmarried guests to stay together. In classic Colette fashion she went to City Hall and were married without fanfare or guests. Ironically, on the Normandie and also headed for New York was Bertrand with a new found love Martha Gelhorn, a brilliant journalist who would later marry Ernest Hemingway. Colette remained married to Goudeket until her death in 1954.

DIVERGENT THINKING

For Colette life was a fantasy with lust playing a major role. She had to experience it all, physically, mentally, and emotionally. Colette was a dichotomy, a bright but irresponsible woman, one with strong urges but once fulfilled not desire to pursue them, and a passionate persona without morals. She was an anomaly, an opinionated atheist in a devout Roman Catholic nation, an intellectual without education, and an actress without training, and a mother who refused to nurture her child. She was wicked, but seldom ruthless. She refused to attend her daughter's wedding or to attend her mother's funeral. Colette was an iconoclast, faddist, hedonist, and seductress. She had no conscience. All these things made her a successful writer since she wrote from the heart rather than the head.

The Paris elite saw her as a social pariah after she committed class treason at the *Moulin Rouge*. She would write, "The music hall made me a tough and honest businesswoman." But her excesses led Jean Cocteau to say, "Everything in art is monstrous. Madam Colette does not escape that rule" (Thurman p. 449). The radical justified her indiscretions with the following definition of her own eccentricity, "Voluptuaries, consumed by their senses, always begin by flinging themselves with a great display of frenzy into an abyss. But survive and then develop a routine of the abyss."

CREATIVE INSPIRATIONS

Colette wrote eighty books. The comic masterpiece *Gigi* is testimony to her insight, resiliency and passion. Her words of lust and living seemed real. Why? Because she had lived most of them and often exceeded what she dared put down on paper. The observation skills of Colette contributed to her ability to relate worldly events to provocative stories and it led to her becoming the first female reporter in France. She was also Literary Editor and Drama Critic for the *Le Martin*. She even ventured into the world of entrepreneurship when she and third husband Maurice Goudeket opened a cosmetics shop in Paris. She had no patience for seeing such a venture to its end and it was short-lived. Detail was not a strength of Colette.

Her most acclaimed works were *Cheri* and *Gigi*, about older women and younger men, an area of expertise. Colette loved life in the penthouse and she was not of the Virginia Woolf school of letters, that the British writer called, "Five hundred a year and a room of one's own." For Colette, life was marginal at *Fifty thousand a year and a villa of one's own, with a great chef, a big garden, and a pretty boy available for your every whim.* An example is her classic *Cheri* with a young gigolo emerging from adolescence to be nurtured and loved by an older woman. The novel personifies her penchant for the unconventional and her interest in reversing gender roles. She often depicted strong females leading weaker males through intrigue and romantic debacles. Colette was Lea in *Cheri*, and Cheri was Bertrand, the boy she had deflowered. But what is lost in Colette's long and often lonely life, was when to bet 'em and when to fold 'em. She was not one to give in or give up and with Bertrand she would have been better served to teach him and let him go. She didn't and it nearly destroyed her.

BABE RUTH – BASEBALL ICON

The Bambino went for broke in the field and all other venues. He did nothing half way and that would be his legacy that still casts a spell over baseball seven decades after he left the sport. In 1999 the Babe was named the greatest ballplayer in history and was named as one of three athletes considered the greatest athletes of the 20th century. Few athletes ever rise to the level of Ruth and seldom has anyone ever so dominated their sport as the Sultan of Swat. He transcended his sport like few others.

Passion and excess defined Babe. Without his hyper-kinetic energy he might have been good, but it is highly unlikely he would have been great. Everything the Babe did was larger than life. Boston sportswriter Burt Whitman wrote, "The more I see the Babe the more he seems like a figure out of mythology" (Creamer p. 37). In retrospect he still is more myth than reality. Sportswriter Ronald Blum (1999) wrote, "Babe Ruth towered over baseball." An HBO special in 1999 described him as an icon without peer. "If Babe Ruth had not existed, it would be impossible to invent him. Ruth is bigger than the myth."

The irony of his myth as a prodigious homerun hitter is the fact he was an All Star pitcher for three years before he was allowed to play everyday as a hitter. In Ruth's first full season in the American League he won 18 games as a pitcher for the Boston Red Sox. The next year he won 23 games and then 24and only after he hit balls out of sight did they begin allowing him to play in the field while not pitching in 1918. For those not familiar with baseball the pitcher wears himself out to such a degree he must rest for three to four days between pitching assignments, therefore playing between taking the mound is just not done despite the pitcher's hitting skills. But the Babe was not ordinary in any respect. In 1919, a year in which he pitched 133 innings, he hit an unprecedented 29 home runs, led the league in runs scored, runs batted in, extra-base hits, total bases, and slugging percentage. The Ruthian legend had begun. His fires would not wane for another twenty years.

SUPERMAN WITH A BAT

The Bambino had Herculean-like stamina. He could stay up all night and go to the park and pitch a shutout. The next day he would play the outfield, hit a homer, and spend all night celebrating in the bars and brothels. He would show up the next day with virtually no rest. The Babe pushed his body like few athletes in history. His dissipation would cost him in the end and there was a home in the Boston area where he went to dry out and catch up after the season. Like others who live life in the fast lane the Babe would drain his system dry and then collapse. Such is the life of the driven personality.

The Babe was like a big kid in a candy shop that he saw as life. His roommates never knew him as he didn't want to waste one minute out of the action. His hotel room was a place to change clothes for the game although his mangers didn't see it as he did and he was continually fined for insubordination. The Babe would stay out all night carousing and show up at the park. He never rested his body or his libido. One teammate told the media, "He was continually with women, morning and night. I don't know how he kept going" (Creamer p. 322). Another roommate spoke to his prolific ability with women. He said, "Ruth made love to a girl, smoked a cigar, then returned to the room, smoked another cigar, and so on through the night." When the player queried Ruth about his times with the lady, Ruth responded, "Seven!" "How do you know?" "I just count the cigars. There are seven so that is how many times we did it."

A LEGEND IN HIS OWN TIME. Ruth not only broke many of baseball's most cherished records, he shattered them. He still holds many of them like the most extra base hits in a single season set in 1921 with 119. There is no telling what he might have done had he began as a hitter or had led a more normal life off the field. Ruth led the league in slugging percentage 13 times, home runs 12 times, runs scored 8 times, and RBI's 6 times. He was the first baseball player to hit 30 home runs, 40 home runs, 50 home runs, and 60 home runs. In the era of the dead ball he hit more home runs than most other teams and in 1921 more than the whole league. When the Bambino hit his 700th home run only two men had hit 300. When the Babe retired he had twice the homers of his nearest competitor. His slugging percentage of .847 in 1920 has never been broken and probably never will.

The shocker is that the Babe was a pitcher for four years during his prime years in which he hit only nine home runs. Had he spent his career as a pitcher he may have been just as overwhelming as he was as a hitter since in 1918 he was the best pitcher in the American League. The Babe dominated baseball more than Michael Jordan did in basketball, Wayne Gretsky did in Hockey, or Tiger Woods has in golf. The Babe had no peers.

PASSIONATE PERSONA

During Ruth's early days a sportswriter named Drabager wrote, "Ruth is the most uninhibited human being I've ever known" (Creamer p. 29). His notorious antics off the field rival those on it. He was an insatiable womanizer and gourmand who could stupefy teammates. They marveled at his insatiable appetite for beer, women, food, cigars, gambling, and fast cars. He lived life at the edge. Other players were perplexed that he could stay up all night and still play ball as if he had been to sleep. And he was equally as enamored with playing poker, driving fast sports cars, betting on horses, smoking cigars, and playing golf. He was able to drink more, love more, smoke more, and eat more than any normal human. Excess defined him.

The stories surrounding the lusts of the Babe are legendary. Claire Ruth, the Babe's second wife, described his behavior in a self-effacing way saying, "He brought out the beast in a lot of ladies the world over" (Wallace p. 392). Irving Wallace included the Babe in a book on *The Sex Lives of Famous People* (1993) with the comment that hardly one day passed when he was playing ball that he did not have sex with at least one woman. And it must be remembered he was married during most of that time.

Baseball biographer Robert Creamer describes Ruth's penchant for women as relentless. He spoke of Ruth's habit of pressuring rookies to let him use their rooms when his wife was on a road trip. She believed he was in a team meeting when he was really having a liaison. But Ruth's philandering did not go without repercussions. He was a frequent defendant in paternity suits one of which was for $50,000 when a teenage girl named Dorothy Dixon accused him of fathering her child. The suit was settled out of court.

MAGNETIC CHARM

Ruth was impossible to dislike. His charm overcame his penchant for trouble. He was infamous for picking up women while stopped at a red light. Biographers describe him leaning out his window at the pretty girl in the next car and inviting her for a drink. Before long she was with him in a lounge or restaurant. Such fearless personalities come to believe they are invisible or indestructible. He was as fearless with women and in the batters box. Nothing seemed beyond him and that is the secret of all great seductions. Psychologists have long since known that the biggest rakes have no regard for time, decorum, mates, or societal rules. They are willing to risk everything for the win and consequently they win more than they lose but lose they do. The Babe was such a man. He scored more than he struck out in the game of romance. Like most philanderers he was willing to go beyond the rules and risk being seen or being caught in a compromising situation. For him rules were made to break on the field and in the bedroom. His engaging smile got him to first base and then he stole his way home metaphorically. Ruth roared through life like a big kid, the products were wine, women and excitement.

Testimony to Ruth's notorious reputation as a womanizer he was roasted at a New York baseball writer's dinner following the 1926 season. Writer Bill Slocum wrote a parody recited by sportswriter Rud Rennie playing the part of Ruth's frustrated Manager Miller Huggins:

> *I wonder where my Babe Ruth is tonight?*
> *He grabbed his hat and coat and ducked out of sight.*
> *I wonder where he'll be*
> *At half past two or three?*
> *He may be at a dance or in a fight.*
> *He may be at some cozy roadside inn.*
> *He may be drinking tea or maybe – gin.*
> *I know he's with a dame,*
> *I wonder what's her name?*
> *I wonder where my Babe Ruth is tonight?*

EARLY LIFE EXPERIENCES

George Herman Ruth was born in 1895 in Baltimore, Maryland. His father was saloonkeeper George Ruth and his mother was of German heritage, Katherine Schamberger. She died when Ruth was 15, but when alive she was unable to control him any more than his managers would later in life. He was a renegade who would today be diagnosed with Attention Deficit Disorder. Her husband was never home and her seven year old son ended up in reform school for refusing to attend school.

Ruth was incorrigible as a young boy until the fathers at St. Mary's just outside his hometown of Baltimore exercised authoritarian control. Catholic Brothers were in charge of St. Mary's and discipline was their forte. But George was too young to stay and was sent home twice to live with his parents. But Ruth was a wild child and was sent to St. Mary's to live permanently at age ten when his mother was unable to control him. The home for wayward boys was run by Brother Mathias, a huge man, who would become Ruth's role model for living and hitting a baseball. Brother Mathias was also father figure, since Ruth had no relationship with his father. Mathias was 6' 6" and weighed 250 pounds. He could hit a baseball out of sight with just one hand and the Babe both revered and feared him.

The years at St. Mary's made Ruth independent, but also gave him a sense of family. He had been sent there for hyperactivity. The experience molded him into a man-boy who loved athletics and the company of men. Ruth admitted that he never saw his real father from the age of eight to eighteen, and told the media that Brother Mathias was his greatest influence. He said, "I think I was a born hitter the first time I saw Brother Mathias hit a baseball." As a Yankee he admitted that his only home was St. Mary's and "Brother Mathias was the greatest man I've ever known" (Creamer p. 37).

St. Mary's instilled in Ruth a passionate love of baseball. Always the rebel, Ruth began playing as a left-handed catcher and third baseman. Then he became a pitcher. For the uninitiated, catchers and third basemen are never left-handed. The mechanics of throwing a ball to first base does not work for a left-handed player like Ruth. But as in most kids games, the biggest kid plays the toughest positions like pitcher, catcher and cleanup hitter.

In Ruth's last year at St. Mary's he won every game he pitched and hit a home run in every game. When he turned 19 the school released him to Jack Dunn the owner of the Baltimore Orioles professional team in the International League. In his first professional game he played shortstop and hit a homerun. In 1914 he was sold to the Boston Red Sox of the American League where they intended to groom him for stardom as a pitcher.

Ruth was a neophyte about life and love due to his long-term internment at St. Mary's. When he was released to play ball he was like a kid gone wild. When he got off the bus in Boston his first stop was to eat and as would happen for the next thirty years he fell in love with the waitress. He was always hungry and struck up a conversation with sixteen year-old Helen Woodford and began a relationship that would end in marriage by the end of the season. When the team sent him back down to the minors for more grooming he was unable to live without his first love and sent for her. They were married in Baltimore on Oct. 17, 1914 in a Catholic ceremony at St. Paul's with his friends from St. Mary's in attendance.

THE GENESIS OF A PRO. The name Babe was given to the young rookie pitcher by the baseball writers during his first year. They saw him as a baby faced player but the epithet was more due to his kid-like demeanor. He looked and acted the part of a Babe and the name stuck. In 1915 Ruth was a pitcher on the most dominant team in Boston history. As a prelude of things to come the rookie pitcher went to bat only 92 times but hit .315 with four home runs. The whole team hit only nine homers. By 1916 the Babe was the best left-handed pitcher in the American League. In that year he finished with nine shutouts, 23 wins, and led the league in ERA – earned run average.

He asked for and got more money since he was a star about to be born and the owner knew it. But the bucks soon altered his lifestyle. The boy who matriculated from reform school now had more money he had ever seen. In 1917 he was paid $5000, a season in which he was even more astounding with 24 wins, 6 shutouts, and 35 complete games. By now he was pinch-hitting in key situations when not pitching, an unheard role for a pitcher who was supposed to rest between starts. He batted .325 in 1917, an average only exceeded by Hall of Famers Ty Cobb, George Sisler, and Tris Speaker.

On May 6, 1918, Ruth took the field for the first time as a non-pitcher. He was asked to play first base against the hated New York Yankees and hit a towering home run witnessed by Yankee owner Jacob Ruppert. After the game Ruppert called the Boston owner and offered to buy Ruth's contract. The Boston owner refused. Then Ruth hit massive homeruns in the next three consecutive games. Within a week he was hitting an awesome .484 and had captured the imagination of all baseball. The Ruthian magic was born and would last another twenty years.

Ruth was now destined to become a Yankee in a deal the city of Boston has never forgotten to this day. On December 16, 1919, Boston sold Ruth to the Yankees for $100,000 a deal that proved to be the worst in the history of sports. The Boston owner was near bankruptcy and used his rising superstar to bail him out of a personal financial jam. Unfortunately, much of Ruth's personal life was bared since the owner justified Ruth's sale due to his off-field antics that were already legendary. The Babe already had a huge following and to save face the owner used his players philandering to justify a deal aimed at bailing him out personally. The Red Sox press release said, "Ruth has become simply impossible and the Boston Club can no longer put up with his eccentricities" (Creamer p. 212). The Yankees recognized the Babe's appeal and paid him an unprecedented salary of $20,000. The money only served to fuel the burgeoning superstar's off-field antics. It is ironic that the Babe's last three homers would be hit in Boston on the last day of his baseball career, for a total of 721 despite a body ravaged by years of abuse.

CRISES & EPIPHANY

Out of an unstable home life was born a free spirit that would become affectionately known as the Bambino. Ruth was born in a sleazy neighborhood and grew up the son of a saloonkeeper who was not into the family scene. That fine line that separates huge success and miserable failure can be found in the early years of Ruth. He was a boy of immense passions that were borderline manic-depression based on the symptoms spoke of by his peers. Ruth was impatient, volatile, manic, risk-taking, and a renegade. He had uncontrollable urges all his life. They got him in trouble as a child and even more trouble as a New York Yankee. As an adult he bought his way out of his scrapes but as a child it was St. Mary's that saved him.

At St. Mary's, Ruth channeled his hyper energy into hitting and pitching baseballs. The onetime unhappy child was transformed into an overgrown teen with awesome strength and power. Brother Mathias was shrewd enough to temper his passions and direct them into something worthwhile. The Babe lived on the edge in all things. Such behavior is acceptable on the ball-field but not so in the parlor. But by this time he was a superstar and was making enough money to pay off his fines and endure his suspensions.

Ruth lived life as if there was no tomorrow. It led to a number of serious illnesses. One occurred in 1926 when his dissipating lifestyle almost cost him his life. He was carousing and womanizing all night and playing ball all day. He landed in the hospital with a temperature of 105 degrees. He was unable to walk and was too weak to get out of bed. Ruth was bedridden for six weeks and some thought his dissipation had cost him his career and maybe his life. But when he regained his strength he was released and went right back to his torturous lifestyle. Breakdown precipitating breakthrough occurred. Ruth returned in 1927 to have the best year of his career and set the homerun record for which he became famous. In that year he hit his record breaking 60 home runs, batted .356, and had 164 RBI's. But hyper-activity would plague him as he drove twice the speed limit, flipped sports cars, and abused his body with bad food, too many cigars, too much booze, and far too many women.

PSYCHOSEXUAL ENERGY

Biographer Creamer called Ruth, "The most flamboyantly successful figure in the history of baseball." Creamer wrote the definitive biography on Ruth:

> *Everything about him reflected sexuality – the restless, roving energy; the aggressive skills; fastball pitching; home run hitting; the speed with which he drove cars; the loud, rich voice; the insatiable appetite; the constant need to placate his mouth with food, drink, a cigar, chewing gum, anything. He loved to win at whatever he did. He received absolute physical joy from cards, baseball, golf, bowling, punching the bag, sex* (Creamer p. 322).

The Babe was a skillful bridge player but insisted on playing every hand himself. He had to win every contest whether it was bowling, cards, hitting baseballs, or winning the hand of a fair lady. Passion pervaded Babe's flamboyant life. H could down more hot dogs, drive cars faster, play the most reckless game of cards, bet on the long-shot at the track, hit more home runs, and seduce more women than most men. Ruth was never faithful. He was responsible for his troubled wife's numerous nervous breakdowns, because he was never home and was a horrible husband. His wife saw him in the newspapers with other women including famous movie stars. In a futile attempt to tame Ruth, Helen adopted a daughter named Dorothy. But even that didn't work and the two lived much of their life estranged and Helen was found dead in a Boston fire in 1929. They had remained married to the end but Helen's death opened the way for the wayward Ruth to propose to his long-term sweetheart, New York model Claire Hodgson. The two adopted Dorothy and lived a reasonably sane life for the balance of Babe's career.

Ruth was incapable of a monogamous relationship with any woman, wife or mistress. When the team arrived in a new town they were told to check into the hotel before doing anything else. If early they were to rest up for the next game or to take in a relaxing movie. But not the Babe! Ruth had his roommate take his suitcase to the room and check him in as he had more important matters to attend to like finding a woman for the three-day stand in that city. In the early years his roommate with the Yankees was a player named Bodie. Bodie checked him in as the Babe took off for the local haunts where he sought out a new woman to sate his raging libido. Bodie says, "He was off looking for a girl he knew, or knew of, or hoped to know" (Creamer p. 222). An enterprising reporter trying to find the source of Ruth's magic asked Bodie about the Babe. Bodie responded, "I don't know anything about him." Thinking Bodie was trying to be smart, the reporter asked, "But you room with him?" Bodie said, "I don't room with him. I room with his suitcase." While in New York Ruth lived a lifestyle that permitted him liaisons. He refused to buy a house and liked the simple life provided by hotel life with catered meals, maid service, and no responsibility. He kept a suite at the Ansonia Hotel in Manhattan for many years.

DIVERGENT BEHAVIOR

Renegades like Ruth ignore traffic signals and all other regulations with the team or society. He was often cited for speeding. Once he was picked up driving recklessly down Riverside Drive in Manhattan and spent the night in jail prior to an important Yankee game. He befriended the New York cops and they provided him a police escort to Yankee Stadium to insure he wouldn't miss the opening pitch.

Ruth was once reported killed in a crash near Philadelphia when he flipped his sports car with his wife Helen and catcher Charley O'Leary in the car. Speed and danger were in his blood. He dismissed narrow misses as part of living in the fast lane. Many of the Babe's traits were those of the bipolar personality. Both wives and teammates described bouts with hyperactivity, grandiosity, and manic episodes. Teammates said he was "always on the go" and a "party animal." Recent studies have found a correlation between high sex drive and a bipolar personality. Babe certainly qualifies.

RISK-TAKER. Fear never dissuaded Ruth from any venture in the ballpark or in life. Casey Stengel played with Ruth and said, "He was very brave at the plate. You rarely saw him fall away from a pitch. No one drove him out." He was unafraid of umpires and once jumped into the stands to chase a fan who called him a "goddamned big bum." He was suspended for his efforts, as he had been for punching an umpire when he tossed Ruth from the game. Biographer Creamer spoke of his fearlessness saying, "In poker games he liked to raise even when cards didn't justify it" (Creamer p. 322).

The Babe was not well-read or well-bred. He could be quite crude in social situations. His comments were amusing when not too offensive, but one had to have a sense of humor to appreciate his naïve sense of style. He could be dining in an elegant restaurant with good friends Douglas Fairbanks and Mary Pickford and announce without fanfare, "Excuse me ladies, I have to take a piss." When something tasted good he would call it "pussy good." Such behavior peaked one night in St. Louis after he won a game with a home run. He walked into a brothel and announced he would have sex with every prostitute in the house. After succeeding in his task he finished off the evening with an 18-egg omelet. His penchant for women reached its peak during the 1928 Detroit World Series when he rented a hotel suite and invited many lady friends, ballplayers and the media. Midway through the evening he stood on a chair and announced, "All right ladies, any girl who doesn't want to fuck can leave" (Wallace p. 390).

MAGNETISM WITHOUT PEER

Few individuals have been idolized like the Babe. The pinnacle of his power occurred during the 1932 World Series in Chicago when he dared point to the centerfield stands and then hit the ball there. In those days the pitchers needed little incentive to throw at a player's head if they thought they were grandstanding. According to many sources, Ruth not only did this once, but twice, and delivered on both occasions. In 1928, Ruth purportedly promised a terminally ill 11-year old Johnny Sylvester that he would hit a homer for him if he would get better, and then had the audacity to tell reporters. Five days later he hit three homers. The *New York Times* reported, "Physicians say that the boy's return to health began when he learned of Ruth's three homers…his fever began to abate at once" (USA Today 1-6-1999).

But the *coup de grace* came one afternoon in 1932 at Wrigley Field when the Bambino called his home run during taunts by Chicago fans throwing lemons at the aging icon. The fans were out for vengeance and calling him an over-the-hill bum. Charley Root was the Chicago pitcher when the Babe looked out to him and called "strike one," then "strike two." Then according to many reliable sources Ruth hit a towering home run into the centerfield bleachers. Paul Gallico, Westbrook Pegler, and the Hearst papers documented the moment for posterity. Headlines screamed of the Ruthian magical feat. The New York World Telegram, printed, "RUTH CALLS SHOT AS HE PUTS HOMER #2 IN SIDE POCKET" (Creamer p. 363). Paul Gallico wrote, "He pointed like a duelest to the spot." Bill Corum of the Hearst papers wrote, "Ruth pointed out where he was going to hit the next one and hit it there." Ruth later was asked about the possibility of striking out. In his inimitable style he said, "I never thought about that" (Creamer p. 365).

The Babe lived big, loved big, and when he lost, lost big. He had a heart of gold, but was totally incapable of suppressing his need for women. The Babe was a man's man, and women's nightmare, but they all wanted to tame him. With the Babe you got what you saw. He would argue with a vengeance over his salary, and then go out and blow the whole thing on some frivolous acquisition or gambling fling. In 1920 he was paid $40,000 for a barnstorming tour in Havana, Cuba, after he had shattered the home run record with 54. He lost the whole thing at the track, and had to borrow the money to return to the United States.

In 1999, sports writer Ronald Blum wrote, "Babe Ruth towered over baseball and is still casting his shadow." Teammate Harry Hooper told the media, "I saw a man transformed from a human being to something pretty close to god" (Herzoz p. 19). Bob Creamer wrote in *Babe* (p. 62):

> *Ruth was the most flamboyantly successful figure in baseball. He was graced with undeniable charm and an infectious appeal. He loved to win at whatever he did and was the biggest man baseball has ever produced.*

8

POWER & PASSION

Charley Chaplin   Jack Kennedy

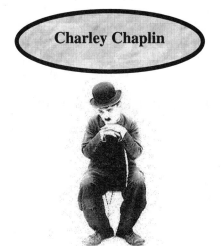

"I am the eighth wonder
of the world"

"Conformity is the jailer of
freedom and the enemy of growth"

"Power is my mistress"
Napoleon

"Power is the ultimate aphrodisiac"
Henry Kissinger

"Sex & Power are inextricably intertwined"
Michael Hutchison

"The Will to Power is man's basic motive in life"
Frederick Nietzsche

"Power is the ability to manipulate or control the activities of others to
suit one's own principles"
Alfred Adler

CHARLES SPENCER CHAPLIN
GREATEST ENTERTAINER OF 20TH CENTURY
b. London, England, April 16, 1889
d. Corsieir-Sur-Vevey, Switzerland December 25, 1977

NOTABLE TRAIT: SHY, MANIC, OBSESSIVE & MACHIAVELLIAN

PHILOSOPHY: "NO ART CAN BE LEARNED AT ONCE; LOVE-MAKING A SUBLIME ART NEEDING PRACTICE"

SELF-ANALYSIS: "I AM THE EIGHTH WONDER OF THE WORLD"

MOTTO: "VIRGINS ARE THE MOST BEAUTIFUL FORM OF HIUMAN LIFE"

MARITAL STATUS: MILDRED HARRIS (16) AT 28
LITA GREY (16) AT 35
PAULETTE GODDARD (19) AT 44
OONA O'NEILL (18) AT 54

RELIGION: ARELIGIOUS

INNOVATIONS: *THE KID* (1921); *CITY LIGHTS* (1931)
MODERN TIMES (1936); *GREAT DICTATOR* (1941)

PASSIONS: OBSESSIVE: TOOK 8-10 BATHS A DAY AND COULD MAKE LOVE SIX TIMES A DAY

AGGRESSIVENESS: "AMERICA I AM COMING TO CONQUER YOU"

THRILL-SEEKING: DARED ANYTHING; SPENT $500K TO PRODUCE *THE KID* IN 1920 – A FOOLISH BET THAT MADE THE LITTLE TRAMP A HUGE SUCCESS

CHARM: *CHAPLINITIS* SET IN FOR 25 YEARS

EGOISM: "I'M MORE FAMOUS THAN JESUS CHRIST"

ECCENTRICITIES: "CHAPLIN'S BEHAVIOR OCCASIONALLY CROSSED THE LINE FROM ECCENTRICITY TO MADNESS" - VOYEUR, M/D, OCD, PANIC ATTACKS

MANIAS: INSATIABLE SEX-MACHINE; ONCE IN MANIC STATE SPOKE NON-STOP FOR 28 HOURS

JOHN FITZGERALD KENNEDY
35TH PRESIDENT OF THE UNITED STATES
b. Boston, Massachusetts May 29, 1917
d. Dallas, Texas November 23, 1973

NOTABLE TRAIT: DARING & CHARISMATIC TO A FAULT; PASSION LED TO *MENAGE A TROIS* ADDICTION

PHILOSOPHY: "THIS ADMINISTRATION IS GOING TO DO FOR SEX WHAT THE LAST ONE DID FOR GOLF"

SELF-ANALYSIS: "A MAN DOES WHAT HE MUST"

MOTTO: "WHEN POWER CORRUPTS, POETRY CLEANSES"

MARITAL STATUS: [DURIE DESLOGE MALCOLM, PALM BEACH SOCIALITE - ANULLED] JACQUELINE BOUVIER AT 36 - CHILDREN CAROLINE & JOHN JR

RELIGION: FAIR WEATHER ROMAN CATHOLIC

INNOVATIONS: BROUGHT YOUTH & STYLE TO POLITICS

PASSIONS: "JACK HAS THE MOST ACTIVE LIBIDO OF ANY MAN I'VE EVER KNOWN" (SENATOR SMATHERS)

AGGRESSIVENESS: "JACK HATED TO LOSE AT ANYTHING"

THRILL-SEEKING: MOST DARING PRESIDENT IN HISTORY CALLED "CRASH KENNEDY" DURING WAR

CHARM: MOST CHARISMATIC U.S. PRESIDENT

EGOISM: "I NEVER MET ANYONE SO COMPLETELY OBSESSED WITH HIMSELF" (FDR JR.)

ECCENTRICITIES: "NO ONE WAS OFF-LIMITS TO JACK, NOT YOUR WIFE, YOUR MOTHER OR SISTER" (BEST FRIEND SENATOR GEORGE SMATHERS)

MANIAS: OBSESSIVE LIBIDINAL DRIVE

MARRIAGE OF POWER & PASSION

Psychotherapist Alfred Adler wrote, "Power is the ability to manipulate or control the activities of others to suit one's own principles." This definition elevates these subjects to the pinnacle of manipulators as well as validating their inner powers. All were control freaks with Chaplin and Kennedy leading the way in this respect. Chaplin abused his star-making power to seduce young aspiring starlets. According to biographers he attempted to seduce every young girl that crossed his path. Kennedy had a similar propensity although his power was political not star-making. But many women felt like they would be more powerful just by sleeping with him. His bed partners read like a Who's Who of Hollywood including such beautiful actresses as Audrey Hepburn, Angie Dickinson, Jaine Mansfield, Sophia Loren, Lee Remick, Zsa Zsa Gabor and Marilyn Monroe. His spell didn't stop in Hollywood as a myriad of Ivy League trained female journalists made it to his bed, enamored with getting laid in the White House.

POWER & SEX

Males typically are more inclined to use their powers to seduce than females. Men often try to get power because of its close tie to sexual appeal. Michael Jordan admitted that he started out to become a great athlete for the sole reason that the top jocks got first call on the most attractive girls. In contrast females spend an inordinate amount of time on their sexuality since they have learned that it is often their means of attaining power. Are there exceptions? Of course there are but in general men use power to get sex and women use sex to get power. Overachievers from each gender know this intuitively. Those in the fast lane have a power that psychologists call "influence potential." Chaplin and Kennedy used influence to seduce. Colette, Duncan and Madonna used their sexuality to open doors, and once inside did what they damned well pleased.

Charlie Chaplin was undoubtedly one of the most licentious men who ever graced a stage. Once he was in power no female was safe. Were his seductions and his success related? Beyond comprehension! He was the most libidinally driven comedian in Hollywood and at the end of the 20th century was voted the most famous actor/comedian in the century. He was astounded by his own success and told the media, "I'm more famous than Jesus Christ." His notoriety empowered him to seduce but also led to his founding of United Artists Studios. As his power grew so did his seductions in a kind of linear growth that were highly correlated.

John F. Kennedy had a different kind of appeal that became power. He had money but also had dashing good looks and a way that mesmerized women of all stations. His success was a function of his appeal that led him to power but once in power, like Chaplin, he abused it by having Hollywood starlets flown in for his pleasure and daring to place two party girls on the FBI payroll. Having a $10 million trust fund didn't hurt but he also was the most debonair of all U.S. Presidents. But with all he had going for him the wild soirees that have recently been uncovered took unbelievable nerve.

Both Chaplin and Kennedy lived on the edge by using power to seduce. Both flirted with venereal disease, romantic triangles, paternity suits, pregnancy, and suicide attempts by their conquests. Chaplin and Kennedy used their positions to win over young damsels. Bertrand Russell used his power to seduce young teachers at his London experimental school. Picasso promised his female targets immortality on canvas. All were a bit different but in the end is was their personal or professional power that allowed them to become some of the world's great philanderers. True they were successful but did the success precede the seductive power or did the power cause their sensuality? It appears they are inextricably tied together in the process of becoming successful. They had what Nietzsche characterized a Superman-like *will-to-power*. Inside they felt special. The world was there to conquer professionally, and the other gender there to capture personally.

SEX DRIVE & POWER

Sex drive and power – known as passion for success - is just one dimension of a duality critical to anyone looking to grab the brass ring. The power of persuasion, the power of attraction, the power of enthusiasm, have their genesis in libidinal drive. All such powers emanate from within a passionate person. Those who have it, know it, and those who don't are left to wonder why not. Those without it look on those with it as degenerate. Those with it are in constant wonder over why others are not so turned on by life and lust. Those with passion are perpetually on the prowl for new conquests. Those without passion wonder why those deviants spend so much time chasing fantasies spawned by their little heads.

Lust and libido are first cousins, so it should be no surprise when successful businessmen are found dating female employees, senators and presidents involved in scandalous trysts, or evangelists become romantically involved with members of their flock. One analysis found that the male professions most guilty of extra-marital affairs was ministers and gynecologists. Why? Because they had the opportunity power, but more importantly were into emotional healing, that goes a long way with female clients. Power is at the base of such intrigues and makes it easier for men to satisfy their lust, and for women to gain power. Power allowed Chaplin and Kennedy to sleep with a different woman almost every night, and sensuality was the fuel used by Cleopatra and Madonna to gain power.

WILL-TO-POWER. Psychic energy or drive from within is what Nietzsche labeled a *superman* persona or *will to power*. He wrote, "The Will to Power is man's basic motive in life." He waxed eloquent over the fact that god was dead and man needed a greater power to live without a higher being to guide them through life in a divisive world. The *will* for Nietzsche was the one difference between an average and eminent man. For him true power was not born of a title or position, which can be ever so fleeting, but that inner striving for control over our destiny.

A powerful *will* was the source of the hyper energy of Charlie Chaplin and John F. Kennedy. Both men were endowed with an inner-knowing and a sense of supremacy, that made them omnipotent in the pursuit of their goals. Such power originates in the psyche and arms the individual with the belief they can do anything and have limitless potential. This internal power is far superior to external powers like muscles, money, and titles, since there is always someone stronger, with more bucks and more authority.

Alexander the Great had such power, as did Catherine the Great, Napoleon, Freud, and Mother Teresa. All were confident to a fault. Their power elevated them above their peers and armed them with something they didn't have. Catherine had little education and spoke broken Russian but took over Mother Russia by taking power and once she assumed it she was given it. Napoleon graduated 45th out of 54 at Ecole Military academy but became the most revered military man in history, not because of anything other than his demanding and getting power. Jung and Picasso had a similar view of their supremacy. Both saw life philosophically and set out to conquer it, not on anyone else's terms, but on their own. Their work has been described as surreal and metaphysical since it was outside the sensitivity of mere mortals. They each saw themselves as a metaphorical superman and their work became a testament to their beliefs. Both were highly influenced by Nietzsche. One author said, "Carl Jung was the charismatic leader of his own mystery cult. He had a God-complex." Jung would not have disagreed. He saw himself as a god-like hero of the Mysthraic Mystery Lions. He was the lion symbolic of his astrological sign Leo. He wrote, "All our concepts are mythological images. All our impulses are instincts" (Noll p. 247). Picasso painted a picture for his mother as he left for Paris signed "I, the King." It was a Nietzschean inspired self-portrait titled *Yo* Rey.

POSITION POWER. Once the titular powers are gone so is the power. Once Chaplin could no longer promise women he could make them a star he stopped being a womanizer and he married Oona O'Neill and settled down to raise a family in Switzerland. Soichiro Honda, the entrepreneurial genius who founded the Hondo Motor empire was known in his youth as the Playboy of Hamamatsu. He resigned as head of Hondo Motors when he said, "I am too old to chase girls so I am too old to manage." An even more tragic example of waning power can be seen in the life of Oscar Wilde. While a successful playwright he had his pick of lovers. When forced to flee Britain for Paris he was relegated to paying for love. He wrote, "My companions are such as I can get, and of course, I have to pay for such friendships. How evil it is to buy love and how evil it is to sell it" (Schmidgall p. 269). Wit and comedy had been Wilde's power when on top. When he hit bottom he wrote, "I have sworn to solemnly dedicate my life to Tragedy."

POWER, LUST & RISK. Harvard psychologist David McClelland studied the derivation of power and found people with power "would rather win spectacularly than regularly" (Lemann p. 95). When playing roulette he found that those with power bet on a number that pays 35:1 odds. The more conservative types bet black or red that pays 2:1 odds. In his research on power people and achievement people he concluded, "High *nPower* people tend to mix together sexually, and value seduction or conquest highly."

Passionate people tend to chase power more than achievement or affiliation. Such people often get their personal and professional goals confused. They roll the dice for the higher odds. Chaplin was infamous for offering attractive young women, with no experience, starring roles in his films. The Little Tramp infuriated his staff by continually signing seductive women with no talent as leading lady. JFK did the same. When he moved into the White House he managed to have a long-term mistress, Pamela Turnure, hired as his wife's press secretary. Jackie was not duped too long. Few men would dare placing hookers on the payroll, but Jack had Fiddle and Faddle on the payroll.

TITILLATION. Most of the subjects in this work were titillated by doing what others saw as insane. Political associates of President Kennedy and Clinton felt their leaders had a death wish due to their wild philandering lifestyle. Fear was not in either man's vocabulary. They got a rush from daring what others feared. For them excitement equaled titillation.

195

Danger fuels the Big T (high testosterone) personality. Men and women like Howard Hughes and Amelia Earhart are not much different when it comes to taking risk. Both were Big T types who lived right on the edge in most things although Hughes had a penchant for seduction that was far greater than Amelia Earhart. But it appears he was more inclined to prove his masculinity while Earhart had no such need. Allure and the thrill was enough for her. Why did she risk her life to go where no one else had been? Because, according to psychologists she was obsessed with thrill-seeking to the detriment of her own well being. Both Chaplin and Kennedy had a similar propensity. The thrill of the chase was far more exciting then the catch for them as it is for most males. The experience of the journey is typically more important for the females.

Was inviting Marilyn Monroe aboard Air Force One worth risking the Presidency when Jack could have had her in any location he pleased? Of course not! But he was titillated by doing what others wouldn't even consider in the same way President Clinton would do some years later. Both were Big T personalities and the thrill was more important than anything else. Both presidents brought women into the White House with their wives in residence and their secretaries nearby. Charlie Chaplin once seduced the fifteen-year old Lita Grey with her mother in the next room and Marion Davies while his wife was delivering Charles Jr. in another room.

Consider the audacity of Jack Kennedy sneaking the high profile Marilyn Monroe into the White House and then having her sing at his birthday bash. Jackie was not naïve and left town rather than be embarrassed by his sexual impropriety. JFK's acts were pure folly. Biographers described them as "reckless and dangerous." The President once had a quickie with Blaze Starr in a closet while her fiancé, Earl Long, the governor of Louisiana, was having a meeting in the next room. That is living life on the edge. But it had little on Madonna's seduction of unsuspecting males in Manhattan's elevators or Carl Jung's inviting his mistress to live with him and his family. It would appear titillation is also coincident with the Big T personality.

SEDUCTION & POWER. There is sexuality in power, and power can be very seductive. But power can take many forms. There is physical power, financial power, knowledge power, the power of will, and what Mao called power at the end of a gun. Many of these sources of power are fleeting since they are externally manifested. There is always someone with more money or more bullets and with more smarts, but if the power resides within it cannot be taken. For women there is always someone younger and with greater physical beauty or charms but if her beauty is internal those external powers are not nearly so important. Anyone who allows their power to be based on some title, position, or house are setting themselves up for a schizophrenic experience or a horrible downfall when they no longer have those things.

Politicians and businessmen turn to financial power to open doors. Hughes liked to say, "I can buy any man or woman in the world," but he was never able to buy happiness since it wasn't for sale. Most great things in life are not and are seldom even appreciated while being experienced. Becoming so immersed in something you love, to follow one's bliss if you will, is the essence of internal power and passionate appeal. Those writers who are attempting to communicate a sensual experience through dialogue often use what they describe the *tumescence test*. If the scene isn't exciting to them then it is not about to be exciting to their readers. The seductive personality has power that they often don't even realize. Mother Theresa was not sure why people were so energized by her presence but they were. Cultists and evangelists have a similar hold over their followers, as do politicians like Kennedy and Clinton. A beautiful young journalist, Gloria Emerson, slept with JFK the night before his inauguration, and would write later, "He was such a stunning figure. He didn't have to lift a finger to attract women; they were drawn to him in the battalions" (Hersh p. 22).

ANOMALY OF PASSION. Why do gorgeous young females flock to the beds of married men? Why did talented young artists sleep with Picasso, a treacherous and abusive man old enough to be their grandfather? For the chance at immortality which is another form of power! One young attractive woman never married and was content to wait for her lover Picasso to show up for a weekly conjugal visit. Marie-Therese was so taken with Picasso she had his child and tolerated abusive insults. When he died, she killed herself, rather than live without him. She was repaid by being immortalized as the nude nymph being carried off by the male Minotaur – his alter-ego – in the masterpiece *The Minotaur Carries Off the Woman* (1937). She offers insight into such power with her comment, "He first raped the woman and then he worked" (Landrum 1996 p. 177). Picasso had cast his spell over her.

CHARLIE CHAPLIN – A LOLITA SYNDROME

Charles Chaplin made himself into an American treasure but was British and never quite made the transition to the nation that made him an international star. He was born in London and didn't emigrate to the U.S. until his mid-twenties. And when he was no longer welcome here he was deported, not just because he was still an alien and had refused citizenship, but due to his reputation with women and socialist sympathies.

Half-century after he had been asked to leave he would be deified as the "greatest comedian in American history." He had made the world laugh, cry, and identify with the underdog and a world in chaos came to see him as their alter-ego. Having lived in the gutters, dealt with mental disorder, emotional trauma, and being hungry he was able to impart these foibles in pantomime and with such deftness he had no peer. Passion would make him great and be what destroyed him. It is ironic that he would become the childhood idol of Walt Disney, and both men would use unrequited passion in the form of manic-depression, obsessive-compulsive disorders, fears, paranoia, and insecurities, to build huge Hollywood empires.

In 1972, Chaplin had been absent from the United States for thirty years, when the aging actor was invited back to accept an Academy Award for Special Contributions to the art. The *Little Tramp* had left in the middle of the McCarthy Hearings in 1953 at age 64 and had never returned. But he entered the country with fanfare at age 83 to accept his award from the Academy of Motion Picture Arts & Sciences. Then in 1975, at age 86, Chaplin was Knighted by Queen Elizabeth and by the turn of the century he would lead all others in voting as the greatest actor in the 20th century.

THE LITTLE TRAMP. The Little Tramp was an icon to three generations of adults and children. He sold happiness in a period when life was dismal and people had little else but fantasy in celluloid. Chaplin had given people a chance to laugh at their anguish and someone else's trauma. He was expert at depicting the tragic as transitory and the helpless and hapless as comedic. The *Little Fellow* was Horatio Alger in reverse. Filmmaker Mack Sennet called him, "just the greatest actor who ever lived." What made him so great? He made people look within, and come to terms with their own insecurities and ineptitudes. His routines transcended classes and ethnic boundaries. He amused the rich and poor, the erudite and illiterate, the well-bred and unfed. George Bernard Shaw admired his work as did Marcel Proust, and Sigmund Freud. Poet Hart Crane saw Chaplin's work "the futile gesture of the poet today" in a 1923 poem. The genesis of the Little Fellow, aka Little Tramp, substantiates the inner powers of persuasion as critical in creative success. Chaplin took what he knew and through creative imagination made it into everyman's identity. Timing was critical to his success. The world was in need of a fantasy escape from Prohibition, the 1929 Stock Market Crash, two world wars, and the Great Depression.

Chaplin's influence was pervasive, crossing many disciplines. Jack Kerouac took to the road like the Little Tramp as a hobo-like character. Walt Disney idolized Chaplin and borrowed extensively from his plots for his own animal characterizations. His influence can be found in John Steinbeck's *Grapes of Wrath*. Then as in a time warp, IBM used the Little Tramp to launch their multi-million dollar ad campaign on the PC in the early 1980's

LIBIDO GONE AMOK. Chaplin had a raging libido that was born of many emotional dysfunctions. He grew up seeing life as cheap and it left him with few scruples and a libido that needed to be sated at any cost. Early in his career, Chaplin had no money and little power, and satisfied his sexual appetites with prostitutes. Once *Chaplinitis* set in his income rose to astronomic levels and so did his seductions. Chaplin's loves and lusts were highly correlated to his income and power.

Chaplin was obsessed with young nubile females writing in his memoirs, "I have always been in love with young girls." He married four teenagers, the last three when in middle age. Mildred Harris was his first conquest when he was 28 and she 16. Her mother was aghast when he took advantage of the young girl at 14 and only when she turned up pregnant did he consent to marry her at 16. The pregnancy was a ruse it turns out but she did become pregnant and almost as if an omen the child was born severely deformed and died. The marriage ended almost before it began, but within two years he was engaged again to Florence Deshon. She had an abortion and then committed suicide after a turbulent relationship with Chaplin.

LOLITA **SYNDROME.** Charlie had three more engagements before 35 when he married his *Lolita* girl Lita Gray. Lita was 16 and the marriage produced Charles, Jr. and Syd, named after Charlie's older half-brother. Chaplin called her his "Age of innocence girl." By 44 Chaplin had become the Big Tramp when he married 19 year-old actress Paulette Goddard. Numerous accounts have him marrying her at sea on his yacht *Panacea,* and then tearing up the ships log record after a night of romance. Howard Hughes did the same on many occasions as this seemed to be a way the powerbrokers in Hollywood got what they wanted without any commitment.

Vladimir Nabokov's *Lolita* had more than just a striking resemblance to the fantasy romances of Charlie Chaplin. In Nobokov's award-winning novel, an older man Humbert, replete with toothbrush mustache, seduces a virginal young girl. The contrast between the story and Chaplin's seductions are far more than coincidental. Chaplin's second wife Lita closely resembles that of Lolita and Lita's name was legally Lillita McMurray. It appears Nobokov had used Chaplin's urges as the basis of his eloquent words and actions. And his most scandalous seduction offer validity to this *Lolita Syndrome* when the scoundrel Chaplin stole the teen daughter of playwright Eugene O'Neill from his two sons who had been courting Oona O'Neill. Oona was an aspiring actress when their incorrigible father entered the scene and after a few dates and the need of some semblance of a family due to a paternity suit he proposed and she accepted. This was his fourth teenage wife and he was now fifty-four and Oona was just 18. Her father was furious.

PASSIONATE PERSONA

Time magazine on June 8, 1998 wrote, "From the start, his extraordinary athleticism, expressive grace, impeccable timing, endless inventiveness and genius for hard work set him apart." The article characterized Chaplin as "the most funny when most afraid." Charlie Chaplin pioneered in showing that speech is the language of adversity and hatred, and how silence is often more romantic than words. In other words, a fantasy is far more exciting than any reality, a fact of life lost on most people.

SATYR. Chaplin referred to his appendage as The Eighth Wonder of the World, since, according to reliable sources, it was far above average. Irving Wallace spoke of him as a "human sex-machine" capable of as many as "six bouts in succession with scarcely five minutes rest in between" (Wallace p. 95). His perversities included voyeurism. The on-screen funny man had erected a high-power telescope in his Beverly Hills bedroom trained on the bedroom of infamous libertine John Barrymore.

Chaplin's conquests are legend. They crossed all political, religious, ethnic, and professional bounds. Chaplin never discriminated in his philandering. He had his way with leading ladies, social acquaintances, hookers, wives of friends, waitresses met on the street, and any other woman who crossed his path. Did he use power for seduction? Absolutely! He was an obsessive-compulsive who had to have virtually every female he met and like Howard Hughes actually proposed to many acquaintances on the first date and offered jobs to any woman who would go to bed with him. A short list of his conquests include: Clare Sheridan, cousin of Winston Churchill, political activist Florence Deshon, actresses Mabel Normand, Edna Pruviance, Lita Grey, Georgia Hale, Pola Negri, Paulette Goddard, Joan Barry, Peggy Hopkins Joyce, May Reeves, Ziegfield Follies star Louise Brooks, British actress Lari Maritza, and William Randolph Hearst's mistress Marion Davies.

The licentious are often victims of their own need. One young aspiring actress, Joan Barry, met him at a screen test and succumbed to his charms. But she wanted more and began stalking him when he tried to jilt her. She showed up at his home at all hours of the night. In May 1943, Barry broke into his home and served thirty days in jail. She had the last laugh when she filed a paternity suit against him on moral charges that would result in a notorious trial that lasted months. His paranoia over going to jail was behind his proposal to Oona O'Neill. Despite his duplicity, the Tramp found himself in a media war of words that left him with names like "svengali" and "lecherous hound." He was acquitted, but was required to pay child support for Barry's child even though it wasn't his. Why? Because it came out in the trail that he had impregnated her twice before and each time had forced her to have an abortion.

As with most men afflicted with satyriasis, Chaplin was never quite able to separate his lusts from his life's work. Leading ladies were fair game for him. If getting them to bed meant signing them up then he gave them a contract. For Chaplin play and reality was an ill-defined line. He had an uncontrollable urge to seduce every woman in every movie, not unusual for the obsessive personality. As a star-maker he was a perverse caretaker but the care was his.

Examples of women who worked for him and became lovers were Mildred Harris, Lita Grey, Joan Barry, and Oona O'Neill. Joan Barry, who would file sexual discrimination charges, had actually failed the screen test and was obviously a troubled young woman who his executives feared. But logic and propriety were way down the list of priorities for Chaplin. When one of his stars turned up pregnant he encouraged them to get rid of the child or forfeit their budding career. In a few instances he suggested they perform their own abortions as in the case of Lita Grey and Joan Barry. Florence Deshon followed his advice and months later committed suicide.

As with most satyrs, once Charlie had a woman he no longer had any interest in her. Lita Grey told a reporter that once they were married Charlie seldom even spoke to her. She told of him arriving home only to get up in the middle of the night and leave her and their two sons. He took no interest in his children. He told lover Georgia Hale, "The one reason I married is because I wanted children. I wanted to look at the little bundle of flesh and feel that it was part of me. And I was sadly disappointed. I didn't have that feeling at all" (Milton p. 285). Chaplin was not a good husband or father but in his defense he had no role model for the job.

EARLY LIFE EXPERIENCES

Chaplin's early life was a series of mishaps that molded him with serious emotional problems including paranoia, bipolar affliction, and obsessions and compulsions. He had gotten them legitimately as his mother was repeatedly institutionalized in London during his childhood for manic-depression and schizophrenia. The King, as his mother called him as a child, was often hungry and without adequate clothes. Charles Spencer Chaplin was born on April 16, 1889 in the squalor of South London to show business parents Charles Sr. and Hannah Hill. Charlie wrote in his memoirs that he never saw his father more than three times before age eight. His mother was a singer and performed with her husband, but he was gone most of the time.

Hannah spent a great deal of time in and out of mental hospitals and his alcoholic father would die of cirrhosis at 37 when Charlie was ten. His mother treated Charlie as a King but since he was forced to wear hand-me-down clothes from older half-brother Syd he hardly looked like royalty. It would be the genesis of the Little Tramp. Charlie and his half-brother grew up in abject poverty and lived in flop-houses, orphanages, and a poorhouse. The cruel reality of life in the gutter was indelibly imprinted in a boy who was without role models or mentors.

Learning to cope proved important for Chaplin's later work as a vaudeville comedian and in Hollywood. When his mother was taken to a mental ward at age six, he was sent to live with relatives and then when that didn't work to an orphanage. When she was released so was he but this churning would take place another three times. He had little formal schooling and was illiterate until his teens, but was taught to read and write at Hanwell Orphanage. It is interesting that once he became successful he would become a book fanatic once and haunted books stores in Hollywood. By ten his formal education was over. His father had influence in vaudeville and arranged to get his boy an acting job in a traveling vaudeville company as a clog dancer. The job with The Eight Lancaster Lads lasted only a few months but groomed him for a life on stage. His hero of the time was French clown Marceline and he often mimicked his hero.

SUCCESS IMPRINTS. Chaplin showed early signs of dysfunctional and anti-social behavior. A refusal to follow instructions succeeded in getting him fired from his first few acting jobs. It is apparent he had inherited his bipolar affliction from his mother. In 1903 he played a newspaper boy Billy in *Sherlock Holmes* and was in the *Casey Circus* before joining the Karno Pantomime Troupe that brought him to America in 1912. A Keystone Film executive, Adam Kessell saw him perform in New York and offered him $125 a week in May 1913.

Early trauma conditioned Charlie to fight for what he got but also to appreciate class differences. His later genius was finding humor in adversity and it was a natural since he had lived his parts. The Little Tramp was Charlie in a survival mode on the streets of London at the turn of the century. Having an alcoholic father is no fun. But for an actor knowing how to play a drunk it can be quite instructive. Who else can understand the nuances of a man trying to talk without slurring words, walk without bumping into things, or keeping ones eyes focused. Charlie was never so funny as when acting the drunk and trying to appear sober as his father had tried when he was a child.

Chaplin's hobo routine dressed to the nines replete with top hat and cane, and attempting to appear chic was hilarious, not because of the tragedy but because of trying to be what one is not. Consider the era. Chaplin's routines were all played out to returning war veterans, vagrants, and people attempting to cope without food or housing in the Great Depression. These were pervasive scenes in the 1920's and 1930's. The *Little Tramp* offered a fantasy escape to a world gone mad and an economy without banks or hope. It is not an accident that his pinnacle occurred at the very height of the world's greatest chaos. Charlie was funniest when portraying hobos trying to act sophisticated, when wearing clothes three sizes too large, hats that didn't fit and shoes three sized too big. All this had been life for Charlie that was not humorous but stark reality.

Charlie also learned from his mother that love and lust were the same and that children were only by-products of pursuing emotional needs. Syd had been named after a man his mother never married, a concept that would be adopted by Charlie in America. After Charlie's birth, Hannah took up with another vaudeville star Leo Dryden, and that short relationship produced another child when Charlie was two. The father took off with the boy and his mother took up with another man before he too left her. Charlie and Syd ended up on the street or in strange homes. Few actors would have found anything funny in wearing clothes retrieved from a trashcan and then trying to act as if they were purchased at Brooks Brothers. But such was the reality of Charlie's early life. He somehow learned to laugh at the impropriety of life since the alternative was to cry. Tragedy was the birth of his humor.

Once when Charlie was five his mother came home drunk. At the theater she was unable to go on and his father in a panic pushed his young son out on the stage and told him to sing. The shocked boy went out and sang "Jack Jones," a song about a pushcart peddler who had taken on airs. His performance was received with huge applause and three pounds of coins, and a star was born. It would take some years for the imprint to gain momentum but the Little Tramp was really born that night when his mother was drunk. The importance of this story is that it was told to his friend Harry Crocker thirty years later at the peak of his success in Hollywood.

The Chaplin mystique was born in the squalor of London and that included his extraordinary athleticism, poetic grace, impeccable timing, indomitable spirit and renegade personality. At the time he didn't recognize what was happening but it did. Without the tragedy of those early years the Little Tramp wouldn't have taken form. All the clothes, body language, mimicry, poignant messages, and rags to riches scenes were a by-product of a tragic childhood that would have destroyed a lesser person.

BIRTH OF A COMIC. When Charlie was 14 he looked ten and it allowed him to play parts otherwise not available like playing the kid in Sherlock Holmes. His years in vaudeville proved important since the whole shtick was to use drunks to get laughs. His transformation into a comic occurred when he was chosen to play a part in Cassey's Court Circus. His character was to wear a top hat, but the hat was too small and kept falling over his nose and covering his eyes. In an attempt to correct the problem the teen stuffed the hat with paper, but while on stage the paper fell out and the hat fell down over his eyes. The unrehearsed scene brought the house down. Years later he related the story to the media saying, "I had stumbled on the secret of being funny – unexpectedly. It works every time. I walk on stage elegantly and sit on a cat. Littler nervous shocks make you laugh" (Milton p. 38).

By seventeen Charlie landed a job as a mime in Fred Karno's Mumming Birds. His roommate was Stan Laurel and the two toured the United States in 1913. During one tour he was signed by Mack Sennett to make one-reel comedies. In the first year he made 35 films, but was disruptive and unruly. He was close to being fired for insubordination when Max Sennett told him "Improve or else." A disillusioned Chaplin told his friend Stan Laurel, "I'm going to get out of this business. I'll never catch on. It's too fast – the cinema is little more than a fad" (Milton p. 60).

During this period Chaplin's abnormal behavior became apparent. He was highly insecure, manic, and compulsive. He seldom went to bed before 2 a.m.

SYBARITIC GENIUS

He blamed others for his failures and was not the favorite actor to work with. The cast at Keystone Pictures told Max Sennet, "Chaplin is an s.o.b., and impossible to work with." (Milton p. 69). While filming the Keystone series he finally told Sennett that he wanted to direct himself and knowing that if it didn't work he would be fired so he agreed to work for nothing. In other words, he bet his salary on his self-belief and told Sennett, "If the film is no good I will pay the $1500 cost of production" (Milton 69). Sennett agreed. His first film as director was *Caught in the Rain*. It was released in late 1914 and was a huge success. The next was *The Tramp* in 1915 and by the time he had made *The Kid* (1921) he was both rich and famous. Within four years he was making more money than anyone in Hollywood history.

CRISES & AN EPIPHANY

Chaplin never had a normal home life or even a home. He almost drowned in the Tames at age eleven. But for him chaos proved to be providential and led to a transformation into greatness. The journey would be slow but the genius of Chaplin was born in the tragedy of life in London slums. As the story goes what doesn't kill you will temper you and this was true for Charlie Chaplin.

When Max Sennet told Chaplin in 1914 to improve or go back to England, Chaplin got a wake-up call. The Keystone Film Company was filming in Southern California on a rainy day when he his true transformation took place. On this day the crew and actors were playing pinochle. The loner Chaplin was never known to fraternize and it wasn't surprising that he was off somewhere pouting on his own. But the hyper Charlie got bored and wandered into wardrobe, donned a pair of old outsized pants, shoes five sizes too big, a cane, and a top hat so large it came to rest on his nose. He painted on a mustache and came out strutting like a drunk trying to appear sober. He kept falling into make-believe manholes and down imaginary steps. On a roll he started acting the role of a bum trying to be chic, a role he knew well, the surreal that was hardly real. The card players including old friend Fatty Arbuckle cracked up. Max Sennett had been watching the whole scene from the wings. He looked at his renegade comic and told him, "Chaplin, you do exactly as you are doing now in your next picture. Remember to do it in that get-up. Otherwise, dear old England is beckoning" (Milton p. 60). What had Chaplin done? He had created the all-time underdog – The Tramp – a born loser that everyone loves. His choice of attire was "shabby gentility" the garb of the hobo who he would make famous.

POWER & PASSION

PSYCHOSEXUAL ENERGY

Only a lecher could marry four teenage girls and not think it was weird. When the media questioned his need for young girls he told them, "Virgins are the most beautiful form of human life. I have always been in love with young girls, not in an amorous way (ha). I just loved to caress and fondle her – not passionately – just to have her in my arms" (Milton p. 45).

Libidinal energy pervaded every aspect of Chaplin's life and work. He was an infamous voyeur and many of his scenes were subliminal attempts at sating his need for sexual titillation. His most famous film was *The Little Tramp* that elicited a comment from film critic Sime Silverman who reported in *Variety*, "Never anything dirtier was placed upon the screen than Chaplin's *The Tramp* (Milton p. 95). Silverman had already demeaned his earlier movie *Work* saying, "The usual Chaplin work of late, mussy, messy, and dirty." When he depicted cross-dressing in *Woman,* the *Chicago Tribune* wrote, "as coarse a film as I have ever seen." Swedish censors banned the film.

By 1918 the entertainment media was hailing him as a "vulgar genius." While Chaplin was producing his masterpiece *The Kid* (1920) he met and fell in love with a socialist actress named Florence Deshon. As was his habit he proposed marriage despite already being married to Midlred Harris. During this period he found time for a trip to England and seduced Winston Churchill's cousin, artist Clare Sheridan. On the same trip he had a liaison with Brit Rebecca West during the same time he was carrying on a torrid affair with Claire Windsor.

Chaplin slept with virtually every one of his leading ladies including Mabel Normand, Georgia Hale and Edna Purviance, as well as secretary May Collins. All left his employee as soon as the affair of the heart had subsided. His affairs were often heartless encounters with him having sex with Marion Davies in the house as his second wife was giving birth to his son Syd. During a divorce trial with Lita Grey he was forced to fire leading lady Georgia Hale because of their affair. He feared her testimony at the trial.

UNIVERSAL APPEAL. *The Tramp* characterization was never completely masculine or feminine making it androgynous and appealing to a wide range of theater patrons. Biographer Milton said, "Chaplin instinctively understood that androgyny was in tune with modern temperament." Chaplin was close to many of Hollywood's gays and had problems with his own gender identity. Gays identified with Chaplin's cross-dressing and adaptable gender roles. Young poet Hart Crane was enchanted by *The Kid* and wrote a long poem on the nuances of the characterization. Hart saw The Kid as a "dispossessed and sexually indeterminate character who Chaplin made heroic" (Milton p. 182).

Hollywood experts were perplexed when Chaplin abruptly stopped using the Little Tramp character. He wanted to make serious movies but his fans longed for more of the underdog. His Archetype was an institution and a license to mint money. He could have made many more films but by the late thirties he dumped the character and never again made a film with him.

Despite an ardent appeal from fans his first serious comedy was *The Great Dictator* in 1939. In this movie he played dual characters, the tyrant Hitler and Jewish tailor, a dichotomy for which Chaplin could identify. Chaplin then acquired the rights to a multiple wife killer movie *Monsieur Verdoux* from the blacklisted Orson Welles and made it into a comical thriller.

DIVERGENT THINKING

Chaplin lived and loved way outside the bounds of convention, mostly due to an early identity with the common folk, a bipolar and obsessive personality, and paranoia that was rampant in all things. He sympathized with the socialist cause and supported the Russian Revolution, not for their ideology, but because they represented the masses not the classes. He adamantly refused to conform or adhere to any social decorum and it came to haunt him. Friend and fellow actor Stan Laurel said, "He was a very eccentric person." Others described him as anti-social, lewd, secretive, shy and Machiavellian. As a prelude to sex he read erotic passages from *Lady Chatterly's Lover* or *Fanny Hill* (Wallace p. 95).

To Chaplin romance was getting laid. Relationships were not something he understood or wanted. He was a control freak in the largest possible sense making sharing a life with someone impossible. Females were there as a conquest and little else. He used women to sate his libidinal drives and when they had they were of no further use. Chaplin went through wild mood swings due to his manic-depression and when up was euphoric and when down morose. When manic he would become a nocturnal animal stalking the streets of Los Angeles. Ex-wives spoke of his obsessive-compulsive nature with him taking 8-10 baths a day. Half-brother Syd described his wild mood swings with biographer Milton sayhing, "He was often too nervous to drive a car." His perfectionism was responsible for missing every movie deadline and not one film ever was released when scheduled. If it wasn't perfect, he refused to allow it to be released regardless of cost.

Chaplain experienced a number of emotional breakdowns caused by his need to push the limits personally and professionally. He worked with such intensity he would be completely drained to the point of physical and emotional exhaustion and would retreat into his own inner sanctum for refuge. Like Howard Hughes and Walt Disney, both manic-depressives, Chaplin would just disappear until reenergized and able to cope with life's debacles.

CREATIVE INSPIRATIONS

The king of silent films made eighty movies. Most were made at his firm United Artists, formed in 1919 in concert with Mary Pickford, Douglas Fairbanks, and D. W. Griffith. This studio produced many of the most famous comedies in history including: *The Kid* (1921), *A Woman of Paris* (1923), *The Gold Rush* (1925), and *The Circus* (1928), *City Lights* (1931), *Modern Times* (1936), and *The Great Dictator* (1941). *Variety* called, *Gold Rush*, "The greatest comedy ever filmed."

His role as the *Great Dictator* was interesting due to the many striking similarities between Chaplin and Hitler. Chaplin was not Jewish or anti-Semitic, but it appears he had an affinity for the Fuhrer's Master Race thesis, although he denied it. Both men were obsessive-compulsive, manic-depressive, small in stature, wore identical mustaches, and were born four days apart in Europe. Both were engaged to the sultry actress Palo Negri, and both were Machiavellian control-freaks who used power to seduce for their own ends. Chaplin was hilarious as Adenoid Hynkel in *The Great Dictator,* but the film never reached the acclaim of his Little Tramp characterizations.

Charlie Chaplin was a satyr. His unrequited ardor without doubt was at the seat of his unscrupulous behavior, but it also was behind his artistic genius. Passion made him rich and famous and a scoundrel. He would never have been named the Greatest Actor in the 20th century if he had been more normal but young women would have been far safer had he been.

JOHN F. KENNEDY – PROVOCATIVE PRESIDENT

A study on the average approval ratings of American presidents in the last half of the 20th century showed John F. Kennedy the clear leader with a 76 percent rating compared to Eisenhower with 69 percent, Jimmy Carter at 62 percent, and George Bush Sr. at 66 percent. Since power in politics comes from the people Kennedy's power was predicated on his image. Where did this originate? Unquestionably, JFK was endowed with good looks, a smile that could melt butter, and charisma. But it was his passion for the moment that separated him from the pack and elevated him to the 35th President of the United States. Did his fervor have a downside? You bet! Was he a more blatant philanderer than Bill Clinton? Absolutely! But what made him a poor husband contributed to his election to the Senate and Presidency. It was also the same quality that armed him for battle with Nikita Khrushchev.

Kennedy made it to the U.S. Senate by age thirty and beat incumbent stalwart Henry Cabot Lodge for a Senate seat in 1952. A year after becoming a senator, he married Jacqueline Bouvier and had three children, Caroline, John Fitzgerald, Jr., and a second son who died in infancy in the middle of his Presidency. He won the Pulitzer Prize for biography with his 1957 work titled *Profiles of Courage*. By forty-three he had become the youngest President in American history. His legacy will be his breakthrough Civil Rights legislation, educational reform, and Peace Corps creation, all part of his Alliance for Progress program. But he will forever be known for the ill-fated Bay of Pigs Invasion of Cuba in April, 1961, and his gutsy stand-down of Nikita Khrushchev during the Fall of 1962.

Jack Kennedy never had to work, take risks, or share his power. But he did daily. Why? Because he had a passion to seek his destiny, to self-actualize, and to play to the hilt the hand he had been dealt. Seymore Hersh wrote of the Kennedy mystique saying, "There was no tomorrow. He was willing to take enormous risks to gratify his obsession with sex" (p. 222). Political associate Lem Billings wrote, "Jack knew he was using women to prove his masculinity and sometimes it depressed him."

A HIGH TESTOSTERONE PERSONALITY

There is a price we pay for electing individuals with passion. We benefit from their insatiable energy, enthusiasm, articulate ability, and temerity to make tough decisions. Such people are not prone to back down in the face of aggression, are innovative, and more intense than less driven personalities.

Such men are capable of persuading Congress and their Cabinet to see things their way. Is here a downside? Of course there is, since our greatest strengths are always our greatest weaknesses and such intensity can spill over into seductions beyond norms or needs.

Electing a Big T personality (high-testosterone & high thrill-seeking) to office brings with it the good and the bad. One doesn't exist without the other, so why do pundits not understand such individuals are not about to change once in office? The leopard does not change his spots any more than Kennedy or Clinton were about to spot sleeping around once in the Oval Office. Big T's come equipped with inordinate creative energy, an aggressive attitude, a penchant for seduction, and the need to live on the edge. You get it all in that same Big T package, not just the parts you like. It is naive to think that electing Pat Robertson to office would cause him to keep his religious beliefs out of his decision-making, just as it was not to be for Jimmy Carter to become a hard-ass once in office, or Reagan to become a hands-on type.

Jack Kennedy had flare. It proved to be his defining quality that attracted legions of voters in 1960. He fit the 60's view of the All-American boy who was brash, young, rich, idealistic, and beautiful. He was all of those and rode the crest of the wave that proved dangerous and exciting. But that was his style, it got him elected and it got him laid and that was what Jack was all about. He never hid his beliefs nor his passions.

PASSIONATE PERSONA

Friend and fellow lothario George Smathers of Florida said of Kennedy, "Jack has the most active libido of any man I've ever known. No one was off limits to Jack, not your wife, your mother or sister" (Hersh p. 1997). Jack was incorrigible. Biographer Thomas Reeves (1997) wrote, "Jack hated to lose at anything." That competitive nature is apparent in his professional and personal life. He hosted wild crazy White House parties that turned into swimming pool orgies with as many as twelve party girls and his closest male friends. Jack actually believed he had to have sex daily or would be unable to sleep, saying "I get a terrible migraine if I don't get laid every day."

In the *Dark Side of Camelot*, Pulitzer Prize winning author Seymour Hersh wrote, "JFK was willing to take enormous risks to gratify his obsession with sex" (Hersh p. 222). Hersh spoke of Jack's addiction to *ménage a trios* sexual encounters. His passion was such that he had secretary Evelyn Lincoln and Press Secretary Pierre Salinger place two party girls nicknamed Fiddle and Faddle on their payroll. Hersh wrote, "When Jackie left he hit the pool with

Fiddle and Faddle" (Hersh p. 238). Both women traveled on Air Force One for the express purpose of sating his needs while on a trip.

CONFIDENT CHARM. Kennedy's charismatic appeal did not stop at women. His appeal transcended age, ethnic groups, and even political parties. Biographer Reeves spoke of Kennedy as a "man's man." He wrote, "The older ladies mothered him and the young ones fell in love" (Reeves p. 79). Columnist Rowland Evans said, "Jack was simply the most appealing human being I ever met." But not everyone was so impressed with his strong sense of self. After a dinner with Kennedy, Franklin D. Roosevelt Jr. said, "I'd never met somebody so completely obsessed in themselves" (Reeves p. 151). Even Jackie told the media, "If I were to draw him I would draw a very tiny body and a very big head" (Reeves p. 144). In another cynical moment in response to attending the opera, she told the media, "The only music Jack likes is *Hail to the Chief*."

EARLY LIFE EXPERIENCES

Jack Kennedy was the second born of nine children to Rose and Joe Kennedy. He had a great role model in his father both for professional success and a philandering lifestyle. Joe Kennedy was a brash entrepreneur who became a billionaire and then Ambassador to Great Britain. Along the way he seduced such famous women as Gloria Swanson. His long-suffering wife Rose survived by running off to France to buy new clothes or art. Many of Joe's trysts took place right in the Kennedy home. Joe once brought a mistress into the Hyannis Port home to live for an extended stay. Jack admitted to Clare Booth Luce, who was writing on the Kennedy clan, "Dad told all the boys to get laid as often as possible." He told Luce, "I can't get to sleep unless I've had a lay." (Reeves p. 41).

The Kennedys have long been associated with Massachusetts politically, but Jack had more affinity elsewhere. He was born in New York and enjoyed life in Palm Beach more than in the Bay State. As a child he lived in both Brookline, Massachusetts and in Riverside, New York. He spent little time in the Bay State except for his days at Choate and Harvard. Summer vacations were spent at Hyannis Port. Each winter the clan went to Palm Beach and the kids came down when out of school.

Jack was the second son. Joe Jr., not Jack, was the one groomed for a political career. Jack was a shy as a child and grew up loving books and considered a career in journalism. He was tested in school with a 119 IQ, some twenty points lower than Madonna in this book. He loved books on history, economics and political heroes. He was one of the first to become a speed-reader and was tested reading at twice the speed of an average person. As President this skill allowed him to scan documents and provide a lucid analysis leaving associates bewildered. He attended Canterbury and Choate prep schools in preparation for an Ivy League education and then enrolled at Princeton, but was forced to withdraw due to back problems. He graduated *cum laude* from Harvard with a B.A. in history, economics and government in June 1940. He then took off for the sun and sand of California and attended Stanford for three months where he shared an apartment with actor Robert Stack, who later recalled, "I've known many of the great Hollywood stars and only a very few of them seemed to hold the attention for women that JFK did. He'd just look at them and they'd tumble" (Reeves p. 54).

Jack had virtually no home life. He had no role model for being a husband or father. Joe was the dominant influence in his life. Rose was off in France looking for art, antiques, and the latest fashions. When not in boarding school the kids were left with servants. Joe was a stern taskmaster and businessman and philanderer, and the only male role model Jack had growing up.

CRISES & AN EPIPHANY

Jack Kennedy was given the last rites of the Roman Catholic Church three times prior to age 35. He was a sickly child and his infirmities grew worse as he aged. Everyone in the family thought he was destined for a short life. A young friend from Choate, Charles Spalding told the media, "He had to live for today, because he didn't think very long in the future."

Jack's first serious brush with trauma came when his younger sister Rosemary was institutionalized for retardation early in life. Then when in the waning days of the war Joe Jr. was killed in the explosion of an experimental bomber in Europe. The heir apparent was dead before thirty leaving Jack to carry on the family mantle. Jack's favorite sister Kathleen was killed in a plane crash in 1949. All this death conditioned Jack to live life in the present and to hell with the consequences. Death and illness had pervaded him personally and instilled a sense of mortality not found in most people until much later in life.

Jack's bad back kept him from playing his beloved football at Harvard. It would also plague him throughout his short life. In 1954 he was forced to have a double-fusion of his vertebrae. During the operation he went into a coma, and according to Joe, twice came within twenty minutes of dying. His back problems came close to killing him since the operation was compounded by malaria and Addison's Disease. There is some conjecture that his back could have been responsible for his death in Dallas. He was in a neck brace that day, and was unable to bend over in any way. The first bullet wouldn't have been fatal, according to doctors, but Jack was unable to react as most men due to his brace. Seymour Hersh felt the brace caused his death.

Kennedy was a valiant soul. Despite his physical disabilities he wanted to go to war and fight. He used Joe's enormous influence to have the Navy ignore his physical condition and give him a commission. Once accepted in the Navy he was shipped to the Pacific Theater and took command of PT-109. One August night in 1943, in somewhat suspect circumstances, PT-109 was cut in half by a Japanese destroyer. His boat was not supposed to be where it was according to biographer Reeves (1997) and in an act of contrition Kennedy swam for four hours in a manic attempt to save his men. He saved three swimming in the open Pacific and was awarded the Navy Cross for valor. Much controversy surrounded the event according to biographers. Most telling were the comments he had made to mistress Ellen Rometsch, "They didn't know whether to give me a medal or kick me out" (Reeves p. 68). Privately, he joked about not being much of a hero for PT-109 and after the Bay of Pigs he told a reporter, "The whole story was more fucked up than Cuba" (Reeves p. 68).

For much of Kennedy's life he suffered from adrenal failure known as Addison's Disease and could not have survived without constant medication. He contracted malaria while in the South Pacific and the combination led to a constant barrage of pills and drugs to relieve the pain. While visiting London he took ill and an attending doctor told female friend Pamela Churchill, "he doesn't have a year to live" (Reeves p. 93). When his friend George Smathers cautioned him to slow down, Jack said, "I can't. The drugs will finish me off by the time I'm 45. The point is you've got to live every day like it's your last day on earth. That's what I'm doing" (Reeves p. 95).

CHARISMATIC INTENSITY

Journalist Gloria Emerson was another one of Kennedy's women. The Ivy League journalist told a biographer, "I was almost hypnotized by the sight of this man" (Hersh p. 22). Marilyn Monroe told her psychiatrist Kennedy was her "commander-in-chief," adding, "He is greatest and most powerful man in the world" (Hersh p. 104). Most biographers agree that Marilyn was in love with Kennedy but for him it was little more than lust for a Hollywood starlet. For her it was romance, for Kennedy it was just a fling, and when she couldn't have him she killed herself.

JFK brought to Washington a magical flair that became known as Camelot. A Choate roommate and lifelong friend Lem Billings told the media, "Jack always could charm the birds out of the trees." Hersh added, "When Jack appeared at a party the temperature went up 105 degrees" (Hersh p. 13). In *My Story* (1977), Judith Campbell Exner said, "He was an amazing man. When you talked to him you felt as though you were the only person on the planet." She and other women who knew he was using them to satisfy his lust agreed that he had a unique ability to look women right in the eyes and forget all else in the room. They felt truly special in his presence and therefore capitulated to his wanton needs.

A LIVE-ON-THE-EDGE LIFE

Jack Kennedy could be a poster boy for the Big T personality. He was in a hurry, fearless, and impatient with anyone so inclined. Kennedy did everything double-time including reading, driving, thinking, talking, and romance. He had a short attention span as do most Type A's. Thomas Reeves related a story of when Kennedy was discharged and told to go to Arizona and read books and rest. A friend was with him and they went horseback riding. Instead of resting his body from a crippling injury, bad back, malaria, and exhaustion he "would charge his horse down the mountainside. He loved speed. He was a daring fellow" (Reeves p. 74). Kennedy's commander in the South Pacific said, "Jack got very wild. Some of my old guys said he was crazy and would get them killed" (Reeves p. 69).

Kennedy's greatest daring took place in his love life. He was incorrigible, and took chances beyond the pale of most men. He indiscriminately slept with women from every socio-economic group and as President had sex regularly with a former Communist Party member. Bright and well-connected women graced his sheets as did socialites, movie stars, and wives of friends. Jack took risks that made Bill Clinton look like a priest. Secret Service agents felt Kennedy's womanizing was a serious threat to national security. Women without clearance walked into the White House. The FBI assigned to security feared Russian plants, blackmailers, or even potential assassins, since his machinations took place at the most heated portion of the Cold War. Former FBI agents told Hersh "the women were everywhere." Most of the agents loved Jack since he was a man's man but they were never allowed to do their job when it came to his women. The agents wanted them checked for guns, recording devices, and lethal drugs.

According to biographers, Hollywood starlets were flown in for the sole purpose of Jack's pleasure. Friend Frank Sinatra and brother-in-law Peter

Lawford, supplied the President with a steady stream of Hollywood actresses. Agent Larry Newman told Hersh, "If she wasn't a starlet, we didn't know who she was." He also disclosed Kennedy's long history with STD's – sexually transmitted disease. Newman commented, "We couldn't even protect the President from getting a venereal disease" (Hersh p. 230). Newman loved JFK, but said his role was relegated to keeping tabs on Jackie so that neither were embarrassed. When the First Lady was on her way back to the White House the phone lines lit up and the party girls left quickly.

MARITAL FLING. One of Jack's early scrapes with disaster occurred during a partying period in the Kennedy enclave in Palm Beach. He had just returned from the South Pacific in 1946 and was being groomed by his ambitious father for a political career. But Jack had just escaped death and was more into partying than politicking. One wild weekend of booze, sex, and partying ended in a marital lark with a much-married Palm Beach socialite Durie Malcolm. According to one of the Kennedy girls, Joe had a "shit fit" when he found out and sent a reliable friend to Palm Beach to have the whole affair removed from the records. Malcolm was an attractive twice-divorced party animal and the two married during a wild drinking soiree according to long-term Kennedy advisor and confidant Charles Spalding. Spalding characterized the whole episode as a "lark," but also confirmed the two appeared before a Justice of the Peace in early 1946 since he was the one Joe sent down to get rid of the evidence. Both Spalding and Cardinal Cushing of Boston confirmed the episode in *The Dark Side of Camelot*.

PSYCHOSEXUAL ENERGY

Passion was the dominating theme in the life and loves of Jack Kennedy. He had few peers when it came to chasing and catching beautiful young women. And one was seldom enough to sate his raging libido. He seriously believed that if he didn't have sex every night with a different woman he would not be able to sleep and told political advisor Bob Baker, "You know, I get a migraine if I don't get a strange piece of ass every day" (Hersh p. 389). On first meeting Kennedy in Washington one seasoned politician said, "He had more fancy young girls flying in from all over the country than anyone could count." Milton Berle's wife was shocked at the White House shenanigans. She told Hugh Sidey of *Time* (Nov. 17, 1997), "If all the women who claim to have slept with Kennedy are telling the truth, he would not have the strength enough to lift a teacup."

The Secret Service watched helplessly as strange women entered Kennedy's White House quarters on a daily basis. They didn't dare make a ruckus as they liked their jobs and admired their fun-loving boss. But the relationship with one gorgeous divorcee Judith Campbell Exner was flammable. Campbell had been introduced to Kennedy by Frank Sinatra during a Las Vegas campaign stop. She was newly divorced, but unknown to Kennedy she was also sleeping with a Mafia kingpin, Sam Giancana. It has since come out that she was often an unwitting messenger carrying packages between the two during the Presidential election. Giancana was helping with the Democratic political campaign in Chicago, so critical to winning the election. The severity of this liaison comes to the fore with Giancana's unsolved murder during the Church Committee's investigation into the Bay of Pigs in 1975.

Associated Press reporter James Baker, assigned to Hollywood wrote, "JFK loved it out here. He was a man who was addicted to sex and if you want sex this is the place" (Hersh p. 329). JFK's Hollywood seductions reads like a Who's Who of Tinsletown including Jayne Mansfield, Lee Remick, Sophia Loren, Marlene Dietrich, Joan Crawford, Audrey Hepburn, Zsa Zsa Gabor, Arlene Dahl, Sonja Henie and Norma Shearer. One of his more dangerous liaisons was with Ellen Rometsch, a high-class prostitute he slept with right through the Cuban Missile Crisis. Kennedy was never aware that she was born in East Germany and had been a member of the Communist Party in her youth. He was aware of her gorgeous body and a willingness to participate in his most outlandish fantasies and was oblivious of her potential for disaster.

Another example of his penchant for disaster was Jackie finding a pair of women's panties stuffed in the pillow on her bed. Obviously, one of his more adventurous female friends thought it would be cute to leave a memento of her visit. Jackie was not amused and walked into his office and said, "Would you please shop around and see who these belong to. They're not my size" (Reeves p. 241). One lovely British tennis star, whom had a number of trysts with Kennedy wrote in her little black address book of his renegade behavior:

> *Jack had much more of an Englishman's attitude toward*
> *women. He really didn't give a damn. He liked to have*
> *them around and he liked to enjoy himself but he was quite*
> *unreliable. He did as he pleased.* (Reeves p. 75).

A MAN FOR HIS TIME

Kennedy became president during a period of "revolt" that permeated the tumultuous 60's. The nuclear family of the 50's was gone. His death was out of synch with reality and quite surreal. It was the stuff of make-believe and the movies. That Camelot era was magic and a magician was sitting in the most prestigious post in the world. His glamorous image attracted women and the consummate iconoclast saw fit to indulge his most perverse fantasies. But his heritage, despite his philandering, will be the nation's first Civil Rights Laws, the New Frontier Legislation that created the Peace Corps, an Alliance for Progress – the Latin version of the Marshall Plan, and standing down Khrushchev in the Cuban Missile Crisis. He believed fervently that, "Mankind must put an end to war or war will put an end to mankind."

DIVERGENT LEADERSHIP

Kennedy said, "Forgive, but never forget." But even more profound was, "Conformity is the jailer of freedom and the enemy of growth." He was a non-conformist and renegade who led by daring what many other political aspirants would not. Conventional politicians live within certain parameters, but renegades like Kennedy see the world outside the box and operate accordingly, to the furor of those steeped in tradition. The definition of innovation came out of Harvard where Kennedy had gone to school with a teacher named Schumpeter saying, "Innovation is creative destruction." That was Kennedy's style to the chagrin of advisors and cabinet members.

One example was Kennedy's disdain for administrative matters. He preceded Reagan in a total disdain for details, and showed little interest in the administrative aspects of leadership. He understood that a leaders job is to provide vision for the future and delegate the little stuff to staff personnel. This flippant disregard for anything quantitative frustrated Washington bureaucrats, White House luminaries, and congressional leaders. Politicians are typically steeped in budgets, crossing all the t's, and dotting all the i's. We now know that Kennedy was right and the bureaucrats were wrong, especially if change is important to progress, which it is in a dynamic world. Kennedy saw budgets as necessary tools to maintain order, but not bibles, as many of his long-term political advisors believed. Fortunately, he surrounded himself with a group of young intellectuals who were more inclined to a progressive posture than a cover-your-ass one.

CREATIVE INSPIRATIONS

Jack lived an enchanted if not a charmed life. He wrote *Profiles of Courage* in 1954 while recuperating from a very serious back operation. If not for the affliction it is unlikely the book would ever have been written. The book was his version of the PT-109 debacle in the South Pacific that helped make him a hero and according to some political pundits one of the reasons he won the presidential election in 1960. His personal assistant at the time was the brilliant Harvard lawyer Ted Sorensen, the one most responsible for the book's lucid style. There has been much speculation that Sorensen wrote it, but that is not the case according to historical records. When the book became a best seller, Kennedy was more shocked than anyone. It sold 125,000 copies in the first two years. He was even more astonished when it won the Pulitzer Prize in 1957. Unquestionably, political power and connections helped make him a success, but his flamboyant style, ability to go where others feared, and to tell it as it is from the heart, led him to the top.

Unquestionably, Jack Kennedy was at the right place at the right time. But a less passionate mane would not have left his adversaries in his wake to win the presidency. When he went after something nothing was spared in achieving his goals. When he decided to go after the biggest job in the nation he did so with unabated passion that left those who saw him as some kind of playboy flabbergasted. His seductiveness was aligned with productiveness. Few people believed a Roman Catholic Yankee could become president in a nation established to keep religion out of politics and everyone saw Catholics as mere puppets to the Pope. Kennedy showed his mettle when he put aside personal feelings and adroitly selected Texan Lyndon Johnson as his running mate. That brought him Texas and southern votes that would have been impossible due to the power of the Southern Baptist faction.

Winning wasn't without its price. Hollywood and Las Vegas friends were crucial to his win. They were instrumental in bringing in both union and blue-collar votes. Johnson brought the South, but it would be the Chicago underground and Giancana who would get him the Illinois electoral votes that won the election. His team had identified the swing votes from day one and concentrated there. Chicago and Nevada helped him beat Nixon by the smallest number of electoral votes in history.

THE DEATH OF CAMELOT. Kennedy's assassination by Lee Harvey Oswald has been beset by controversy. It is not a big stretch to show that Kennedy was a victim of a plot by the crime lords that helped elect him. The murder of Oswald before he could be legitimately interrogated is a common ploy among the mobs. They would never allow Oswald to be interrogated. Even more suspicious are the unsolved murders of long-term mistress Mary Pinchot Meyer, followed by the mysterious deaths of mafia kingpins Sam Giancana, Johnny Rosselli, and Jimmy Hoffa.

JFK's legacy will be passion without prudence. Did he exceed reasonable and prudent limits? Of course he did. But energy is the fuel of progress. Kennedy, like others in this book, were unable to turn off their ardor, once on top. Passion was the ticket to success and it would prove to be at the bottom of his contributions and to his failings. But in the end, Kennedy gave more than he took. He was undoubtedly, a man on a mission, one who took few prisoners. Such an approach seldom appeals to the temperate or faint of heart. It must be remembered that Kennedy expected to die young, and was dedicated to experiencing all he could before he expired. Hedonism defined him, but so did a deep respect for the common man.

In many respects Kennedy was dealt a better hand than most, but in another sense he had been dealt one of chaos. The chaos part took precedent, at least relative to his need to live life on the edge as if he wouldn't be alive next year. Such a mentality led him to live a life of debaucher that made him a horrible husband and often absent father. While Jackie was having an emergency cesarean operation with their fist child, born stillborn, Jack was cavorting on the Mediterranean with a bevy of girls and his friend senator George Smathers. Jackie came close to dying and never forgave him. Joe was forced to give her a $1 million gift to stay with him for his Presidential bid.

Perversity and philandering were his way of living with his destiny. But contrary to popular pundits, his perverse zeal seldom interfered with his ability to perform his Presidential duties diligently and elegantly. No question he lived life on the precipice, one that jeopardized his marriage and political career, but he saw it as necessary to maintain his sanity. For him life without passion was akin to not living and the risks he took were preferable to the alternative. His life and loves are but a prologue for political perversity but also an instructive look at the power of passion in the process.

DYSFUNCTIONAL PASSION

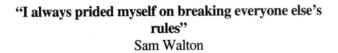

"I had certain peculiarities and customs"
Mark Twain

"I always prided myself on breaking everyone else's rules"
Sam Walton

"The gifted tend to question, challenge, or defy traditions that his peers take for granted"
(Kohlberg)

ABNORMALITY & EMINENCE

Are eminent and highly successful individuals abnormal? Yes! But they are abnormal in many of the same ways that appear to be crucial to rising to the very top in many disciplines. And besides what is normal? Normal is what the majority in any given society agrees is normal? In some parts of Africa that includes eating your enemies. In Haiti voodoo is considered a science. In ancient Egypt incest was an acceptable and encouraged practice. In Greece virile men were expected to engage in sex with each other. In Asia it is okay to eat your pet dogs and cats. In Saudi Arabia wives expect to be killed by their husband if they allow another man to see their face.. In psychological terms, abnormality is any "mental, emotional, or behavioral activity deviating from cultural norms."

Is abnormality bad? Hardly! *Abnormal* means that you are not adhering to some accepted convention. But in the world of creativity and innovation abnormality should be worshipped since normality leads to failure. Breaking new ground and altering paradigms are a function of going outside accepted customs for that given area. It is why Isadora Duncan had to defile ballet, Picasso had to challenge the old masters in art, Carl Jung had to break with Freud, and Larry Ellison had to run Oracle like a philosopher rather than a businessman.

CREATIVE DESTRUCTION. All change demands destroying what exists. That takes defiance of tradition and established ways. The textbook definition of innovation is "creative destruction," since any thing that is new demands getting rid of the old. And the destroyers must violate those cherished norms. The *Journal of Creative Behavior* (1994 p. 202) wrote, "We believe entrepreneurs are not normal people. They are more than mildly non-conformist, they are mildly sociopathic." Since *change* demands destruction, change artists must be renegades, and the greater the creativity the greater the eccentricities.

We now know that virtually all creativity comes from the fringe. That is why no creativity is found in any bureaucratic environment. It is why IBM did not invent the PC, the Postal Service did not invent overnight package delivery, and why the Internet was born of a bunch of young innovators in Silicon Valley. Large organizations not only discourage change, they fear those who try to enact it. Bureaucrats abhor change, since they worship at the altar of status quo. Tradition is godly and budgets become bibles in the old line firms. But the truth is that tradition and budgets are often the enemy of all progress and technological innovation. Creativity for such organizations is contra to control. Change forces a bureaucrat to deal with the complex, and destroys their power, consequently they will resist change even when it is beneficial to the organization.

CREATIVITY DEMANDS ABNORMALITY. *Normal success emanates from a normal person; abnormal success emanates from an abnormal person.* Why? Because abnormal success demands abnormal drive, abnormal work ethic, abnormal risk, abnormal tenacity, abnormal charm, abnormal confidence, and passion! George Bernard Shaw said it far more eloquently, "Reasonable men adapt to the world. Unreasonable men attempt to adapt the world to them; therefore all progress depends on the unreasonable man." Were these subjects unreasonable men? Off the scale! Were they abnormal? Beyond the definition! Did they pay for their defiance? Big time! The same powerbrokers who poisoned Socrates were the types who prosecuted Oscar Wilde, banned Isadora's performances, imprisoned Bertrand Russell and banned his teaching in America, called Jung's work mysticism, deported Charlie Chaplin, ridiculed the work of Bucky Fuller, and boycotted Madonna's concerts.

Is Michael Jackson eccentric? Yes, and his eccentricities – white glove, white socks, sunglasses, and crotch-grabbing – have all contributed to his success. He told the media, "My attitude is that if fashion says it's forbidden, then I'm going to do it" (Landrum 1997 p. 199). He is one more example of an abnormal person - in the eyes of the establishment - becoming one of the most famous entertainers of his era. Picasso had much the same attitude. He told the media, "I always try to be subversive" (Landrum 1996 p. 181). Even President Kennedy was radical for a politician. He refused to take the advice of all advisors especially in his combative dealings with Nikita Khrushchev. Posterity has seen fit to validate his moves but at the time the press blasted him for his daring.

The abnormal take more risks and have more passion than the normal. Their zeal transcends work and even their life. It pervades the boardroom and the bedroom. Are the psychosexually driven abnormal to the point of endangering others? No doubt! But not to the degree the religious right would have us believe. Should Oscar Wilde have been destroyed for what is now called a victimless crime, when everyday murders, rapes, and worse are taking place? Did Isadora Duncan, Babe Ruth and Carl Jung exceed prudent limits? Sure they did, but were their dalliances worse then their enormous contributions to society? The answer will always be answered in context to some moral dictum or ethical predisposition that are prejudiced by definition. One thing is sure. These fourteen subjects were never dull and certainly made the world a more interesting place to live. But their contributions did not justify their abuse of power or taking advantage of the young or disenfranchised. But it also didn't justify persecution just because they were different. For once you begin to say one cannot succumb to the charms of another, the next day a law can be enacted saying you cannot ask someone for a date, and the next day you can be imprisoned for just looking at someone and finally, like in some Middle Eastern countries a woman may be killed for daring to speak to a strange man.

RENEGADE PASSION

Renegades are passionate people. They violate sacred dogmas and pay dearly for their audacity to be different. Socrates was poisoned for teaching people to think. Galileo was imprisoned for saying that the sun, not the earth, was the center of the universe. Guttenberg was ostracized for inventing movable type, Charles Darwin was charged with heresy for proposing a theory of evolution, and Thoreau was jailed for having ecological values. Freud was despised for saying we had unconscious longings, and Edison was ridiculed for his electric light bulb. Ford was called "mad Henry" for pricing the Model T for the masses. Even the banker J..P. Morgan saw fit to call Bell's telephone idea "of no commercial value."

In 1902 the *Scientific American* called the Wright Brother's flight a "hoax." In 1925 inventor Milo Farnsworth walked into Motorola with a new invention - a radio that displayed pictures (first TV), and the head of engineering sent a secretary down to dismiss him with a warning to look out for knives and guns since the man was an obvious kook. Walt Disney's first full-length animated film *Snow White,* was labeled 'Disney's Folly,' and no bank would finance the stupid idea. Bureaucrats at the millennium attacked Bill Gates for being too good. If Gates were in Japan the politicians would have been standing staunchly behind him, imploring him to "go get em." In the myopic world of traditionalists, Gates is perceived as a threat. A similar myopia led twelve publishers to turn down the Harry Potter books by Joanne Rowling since they were such a departure from tradition. Her books have now sold close to 50 million copies.

DYSFUNCTIONAL PASSION

What is the message in all this? The price we pay for being innovative, for daring to challenge the establishment, and daring to pursue our personal passions is very high. Unless we are prepared to earn the enmity of friends, family, and adversaries, creativity will escape our grasp. To be creative one must come armed for a fight against the tyrannical forces determined to keep change at bay. And for that to happen passion must be such that it overcomes all attempts to dissuade and destroy. It must be so strong that no price is too great and no adversary will be able to stop the trek to the top. The change artist must come armed with ardor without peer. They must remember that the world they want to change is not the same world their adversaries see. The creative genius sees a world in pictures and principles, one of philosophical truth while the bureaucrat sees a much more restricted picture. Passionate people should never conform. They will never be accepted but they will also never be digitized in an analog world. The world according to Landrum is not the same as it is to many trying to convince us to get in the box, a box of mediocrity that is contra to progress, since:

> *The world is not digital it is analog; it is not quantitative it is qualitative; it is not constant it is dynamic, it is not limited it is boundless, and the path is inductive not deductive.*

SELF-DESTRUCTIVE GENIUS

The creative genius tends to live life on the edge. The tragic life and deaths of Oscar Wilde and Isadora Duncan offer testament to this axiom. Both were revolutionaries in their chosen fields and both paid a horrible price for daring to challenge society. Both were self-destructive in the sense they would rather die than submit to their oppressors. Duncan lived and died for freedom of the dance and her lifestyle. The dance she pioneered is the personification of her life and lusts. Freedom and passion made her and destroyed her. But the Puritanical Pagan insisted, "If one wants to do a thing, why not do it."

Wilde refused to be intimidated by the judicial system or the father of his lover Lord Douglas. His ego got in the way of his common sense when he took on the whole established system in London and his temerity destroyed him. He could have ignored the insult by the Marquees of Queensberry, but he didn't and it led to his sodomy trial and the end of his career as a novelist and dramatist. The two year sentence and promise of continued imprisonment if he was ever again found with another man led to his exile. His notorious trials rivaled the American O.J. Simpson trial 100 years later and after two years in Old Bailey he was a broken man. *Contemporary Authors* (Vo. 119 p. 409) wrote, "Imprisonment for homosexuality was a particularly tragic end for an artist who believed that style – in life as well as art – was of utmost importance."

Charlie Chaplin paid a similar price for daring to arouse the ire of the government caught up in McCarthy hysteria. When he refused to submit the ex-patriot was forced to leave a nation that he loved and had been good to him. But freedom of choice and words were important to him and he paid the price for saying, "Patriotism is the greatest insanity that the world has ever suffered." Those were unacceptable words in the middle of the Cold War period. Suddenly his pictures were boycotted and when he left for a trip to Europe he was not allowed back.

ABNORMAL BEHAVIOR & SUCCESS

An enormous body of work exists on why success comes from the fringe. In *Strange Brains & Genius* (1998) Clifford Pickover wrote, "Almost all mad geniuses have had an irreverence toward authority, and a self-sufficiency and independence." Adlerian psychologist, Lawrence Kohlberg found, "The gifted are likely to question, challenge, or defy tradition." Researchers have discovered that the gifted are intolerant of useless conformity and therefore operate well outside that imaginary box that is conformity. The mad genius isn't necessarily insane, but appears so to the more grounded who see such people as a menace to society and a threat to honored traditions.

The dysfunctional characteristics of these subjects are shown in Table 7 below. All classifications are based on data from their autobiographies, other psychological works or analysis, and the comments by biographers and friends. Six categories were chosen for the analysis. They are: Hypomania, Obsessive-Compulsive behavior, Manic-depression, Type A or B behavior, Machiavellian propensity, and Risk-Taking propensity (Big T high testosterone).

All were obsessive and/or compulsive in sexually or professionally. The same was true for their aggressive nature as all were Type A personalities. Similarly, all were willing to bet it all for their dreams and were classified Big T's. Eighty-six percent were hyperactive, forty-three percent manic-depressive, and fifty-seven percent had Machiavellian tendencies. Normal they were not, but they were abnormal in the same ways.

Their dysfunctional characteristics were well-suited to their role as change masters. As renegades they were ideal candidates for breaking new ground in the arts, sciences, politics, entertainment, and humanities. But their odd behavior also contributed to them being poor mates. And although most would have said they were living a life they loved none were happy in the classical sense.

225

DYSFUNCTIONAL PASSION
TABLE 7

DYSFUNCTIONAL BEHAVIORS
American Psychiatric Glossary DSM-IV Diagnostic and Statistical Manual of Mental Disorders

HYPOMANIA: A mood disorder of excessive elation, inflated self-esteem, grandiosity, hyperactivity, agitation, and accelerated thinking

OBSESSIVE/ COMPULSIVE An anxiety disorder characterized by obsessions and compulsions; "Sexual behavior is compulsive when it interferes with other aspects of a person's life" (Mayo Clinic)

MANIC-DEPRESSIVE: A mood disorder featuring a *manic* episodes of manic or depressive in nature (also known as bipolar disorder)

TYPE A BEHAVIOR: Excessive drive, competitiveness, sense of time urgency, impatience, unrealistic ambition or obsession for control

MACHAVELLIAN: The ends justify the means; get em before they get you syndrome

BIG T'S (high testosterone): High thrill-seeking, divergent thinking, risk-taking, aggression, creativity, and a high sex drive

SUBJECT	HYPO-MANIC	OCD	M/D	A/b	HIGH MACH	BIG T
1. BABE RUTH	H+++	OCD	NO	A+++	NO	T+++
2. ALBERT CAMUS	H++	C	CUSP	A+	NO	T++
3. *COLETTE*	*H+*	*OCD*	*NO*	*A+++*	*M++*	*T+++*
4. CHARLIE CHAPLIN	H+++	OCD	YES	A+++	M+++	T+++
5. *ISADORA DUNCAN*	*H+*	*OCD*	*YES*	*A*	*NO*	*T++*
6. LARRY ELLISON	H+++	OCD	CUSP	A+++	M+++	T+++
7. BUCKY FULLER	H+++	O	NO	A+++	NO	T+++
8. HOWARD HUGHES	H+++	OCD	YES	A+++	M+++	T+++
9. CARL JUNG	NO	C	NO	A++	M+++	T++
10. JOHN KENNEDY	NO	O	NO	A+++	M+++	T+++
11. *MADONNA*	*H+++*	*OCD*	*NO*	*A+++*	*M+++*	*T+++*
12. PABLO PICASSO	H+++	O	NO	A+++	M+++	T+++
13. BERTRAND RUSSELL	H+	O	NO	A+	NO	T++
14. OSCAR WILDE	H++	OCD	CUSP	A+	NO	T+++
TOTALS - ADDICTS	**H/M=12** **86%**	**C=14** **100%**	**MD-6** **43%**	**A=14** **100%**	**M=8** **57%**	**T=14** **100%**

DYSFUNCTIONAL PASSION

HYPOMANIA. Twelve of this book's subjects were hypomanic, meaning they were in a hurry in all things, including their personal and professional lives. Most operated as if double-parked at a busy intersection. Bucky Fuller is the consummate example of a man suffering from a kind of *rushing sickness*. The futurist slept wherever he found himself for a large portion of his early life. Later he concluded that all success was a function of "achieving more and more with less and less," a concept labeled "Ephemarelization." He followed his own beliefs by altering his sleeping habits, which he believed to be a "waste" and developed a highly refined system called Dymaxion Sleep or Power Napping. Fuller taught himself to induce sleep within 30 seconds, sleep for 30 minutes and then work for six hours, induce another nap, and then work for another six hours and so on for long periods of time. It enabled him to outwork and out-produce much younger men. Bucky worked had a compulsion to work constantly, often all night, and admitted that even when in bed he would lie there thinking about the ideas rampaging through his head.

Hypomania helped Picasso become the most prolific painter in history and Charlie Chaplin to produce an enormous output of work. Hyperactivity aided Larry Ellison in building Oracle into the world's second largest software firm. He was prone to euphoria and a "tirade of whitewater words." One associate said, "He speaks with no commas or hyphens, fast like a search engine gone haywire" (Wilson p. 3). Ellison's first wife said, "He is extremely intense. I'm a Type A and he wore me out." Mania was also the fuel that drove Madonna. She told the media, "I'm a workaholic and I have insomnia. It is the reason I'm not married. Who could stand me."

OBSESSIVE-COMPULSIVE BEHAVIOR. Obsessions are ideas or impulses that impede one's ability to function normally. The tics and eye twitches of Howard Hughes emanated from within a demonic psyche. Hughes had a hand-washing fetish. He could stand in front of a washbasin for hours, but it would never assuage his obsessive need for cleanliness. He was a voyeur and obsessed with female breasts. It would dominate his movie *The Outlaw* starring big-breasted Jane Russell. An obsessive fear of germs dominated his life and ultimately led him to a reclusive lifestyle. Hughes became one of the world's all-time control freaks but in later life was unable to even control his own behavior. Hughes was so obsessive he once kept Gina Lollobrigida held captive in Hollywood for his own perversion until she escaped and returned to Italy. One Hughes aid claims he had 108 files on potential candidates for his personal pleasures and this was in 1960 when he was impotent.

Perfectionism and hyper-sexuality are symptoms of obsessive personality. Neither are problems until they come to dominate behavior, interfere with a rational lifestyle, or become debilitating. According to sexual behavior expert Al Cooper, working at the San Jose Marital & Sexuality Center, "Compulsive sexuality means being motivated to engage in sexual activity time and time again in hopes of finding some sort of fulfillment." He adds, "Such people use sex as a form of physical and psychological release." That is precisely what these subjects did for much of their life. Only four appeared to be clinical cases of OCD, but all were very obsessive in their work and sex lives compulsive in some way. Author Irving Wallace (1981) described Charlie Chaplin as a "human sex machine," a man who "had six bouts of sex in succession." Like Hughes he would take eight to ten baths a day. Wallace described Bertrand Russell as a man with "galloping satyriasis," and Picasso as "obsessively possessive." Bucky Fuller had a Chronofile of every single press clipping – 37,000 items, 50,000 slides, 64,000 feet of film and a plethora of every detail of his life. He was obsession gone amok.

MANIC-DEPRESSION. This is a mood disorder also known as bipolar disease. In the manic state the individual becomes talkative, goal-directed, may go on buying sprees, participate in sexual excesses, have a decreased need for sleep and can become highly grandiose in their thinking. Nothing is impossible in such a state according to Kay Jamison who wrote, *Touched with Fire* (1993). She found, "High energy levels and boldness are clearly essential to virtually all creative endeavors. They tend to be characteristic of manic-depressive temperaments. Who would not want such a disease that allows sharpened, unusually creativity, and increased productivity" (Jamison p. 103 & 114). When manic, enormous productivity occurs, but when depressed, virtually nothing is achieved.

Depression sends a person into a netherland of ineptitude. Duncan, Chaplin, Hughes, Ruth, Camus, and Larry Ellison would drive themselves until they became close to breakdown and often did. Hughes and Chaplin both disappeared mysteriously when they became depressed to the point of incapacitation. Ruth would be sent to a remote Boston home for a rest cure. Other symptoms are moodiness, weight loss, disorientation, and extreme fatigue. Wild mood swings dominate the lives of such people who will become anti-social as did Chaplin, Picasso, and Hughes. They could be ebullient in one moment and caustically irreverent in the next. Biographer Milton (1996) said, "Chaplin was a manic person addicted to the pursuit of women, money, and petty legal battles" (183). Fellow actor Stan Laurel said, "He was a very eccentric person." Isadora Duncan experienced wild swings in temperament and considered suicide. She wrote, "I have thought of it, but something always holds me back." Manic-depressives have abnormally high suicide rates. When up they are capable of extraordinary achievement. When down they are unable to function. Eight had seriously considered suicide and Jung, the psychotherapist, kept a loaded pistol under his pillow so that that he could use it the moment he felt himself slipping into insanity.

TYPE A's. Such people confuse self-worth with achievement, and must e productive to feel whole. All these subjects were Type A's. They walked fast, talked fast, thought fast, ate fast, worked fast, and even slept fast. It was their edge. They were afflicted with a kind of rushing sickness and could not take a vacation without feeling guilty. They were incapable of waiting in lines and were highly impatient. Colette wrote, "I could not live without great intensity," and Madonna told the media, "You have to be patient. I am not." Chaplin got so nervous he was incapable of driving a car." JFK said, "I can't wait," and Fuller wrote, "Progress means mobility."

Type A's schedule more than is humanly possible to complete. Having many balls in their air excites them while it causes anxiety in more normal people. This makes them impossible mates but highly productive professionals. Such people can hold a conversation while reading a magazine and listening to the radio. Babe Ruth was unable to have one woman, one vice, or one goal. One teammate commented, "I don't know how he kept going."

MACHIAVELLIAN BEHAVIOR. Such personalities must be in control or they don't want to play the game. Charlie Chaplin refused to be directed even though he didn't know how to direct a movie in the same way Hughes refused to listen to anyone when making movies and became his own producer and director. Both ran their firms with a "my way or the highway" attitude and manipulated leading ladies, partners, wives, and business associates. The bottom line is the only thing sacred to the Machiavellian personality. Picasso was the quintessential High Mach. He refused to allow a person to be his friend unless he slept with their wives. He said, "I would rather see a woman dead than see her happy with someone else" (Huffington p. 56). Madonna used and abused managers like few others in history with a management approach of, "Get em before they get you." She told the media, "All those men I stepped over to get to the top – they still love me." Larry Ellison played the press like a yo-yo in defiling archenemy Bill Gates and operated Oracle with a motto, "Those who lay together stay together."

Big Mach' have an operating style of the ends always justify the means. They are self-serving and manipulate and control to attain their goals. Politicians are infamous for such practices and Kennedy was no different. Jack used his power of persuasion to succeed in politics and in the bedroom. Marilyn Monroe's tragic death is one his more ignominious legacies. Carl Jung used his magic persuasion to attract a cult-like following of women in one of the more sophisticated cases of

DYSFUNCTIONAL PASSION

Machiavellian behavior. Jung threatened to drop women from his cult-like group if they did not conform to his way of thinking. He wrote, "The prerequisite for a good marriage is the license to be unfaithful" (Wallace p. 247). When disciple Constance Long found a new guru he wrote to her and said, "Foreign gods are a sweet poison. You should not make totems of foreign trees" (Milton p. 256).

BIG T's. A Big T has high testosterone and enjoys thrill-seeking. They are normally male since males have higher testosterone than females but all three women in this book were very high Big T's. All lived on the edge and find risk exciting rather than something to fear. Virtually no risk is too great for the Big T. Psychologist Frank Farley says, "Big T's as a group, tend to be creative, extraverted, take more risks, have more experimental artistic preferences, and prefer more variety in their sex lives than do little t's" (*Psychology Today* 6-86). High testosterone has been linked with creativity, aggression, divergent thinking, hyper-sexuality, and high risk-taking. It was Big T's who founded America as the Little t's stayed in Europe. The Big T's are one reason America continually rate highest in risk-taking, independence, produce a full fifty-percent of all Nobel Prizes in the world, and lead in product innovations.

In contrast Little t's avoid risk, outside stimulation, and are not easily aroused. They are the flipside of these subjects. Big T's thrive on new risky ventures, and love stimulating situations and are easily aroused. They are twice as likely to get a traffic ticket, engage in more fights, enjoy more sexual partners, dislike structure, and are energized by uncertainty. Silicon Valley is a stronghold for Big T types, and is one reason it has been the hotbed of new high-tech innovation like IC chips, the microprocessor, video games, PC's and the Internet. It is no accident that 50 percent of American Nobel Prizes for Science have come from those fruits and nuts in California.

These subjects were high Big T's. They drove fast sports cars, raced boats, and flew their own planes. Many went through life as if they had a death wish. Their mates were convinced they did. Wilde, Chaplin, Ruth and Ellison had a plethora of paternity suits. Jack Kennedy was nicknamed "crash Kennedy" during his PT-109 days in the South Pacific. Only a Big T could have two hookers placed on the government payroll. Larry Ellison broke his neck body surfing in Hawaii and when not engaging in mock dog fights in his jet plane he is racing his yacht in dangerous ocean waters. Hughes had seven plane crashes. He was afraid of a fly, but a fearless test pilot. Were they dysfunctional? Off the scale! It made them different, and also made them great. It will go down in history as their legacy. Passion fueled their trek to the top and it led them into many travails. Without it they would have been average. With it they were renegades superstars.

10

PASSION & THE FAMILY

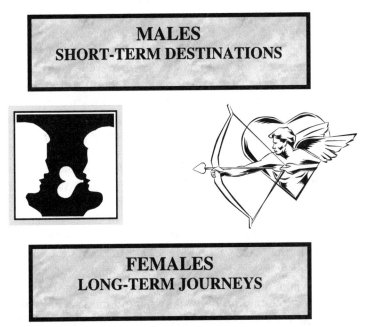

MALES
SHORT-TERM DESTINATIONS

FEMALES
LONG-TERM JOURNEYS

"Sex is the curse of life, I can only be true to myself"
Frank Lloyd Wright

"Margaret Mead has never performed a domestic task"
3RD Husband Gregory Bateson

"Margaret Thatcher is an unbelievably successful politician but an unsuccessful mother, and she knows it"
Long-time female friend of Prime Minister Thatcher

CAN YOU HAVE IT ALL?

Not if you are determined to make it to the very top. Being the very best at anything demands sacrifice and more often than not it is the personal life that is sacrificed for the professional with family and loved ones who lose. Did Leonardo da Vinci or Napoleon have a family life? No! How normal a life did Madam Curie or Mother Teresa have? Not! Babe Didrickson Zaharias achieved her dream of being the world's greatest female athlete. The price was family and friends. Three people showed up at her funeral. Do teenage tennis phenoms or Olympic gymnasts have a well-rounded childhood or adolescence? No way! They must be on the court or in the gym every day while their friends are hanging out at the beach or taking in a ballgame. Did Oprah Winfrey have to sacrifice to become the Queen of Talk Shows? She admits she did, and a traditional family was the price paid for huge success.

Passionate people are endowed with energy and enthusiasm. The price they pay is lack of leisure, inability to relax, a feverish existence, and often the alienation of friends and family. Such people have it all for short periods but even that is seldom found in the frenetic lives of the passionate. Success in the fast lane brings with it all the baggage found is such a life and many bodies are left in the wake. The individual often pays the biggest price for their tortuous lifestyle as in the case of Wilde, Camus, Duncan, Kennedy, and Chaplin all of whom died or were destroyed by the very thing that made them and all had a horrible family life. Many paid in terms of nervous afflictions, breakdowns, and even suicide. Carl Jung slept with a loaded pistol under his pillow for the last fifty years of his life to use to blow out his brains the minute he felt himself slipping into insanity. On the surface these individuals were rich and famous but a closer look reveals great suffering and their families were often the ones who suffered most.

LUST VS. LOVE. Free love proved not to be the friend of marital bliss in the lives of Colette, Duncan, Russell and Jung, all of whom practiced it with a vengeance. And even though the others practiced it without admitting so were also caused great pain for their frivolous lifestyles. Those who live well outside convention, a necessity for breakthrough creativity, the price is alienation of the establishment and often alienation of family and friends who are not so daring. A normal lifestyle was not possible for these subjects even though many like Camus pleaded for one. Despite his words, his actions never permitted one, and drove his wife to attempted suicide.

Picasso's habit of sleeping with his friend's wives certainly didn't endear him to them and the wives were not thrilled either despite being immortalized in art. And even though Carl Jung's long-suffering wife accepted his mistress in their home, it hardly made for an idyllic family environment. Bertrand Russell's open marriage backfired when his second wife Dora Black had two children by one of her lovers leading Russell to file for divorce. Russell said the prenuptial arrangement had been broken, "If she should have a child that was not mine there would be a divorce." The free love advocate wrote, "Any marriage should be terminable by mutual consent" and was convinced, "If marriage and paternity are to survive as social institutions, some compromise is necessary between complete promiscuity and lifelong monogamy" (Russell 1987 p. 223). Albert Camus was cynical on traditional family life writing "We always deceive ourselves twice about the people we love – first to their advantage, then to their disadvantage." He said, "Wives inspire us to create masterpieces and then prevent us from completing them."

Oscar Wilde was the most cynical about marriage since he had decided to pursue boys after his two sons were born. He described marriage as a lonesome and impractical institution writing, "In marriage three is company and two is none." Wilde wrote extensively in his plays about the marital plight as he saw it, "The only way a woman can ever reform her husband is by boring him so completely that he loses all possible interest in life." He had a plethora of aphorisms on the plight of man in long-term sanctimonious relationships that he believed were destined to fail. One of his more profound lines went, "A cynic is a man who knows the price of everything, and the value of nothing." Wilde had little confidence in family and therefore did not have one after he made his affair with Lord Douglas a cause to defend.

Camus described this existentially through his character Jean-Baptiste Clamence who he has say, "True debauchery is liberating because it creates no obligations. In it you possess only yourself; hence it remains the favorite pastime of the great lovers of their own person." That proved the defining element in an egocentric attempting to have it all – family and super achievement. All were egoistic to a fault and it is the reason none had a great family life or personal happiness.

GENDER, PASSION & POWER

The males in this study used their power to seduce. The females used their sexuality to gain power. The males were physically aggressive. The females were emotionally aggressive. The males were seldom interested in any long-term relationships contrasting the females who wanted them but often destroyed them once in hand. The men seduced and as soon as they had their conquest didn't want them. They were destination driven and could care less about the journey which was the dominating characteristic for the women. Colette, Duncan or Madonna spoke of long-term relationships but were so dedicated to work, destroyed any chance at them. The men also placed career way ahead of all else including wives or children but also placed their mistresses and love affairs way ahead of them as well, which wasn't quite so true of the females. But after age forty the females mellowed relative to the norm but were still in netherland compared to the average female.

Sexual conquest for the males was often just another notch on their bedpost or fuel to prove their manhood. Seduction for the females was far more romantically inclined but not in the same sense as the average woman. Colette, Duncan, and Madonna were provocative beyond compare. Chaplin was insatiable when young and had sex with six women in succession. Such a quantitative conquest was never of interest for the females. None would have considered renting out a whole brothel as Babe Ruth did in St. Louis one night to prove how prolific he was. But in contrast was the equally decadent seduction by Colette of her stepson. She justified the act as helping the boy enter manhood and came to couch it as a romantic liaison with a stronger older woman giving tutelage to a weaker younger man. Only Colette of the females were driven like Kennedy to sleep with someone each night although with Kennedy it had to be some new woman for titillation. Both Duncan and Madonna were as prolific at times but not as an addiction like Kennedy.

In general, the orgasm takes a distant second place to a romantic interlude for women, where it takes precedence for the destination driven males. For them it is the only reason to chase whereas the women had some ulterior motive or at least a romantic interlude in mind. Cleopatra undoubtedly seduced Caesar for power not any sexual gratification. This contrasts Kennedy seducing Hollywood starlets as a conquest. Cleopatra's deed was based on survival, his on egoistic fulfillment. Her siblings wanted her dead and Caesar was but a tool, albeit an important one, in her trek to become the Queen of Egypt. Her ploy worked despite her reputation as a seductress of the first order.

Another gender difference noticed in this work was the methodology of men and women. The women were far more exhibitionistic and the men more voyeuristic. Carl Jung spoke of this at length in his work, labeling women with an unconscious "eros and soul" and the men with "spirit and logos." He was ascribing ethereal romance to females, and aggressive rationality to males in his Syzygy concept.

PASSION AS JOURNEY. Females tend to be relationship driven. They would rather not play a game than risk destroying a valued relationship on the way to the win. They play the game for the interplay, not the win, whereas most men play to win and to hell with the broken relationships on the way to victory. Are there exceptions? You bet! Colette destroyed any chance at saving her marriage to Baron de Juvenel when she seduced his son. But a closer look into her motivations makes it obvious the aging star was on a mission to preserve a fleeting youth by proving she was still appealing to a teenager. The 16-year old Bertrand de Jouvenel was but a pawn for a grand dame nearing fifty. Was she interested in the boy as a conquest? Hardly! But such liaisons have a short life and he soon left her for a younger woman. Isadora and Madonna also used many males to further their professional careers and then discarded them when their usefulness ceased.

PASSION AS DESTINATION. Males are far more interested in hitting the target than the pleasure attained at getting to it. Relationships are a long way down their list of importance in the trek through life. Oscar Wilde wrote, "When a man has once loved a woman he would do anything for her except to continue to love her." Larry Ellison, like every other male in this book, cared nothing about finding a nurturing relationship. Women were just something needed to make him feel whole. He admitted, "Love is the enlightened pursuit of happiness, but I don't understand love or people bonding" (Wilson p. 38). Such attitudes lead to conquests, and most men will destroy a valued relationship to win the game. This is a huge difference in the two genders and separates the truly driven man from the most hardened female overachiever.

MEN TALK - WOMEN DO. Locker room talk is replete with Herculean stories of sexual conquests in cars, on the beach, trains, and with a secretary lingering outside the door, as in President Clinton's case. Danger is not only part of the puzzle for men it is part of the motivation. But when it comes to performance in high heat women are the masters of the universe. Men talk a big game but when it comes to performing, and when sufficiently aroused, women do it – anywhere, anytime, in any venue. Just as Cleopatra crawled out of that rug and Lewinsky played with cigars, the aroused female has a huge edge over males.

Men portray themselves as macho dandies in the face of any danger. But in socially dangerous venues the female can and will perform with uninhibited lust leaving the male wondering what happened to his machine gun suddenly gone blank. Women are omnipotent when it comes to romantic conquests just as men are when it comes to unemotional venues like physical combat. Women take emotional risks, men take physical ones, and each get lost in the others playground. A woman can block out the universe when sufficiently charged. A male can block out all emotional feelings when in a battle. Both are strong, but their strength comes to the fore in different venues. Women are powerful in emotional settings, while men are fearless in rational ones. These females only risked for an experiential journey. The males risked when they saw the chance for a conquest that set them apart as special. These women already felt special and offered their bodies and souls for a chance at a future relationship. For the men the thrill of the moment was far more important. The trip was far more important for the women.

POWER AS APHRODISIAC

What motivated Marilyn Monroe, a woman who could have had virtually any male in the world, to end her life because she was unable to have a very married Jack Kennedy? Why did the most beautiful and famous Hollywood stars jump into bed with a dirty and abusive Howard Hughes? What about the crass Babe Ruth could have appealed to well-bred socialites? And what motivated Edith Rockefeller, the enormously wealthy daughter of John D., to leave her husband and children to be near Carl Jung in Switzerland? Why would an extremely talented and beautiful artist, Francois Gilot, a woman fifty years younger than Picasso (who would later marry Jonas Salk) allow the Father of Cubism to ruin her life? It certainly wasn't money, security, or even fame. They were all driven by something else. Marilyn and Edith Rockefeller McCormick had more money than they could ever spend, as did starlets like Ginger Rogers, Katherine Hepburn, and Cary Grant.

The answer to the above is Power. The same power Henry Kissinger called the ultimate aphrodisiac. It was power of persuasion and the power of seduction that fueled these individuals to the top of their chosen fields. How did they get such power? Passion! It pervaded their very being and made them special. It was their greatest strength and their greatest weakness. JFK is the consummate example. Women didn't succumb to his charms just because he was President. They climbed in bed with him when he was just the rich son of Joe, when he was a lowly Congressman and Junior Senator. They succumbed to his charms because he was a powerful man with a powerful presence. He was magic. Such power incites smart women to do stupid things. In a similar way young aspiring starlets were mesmerized by the power of Chaplin, Hughes, and Camus. Picasso used the power of immortality in paint to seduce a long list of young nubile females.

What was the genesis of their power? Was it passion alone? In many senses it was. They were possessed of a super psychic energy and vitality that was contagious and mesmerizing. They had what philosophers have called a *will-to-power*, Shaw called a *Life Force*, and Henri Bergson called a *vital force* or *Elan vital*. The groupies who throw themselves at rock stars get caught up in this emotional lust and so do many normal human beings.

PERSONAL VS PROFESSIONAL

No one can serve two masters at the same time. It is difficult to serve them at different times but these subjects give testimony to the impossibility of having it both personally and professionally. Many of these subjects chased three masters – professional dream, lust, and a normal family life. Did they succeed? No! Two of the three would have been difficult, all three proved impractical. Most gave lip service to their families while spending seven days a week perfecting their craft. Lust pervaded their souls, which as has been discussed at length. Passion was crucial to their professional success, but it was an adversary for any chance of a normal family life.

Babe Ruth was equally proficient at hitting home runs in the bedroom as the ballpark. That left little time or energy for his wife Helen who had a nervous breakdown and finally left him. Bucky Fuller virtually never went home during his early creative years. Picasso became perturbed when young mistress Francoise Gilot asked that he spend time with her and the children, "I sacrifice everything to my painting, you Francoise and everyone else." Albert Camus was similarly inclined writing, "Sensuality alone ruled my life. For a ten-minute affair I would have renounced my parents. One must live with her and shut up, or sleep with them all." In any view, the families of these subjects were way down on any list of priorities.

Most loved their children but didn't want them interfering with their work or lusts. Colette didn't have a child until age forty. She immediately hired a nanny to raise her and was a horrid mother. Most protested love for their children but just were not there for them or their mates. Hughes never wanted any children and forced a number of women into having abortions, as did Chaplin during his early days in Hollywood, although he ultimately fathered a brood of eleven children. Madonna chose abortion while young but in 2000 had her second child by a mate very methodically selected for the job. See Table 8 for an analysis of their children and ages when married.

AGE WHEN MARRIED

Four didn't marry until over thirty. Isadora was the oldest at 44 and only married the mad Russian poet Esenin so he could accompany her on a trip to

America. By the time they returned they were no longer a couple. Three married at 19, Colette, Babe Ruth, and Howard Hughes. JFK was officially married once, but much evidence indicates otherwise. Seymour Hersch says he married Palm Beach divorcee Durie Desloge in 1946 some six years prior to his marriage to Jackie. Russell and Chaplin were married four times. Hughes was only married twice but was infamous for arranged marriages aboard his yacht outside the legal limits in Southern California. Chaplin's last trip to the altar was at 54. Both Picasso and Russell were married at age 80. Colette married three times but lived in a committed relationship with a number of women and men in her long and tumultuous life.

AGE OF FIRST & LAST CHILD

These subjects had children when much older than the average parent. The average age for parenting their first child was thirty-five. Colette didn't have a child until forty, Bertrand Russell didn't have his first until 49. Kennedy's daughter Caroline was born when Kennedy was 39. Madonna and Picasso were both 38 before having their first child. Chaplin's last child was born when he was 73. Picasso had his last child at 68 and Russell at 66.

MIXING WORK & PLEASURE. Most of these subjects integrated the personal with the professional to the consternation of family, mates, lovers and business associates. Chaplin and Hughes were notorious for signing young beautiful starlets to contracts in order to control them for their own pleasure. Hughes allowed his friends to fly free on TWA. Ellison regularly dated and slept with Oracle employees. Russell slept with his teachers at his progressive school in London. Camus slept with most of his leading ladies. Isadora and Colette had a similar propensity, as did Madonna.

Larry Ellison was notorious for mixing work with pleasure and dated a long series of females at Oracle and married one, Barbara Boothe who is the mother of his two children. In the early 90's he had a disastrous affair with fortune-hunter, Adelyn J. Lee at the same time he was dating two other employees. Lee had ulterior motives, and had confided with female friends that she intended to take him for $1 million dollars. After a brief liaison she file a sexual discrimination lawsuit and won a judgment of $100,000. He discovered her ruse and filed criminal charges for perjury. He won and Lee was forced to repay the $100,000, and served jail time for her duplicity.

TABLE 8

MARRIAGE & FAMILY

AVERAGE # CHILDREN = 3
AVERAGE # MARRIAGES = 2
AVERAGE AGE OF 1ST CHILD = 35
AVERAGE AGE OF 1ST MARRIAGE = 27

Subject	1ST Marriage	AGE # Marriages	#AGE 1ST Child	# Children
BABE RUTH	19	2	-	0
CAMUS	20	2	32	2
COLETTE	19	3	40	1
CHAPLIN	29	4	30	11 (LAST 73)
DUNCAN	44	1	27	3
ELLISON	23	2	39	2
FULLER	22	1	23	2
HUGHES	19	2?	0	0
JUNG	28	1	30	5
KENNEDY	36 (1st 30)	1 or 2	40	3
MADONNA	27	1	38	2
PICASSO	37 (LAST 80)	2	38	4 (LAST 68)
RUSSELL	22 (LAST 80)	3	49	4 (LAST 66)
WILDE	30	1	32	2
AVERAGE	**27**	**2**	**35**	**3**

Colette had more nefarious affairs with cast members than Ellison had with employees. She slept with both male and female members of her troupe as did Madonna some years later. Colette married her business partner who was sixteen years her junior. Babe Ruth slept indiscriminately with the wives of his teammates, friends, and any other attractive female. Jack Kennedy was even less discriminating. He slept with Jackie's Press Secretary Pamela Turnure, Gene Tierney, the wife of family friend Oleg Cassini, and Blaze Starr who was engaged to political backer Governor Earl Long of Louisiana.

TYPE A MATES. Type A personalities get things done, but they are impossible to live or work with. All of these subjects qualified as Type A's. They were in a hurry and confused self-worth with achievement. All were obsessive overachievers, arrogant, impulsive, intolerant and high risk-takers. Such traits are inconsistent with maintaining long-term relationships.

Wilde wrote, "Nothing is serious except passion." Bertrand Russell admitted, "I have abnormally high sexual urges." Colette wrote, "I realized I would not be able to live without great intensity." A friend of Isadora Duncan wrote, "She slept little, and acted like a person demented that nothing could stop" (Desti p. 133). An ex-wife of Ellison said, "I never met anyone like him. It was like going straight up in a fighter jet." Bucky Fuller developed a whole philosophic system around speed that he labeled, "Progress means mobility." Madonna told *Vanity Fair*, "I'm a workaholic, and I'm a control freak. That's why I'm not married. Who could stand me."

PHILOSOPHY OF MARRIAGE. Bertrand Russell believed "Very few adults can preserve instinctive happiness in a state of celibacy." Wilde felt, "The only way to get rid of temptation is to yield to it." Isadora Duncan believed marriage was contra to happiness and wrote, "How stupid for an artist to be married." But she did need men as noted by her words. "I fell in love with males at eleven and I have never ceased to be madly in love." Colette's whole philosophy of marriage was couched in bisexuality. She didn't want any permanent commitment with either sex. Her philosophy of relationships went, "Androgynous sex is powerful." She inverted the sex roles of her protagonists in both *Cheri* and *Gigi.* Madonna told the media, "All those men I stepped all over to get to the top – every one would take me back because they still love me and I still love them. Pussy power alone rules my life." Chaplin admitted in his memoirs, "No art can be learned at once and lovemaking is a sublime art that needs practice." He spent his life practicing what he preached. Jung wrote, "Free love will save the world." He truly believed, "Sexuality is the *sine quo non* of spirituality."

SYBARITIC GENIUS

WORKAHOLICS - CONTRA TO MARRIAGE

An obsession with work leaves little time for mates or children. Hedonists like Colette indulged her every whim, and destroyed every valued relationship in her life. The radical novelist followed her passions to wherever they led and be-damned the needs of others and that included her daughter and beloved mother. She didn't take the time to attend her daughter's marriage or her mother's funeral, and although she named her daughter Colette, she had no time for her causing her daughter to tell reporters, "My mother cared more for her stepson than me. She was like a mother cat who tells her little one to shift for herself" (Thurman p.313). Oscar Wilde had a similar disdain for family. He loved his two sons but was too busy chasing lover Lord Douglas to spend any time with them. He did dedicate two classic fairy tales - *The Happy Prince* (1888) and *A House of Pomegranates* (1892) - to them. By the time they were eight and ten he had been convicted of sodomy, imprisoned, and never saw them again.

FAMILY LIFE. For the zealous, family is often but a possession, something expected to have but not necessarily to cherish. These subjects occasionally showed up for holidays and other family venues, but did not expect the family life to interfere with their professional one. John Kennedy Jr. was born three weeks after his father had been elected President of the United States in 1960. His sister had been born three years earlier when her father was a Senator. Both children lived an idyllic life in the White House but JFK was seldom there. To Kennedy's credit he tried to be a good and nurturing father and was notorious for allowing both kids to roam free in his White House office. But more often than not they were with their mother Jackie in France.

Bertrand Russell's first two children were raised by a nanny/teacher in his progressive Beacon Hill school. He was sleeping with the nanny, among others in his entourage. When his open marriage to Dora Black came to an end he married nanny Patricia Spence when 65. She bore him a son during his 66th year. He was convinced marriage could only work if it were open to outside affairs, and defended his stance in *Marriage and Morals:*

> *A businessman who is generous with his employees but falls in love with his stenographer is wicked; another who bullies his employees, but is faithful to his wife is virtuous. This is rank superstition.* (1929 p. 154):

PASSION & THE FAMILY

Oscar Wilde is today known as the "gay icon" because of his tragic suffering at the hands of a homophobic society. But Wilde was the first to admit, "I am a perverse and impossible person." Speaking to the overt naivety of his wife Constance he wrote, "Women have a wonderful instinct about things. They can discover everything but the obvious." In the *Ideal Husband* he wrote, "There is only one thing worse than an absolutely loveless marriage. A marriage in which there is love, but on one side only."

FAMILIAL TRAGEDY

For the most part the children of these subjects turned out badly. They not only lived in the shadow of their famous parents but were disenfranchised at an early age and left to find their own way in the world. In their defense the children had a tough act to follow. Colette was the Mistress of fiction in France, Chaplin won an Academy Award, Russell and Camus won Noble Prizes, Fuller became an icon of creativity, Ellison the second richest man in the world, Picasso the most renowned painter in history. JFK became president, Jung the world's most renowned psychotherapist. Because of their parent's success they had little hands-on nurturing and many had life too easy to make it to the top of anything.

Oscar Wilde flagellated the marital state with comments like "I was bored to death with married life... How marriage ruins a man. It is as demoralizing as cigarettes." Oscar Wilde's son died as a teenager not long after his father's early demise at age 47. Bucky Fuller lost his first daughter to polio at four. Chaplin had two children die in childhood. Isadora lost her son and daughter in a tragic car accident, and another died in early infancy. The barefoot Contessa herself died tragically when her free-flowing scarf caught in the axle of a sports car and snapped her neck. Jack Kennedy lost two children just after childbirth, and his son John Jr. died in a plane crash in 1999 before he was able to begin his own family.

Picasso's perversity knew few limits. Both his wife and mistress Dora Marr were institutionalized. Long-term mistress Marie-Theresa committed suicide shortly after his death, as did second wife Jacqueline. His first son Paulo became an alcoholic bum and his grandson killed himself when not allowed to attend his grandfather's funeral. Such is the power of passion without peer. Passion makes them great and destroys most else in their frenetic life.

11

SUCCESS & SEX DRIVE

"Find, if you can, a single man, in all history of civilization, who achieved outstanding success in any calling, who was not driven by a well developed sex nature"
Napoleon Hill (1960)

"Psychic health depends on orgiastic potency"
Wilhelm Reich (1973)

"Within the power of our will lies the power to do essentially anything"
Evan Harris Walker, *The Physics of Consciousness*

IS PASSION CRITICAL TO GREATNESS?

It isn't just important it is imperative. Nothing great will happen without a zealot making it so. Confirmation comes from two men who looked into the role of passion. Napoleon Hill and Wilhelm Reich came from different schools but arrived at the same conclusion. Hill interviewed Teddy Roosevelt, George Eastman, King Gillette, Andrew Carnegie, Henry Ford, Henry Firestone, Thomas Edison, and John D. Rockefeller in an attempt to uncover the common characteristics of greatness. In his classic work *Think & Grow Rich* (1960) Hill wrote, "Men who accumulate large fortunes, and attain to great heights of power and fame, do so, mainly to satisfy their desire to please women" (p. 194). In a more recent interview Michael Jordan admitted he took up sports as a young boy only to impress the girls.

SYBARITIC GENIUS

Wilhelm Reich spent his life looking into the inner dynamics of man's need to strive and achieve. This Freudian psychotherapist and researcher was a renegade who concluded, "sexuality is the center around which the life of society as a whole as well as the intellectual world of the individual revolves" (Reich p. 21). Hill wrote, "Highly sexed men are the most efficient salesmen, *personal magnetism* is nothing more nor less than sexual energy." Reich was a bit more universal in his assessment of the role played by passion in eminence. In the *Function of Orgasm* (1973) he wrote, "The process of sexual pleasure is the life process per se. This is not a manner of speaking; it is an experimentally proven fact."

PASSION AS PANACEA

The defining difference between the executive and the business tycoon is the passion each has for their job. The same can be said for those making it to the Big Leagues versus those mired in the Minors, the club singer and the superstar, or the journeyman politician and the President. Passion is the difference between mediocrity and eminence. Those with passion are eminently more *persistent, productive, popular, provocative, and persuasive.* Those without it tend to be more *pernicious, peculiar, perverse, perilous, palpable, and prickly.* There is a price for ardor and it is not slight, but if one sets their sights high the passion must be accordingly high.

CONSCIOUSNESS PHYSICS & SEDUCTION

Vitality and intensity are key elements in high achievement. Those with this special quality seem to possess some special aura that separates them from the pack. Simply put, passion is contagious, as is enthusiasm. Consciousness physics is a new controversial concept that says there are no accidents and we are all master of our destiny. Consciousness is our dreams, desires, and ardor manifested in thoughts and actions. Evan Harris Walker in *Physics of Consciousness* (2000) says the observer can be affected by what they observe through the power of just being and thinking. He believes the *will* is transcendent and the basis of all "Omnipresence, Omniscience, Omnipotence" (Walker p. 336). Consider the magnitude of this statement. The observer, through their own thought processes, a kind of osmosis of the mind, can influence their life and those around them. Such an aura was evident in Mother Theresa. When she entered a room it lit up with her presence. Teammates of Michael Jordan spoke of becoming better through association. Babe Ruth was pure majesty at bat as was Isadora Duncan on stage and Bucky Fuller lecturing.

Consciousness physics suggests the greats influence their adversaries and fans through the power of the mind. It was the reason for Kennedy's win over Nixon. Walker wrote, "Experimental evidence increasingly suggest the observer and the observed are tied together, the act of envisioning reality plays a role in the collapse of many states at once into reality." This work is but an extension of the pioneering work by Carl Jung in the area of *synchronicities*. Jung firmly believed there were no accidents and each of us are truly the masters of our destiny.

POWER OF *WILL*. Why do some people attract while others repel? Some label it chemistry, others charisma, Freud called it the Pleasure Principle, and Nietzsche defined it as a *will-to-power*. George Bernard Shaw defined it as the *Life Force*. No matter the name we are in control and our will flows from within to those around us and is manifested in all we do both positive and negative. We cannot hide our true self, as this inner psychic energy is inextricably wrapped into our words, actions, behavior, and works or art. These subjects made it not because of their innate talent which often was quite good but at times not so good, but because they willed success more than peers and adversaries. A consummate example of this is the statement by French poet Jean Cocteau on the inner power of Picasso. "He had a discharge of electricity, rigor, flare, showmanship, and magnetic radiance. He radiated a cosmic and irresistible self-confidence. Nothing seemed beyond him."

Kennedy could have been the poster boy for ethereal seductiveness. His very presence altered the chemistry in a room and women lost reason when he proposed an illicit liaison. Kennedy was a married man with two children living in the White House and yet able to seduce bright, educated women. What was this power? The power of right! These subjects actually believed it was their right to seduce. They believed and it worked. Such men operate in that omnipotent zone that has few limits. Their power is a function of their *will*. They come to believe they are special and endowed with extraordinary powers and they are given them.

Some call such power arrogance. It is! Others will call it guts! It is! Nietzsche described it as power acceding to he who takes it. It is! But those who dare take it, get it, and that is the bottom line. Men like Kennedy dared invite Marilyn Monroe aboard Air Force One for a liaison. She came and he conquered. This instilled him with the confidence to test his mettle in trysts like the one with Gene Tierney in the White House while Jackie was five months pregnant. Charlie Chaplin convinced William Randolph Hearst's mistress Marion Davies to have sex with him while his wife was in another room delivering his child. Ruth would show up in public with cameras flashing knowing his wife would see the pictures. Camus did the same in France years after Colette shocked and seduced her way to the top. Madonna dared what others couldn't conceive and pulled it off through sheer audacity. Such people come to believe they are invisible, invulnerable, or indestructible. They live outside the bounds of ordinary mortals. They operate in a kind of netherland and seem to be protected by some kind of guardian angel who watches out for the dim-witted and the wicked. Rules are there to violate and they dare anyone to deny them that right.

PASSION IN TERMS OF ECONOMICS

Passion empowers. It arms people with focus and fuels them with more intensity. Failure is not a possibility for such people. Businessmen become more daring, the artist is more insightful, the writer more incisive, the entertainer more exciting, and the politician more engaging or believable. Passion separates winners from losers like no other quality. With it one can conquer the world. Without it nothing is possible. Does that mean passion will guarantee success? Not at all! Correlation is not causation. Just because passion is highly correlated to success doesn't mean it causes success. But with it success is very probable and without it success is improbable.

What are the qualities that must accompany passion if success is to be achieved? Remaining healthy is critical, as is a slightly above average intelligence. Beyond these it takes hard work, imagination, temerity, intuition, diligence, charm, timing, drive, and tenacity. But in the end nothing happens until someone gets excited. An example is the relationship between passion and money. Any investment banker or venture capitalist knows few investments in start-up ventures are made rationally. If you have the most awesome E-commerce venture it will not be funded until someone believes in it no matter what the numbers say. If the passion exists it will be funded even if it doesn't make economic sense. If it makes economic sense and there is no passion for it the project is destined to go without funding. That is the sad commentary of new venture funding as it is with all other facets of business.

All investment opportunities are a trade off between fear and greed, the greed to make a fortune, versus the fear of losing the investment. Therefore, it takes an emotional investment before any financial one takes place. In simpler terms, until a potential investor is sufficiently aroused by the potential, no risk will be taken. This is true of any risk including attracting a mate. Regardless of qualifications, until there is heat in the heart the head won't take action. Does an investor need to know the return on investment, or a suitor the baggage involved? Of course they do, but only to justify an emotional need to

246

move forward. The numbers merely justify a predetermined decision to act. Investments are but a linear function of the passion for the project.

SEX DRIVE & CREATIVITY

Many of the world's creative geniuses, such as Leonardo da Vinci, Michelangelo, Nikola Tesla, and Hemingway believed sexual activity and creative output were a direct tradeoff with creative output dropping off in a linear relationship to the amount of sexual activity. These individuals were convinced romance was the mortal enemy of the creative process. Freud agreed saying, "man will make no progress if he could obtain fully satisfying pleasure." A raging libido needs an outlet and these subjects defied the Freudian principle although it is hard to dispute the awesome creative output of Michelangelo, de Vinci, and Tesla.

These subjects were satyrs as well as highly creative. Ruth feared going to bed in case he would miss out on some new female conquest. Kennedy spent an inordinate amount of time each day trying to sate his immense sex drive but still won a Pulitzer Prize for *PT-109*. Bucky Fuller admitted to sleeping with 1000 prostitutes while still in his 20's but was unbelievably productive. Isadora Duncan, Colette, and Madonna were called nymphomaniacs but achieved enormous creative success. Picasso's hyper-sexuality didn't deter him from becoming the most prolific painter in the 20th century. And Hughes stable of women didn't keep him from becoming the wealthiest man in the world, nor did Ellison's womanizing keep him from accumulating $50 billion and building the world's second largest software firm.

SEX DRIVE & MONOGAMY

Psychotherapist Carl Jung believed, "The prerequisite of a good marriage is the license to be unfaithful" (Wallace p. 247). These libertines were not all so out front with their beliefs but all chased work and romance with a similar passion. None allowed work to interfere with their seductions, nor allowed family, social mores, or their lovers to interfere with their work. All were driven passionately but it was work in a close to with sex drive, and families and friends a distant second. Monogamy was not important or even a consideration as they had to appease their inner drives no matter the casualties and there were many. Their lives and lusts were summed up by Colette, "When a woman is earning money, has pretty clothes, a man to fuck her, another begging to fuck her, a third gigolo making the same proposition – that woman should be happy" (Thurman p. 294).

SYBARITIC GENIUS

SYZYGY & SEX DRIVE

This term relates to the conjunction of female qualities in the unconscious of the male, and male qualities in the unconscious of the female. Jung coined the term to describe the repression of our opposite gender. The more macho the male the more they have repressed their female qualities, and the more sensitive the female the more she will have repressed aggressive and risk-taking behaviors. Jung felt the way to be whole was to get in touch with that repressed opposite. The reason for this discussion is that it is obvious these subjects did so more than most. The women offer validity for Sophocles famous adage, "When woman becomes the equal of man she becomes his superior." The males were more sensitive than the average male.

Were Isadora, Colette and Madonna ever accused of being submissive housewife types? Never! In fact not one ever cooked, cleaned or did the dishes. In fact, if asked they probably would have broke the dishes. Care-takers they were not but many females were attracted by the high-strung sensitivity of Wilde, Chaplin, Hughes, Picasso, Fuller, and Camus. The three females were highly competitive, aggressive, and risk-takers beyond the pale of any traditional definition of a woman. One key example is decision-making. In the Western world about two-thirds of females test as making *feeling* type decisions with males making *rational* and *impersonal* decisions. But not these three! All were prone to making *rational* or *impersonal* decisions. In contrast, Wilde, Chaplin, Jung, Camus and even Picasso were more inclined to making decisions emotionally.

University of Chicago psychologist Csikszentmihalyi wrote in *Creativity* (1996), "Creative individuals are more likely to have not only the strengths of their own gender but those of the other. Creative individuals escape rigid gender role stereotyping and tend to androgyny" (p. 65). What does this bode for the ordinary person? Be what you are and also be what you are not. That is the panacea of greatness based on the finding in these subjects. Virginia Woolf wrote, "It is fatal to be man or woman pure and simple; one must be woman manly or man womanly." Csickszentmihalyi offered further insight with his admonition, "When an extravert learns to experience the world as an introvert it is as if he or she discovered a whole new missing dimension." One biographer said of the Little Tramp, "Chaplin understood instinctively that androgyny was in tune with the modern temperament" (Milton p. 1810). Colette offered further confirmation with her words, "I struggle to be a real woman while feeling like a hermaphrodite" (Thurman xv).

SYBARITIC GENIUS

PASSIONATE PEOPLE IGNORE EXPERTS

Why? Because an *expert* has such an investment in what *is* they are seldom capable of seeing what *might be*. Cite the work of the great cartoonist Charles Schultz. The creator of Peanuts, Lucy and Charlie Brown was in tune with kids and their environment. When he first submitted his insights on children to publishers they were summarily rejected by experts who didn't think he was qualified to draw cartoons about children. But Schultz wanted to portray children as he perceived them and refused to be denied. Had he accepted the expert opinion the world would have been worse off. A similar rejection occurred in the life of Ted Geissel, better known as Dr. Seuss. Geissel, like Schultz, loved to portray things in an altered state of reality aimed at the juvenile mind. His work was demeaned for years and he wasn't able to create his classic *Cat in the Hat* until his mid fifties. Had he listened to the experts he would never have revolutionized children's books and killed Dick and Jane readers. He lasted all of a few hours in art school. Why? The teacher told him, "No, Theodore. There are rules that every artist must abide by. You will never succeed if you break them" (Morgan p. 31).

What has this to do with passion? Everything! Passionate people operate outside the box and are intolerant of useless conformity. Traditionalists make rules destroyed by creative types like Schultz and Dr. Seuss. That is why all innovative breakthrough demands a change master who defies the rules. All paradigm shifts are created outside conventional boundaries. This was the basis of Isadora's creation of modern dance. She hated ballet so much she was motivated to create a whole new form of dance. Odd duck Charlie Chaplin did the same for the film industry, as did Hughes for the airline industry, and Picasso in art via Cubism. Seeing *Les Demoiselles d'Avignon* Henri Matisse said, "Picasso has an all-consuming urge to challenge, shock, and destroy and remake the world." Larry Ellison found similar success in developing a billionaire dollar software empire. He offered the basis of his success as, "I never accepted conventional wisdom." Bucky Fuller approached creativity in a similar fashion developing a whole philosophical concept labeled, *antiestablishmentarianism*. In a similar way President John F. Kennedy was unconventional saying, "Conformity is the jailer of freedom and the enemy of growth."

BEHAVIOR OF PASSIONATE GENIUS

What is the derivation of creative genius and passion? It is many qualities, conditioning, and success imprints from early life and behavior characteristics and idiosyncrasies as adults. Some are intrinsic (internal factors like birth order, parental influence, books, crises, etc.) and others are extrinsic (external personality traits like charisma, risk-taking, Machiavellian, and Type A behavior). See Table 9 for detail on the following qualities.

BIRTH ORDER. The order of birth in a family is important to success but only marginally. Eight of the fourteen subjects were born first. Russell and Colette had older siblings but were effectively raised as only children since their siblings were over seven years older. The order of birth is not as important in our development as the way we are treated at an impressionable age. First borns are often doted on and treated *special* and raised as the leaders of their clan. They tend to have higher IQ's, more likely to become leaders (First 17 astronauts were first born and every leader during WW-II), and have more expectations laid on them by parents. Two subjects – Howard Hughes and Larry Ellison - were only children. Isadora was the only last born. It appears from the research that being first born is more important to later success for men than women.

SELF-EMPLOYED PARENT. Twelve of the fourteen had self-employed fathers. Why is this important? Because when a child looks up at their prime role model in life and sees someone not dependent on others for their livelihood and not punching the proverbial time-clock it instills independence, coping skills and self-sufficiency. All but two had parents who were independently employed in some capacity. Their parents did not punch a time clock and neither did they. When such people reach adulthood they are more likely to lead in periods of change since that entails being out in front of the pack and such a position demands independence. They have already been conditioned to being alone and responsible for their own destiny.

BOOKS & EDUCATION. Is knowledge important? You bet! But it doesn't have to be formal knowledge. It can be self-taught or come from books which much of the learning did with these subjects. Duncan, Chaplin Colette, Picasso, and Hughes had little formal education but were voracious readers. Isadora Duncan was called the world's most "erudite woman" by no less a person than Auguste Rodin. She only made it to the 5th grade in school but read the Greek Classics extensively and was highly schooled in philosophy, the arts, and poetry. Chaplin had virtually no formal education but became a book-a-phile in Hollywood. Picasso barely made it out of grade school but was highly steeped in Nietzschean philosophy. Bucky Fuller would hold a chair at Harvard but had been kicked out of the institution, not once but twice, but he went on to master such disciplines as architecture, physics, engineering, math, poetry and the social sciences. One-third finished college. Jung and Russell held doctorates and Camus had a Masters Degree.

TRAVEL & TRANSIENCY. Early travel, moving, boarding school education, or being raised in foster homes appears to have armed these individuals with a special temerity and self-sufficiency. Those raised in boarding schools had no one to fight their battles but them. The majority traveled extensively or moved often. This forced them to cope with the new and foreign. Jack Kennedy lived in three states by age ten – Massachusetts, Connecticut and New York, and vacationed extensively in Florida. From age eleven he lived in a prep school. Wilde, Jung, Hughes, Russell, and Fuller were raised in boarding schools with Ruth and Chaplin in reform schools. Camus was raised in a long series of foster homes, Ellison was born out of wedlock and raised by foster parents in Chicago. By age 17 Duncan lived in San Francisco, Oakland, Chicago and New York City. By 21 she had worked her way to Europe on a freighter. Finding yourself in such new venues requires adapting to new teachers, friends, and cultures. This molds the child with a special strength and ability to cope with the unknown. They learn self-sufficiency and how to deal with ambiguity.

FREEDOM TO ERR. These subjects were independent very early in life. Most were allowed the freedom to roam and discover the vagaries of life. They were allowed to err without remorse and to assume responsibility. Duncan wandered the streets of San Francisco as a young girl and wrote in her memoirs, "I could wander alone and follow my own fantasies, it is certainly to this wild untrammeled life of my childhood that I owe the inspiration of the dance I created, which was but the expression of freedom" (Duncan p. 11). Charlie Chaplin was pushed onto the stage in place of an inebriated mother and told to sing. By twelve he was a vaudevillian. Camus was writing an article for an Algerian magazine by age sixteen. Freedom allowed them to learn early how to cope and molded indomitable spirits.

CRISES & TRAUMA. Staring mortality in the mirror armors one for the tough fights in life. Few people make it to the very top without a visit to the bottom. Why? Because the trip arms you with a certain resiliency and having stared mortality in the mirror little else can instill fear. Madonna told the media, "Surviving rape made me stronger" (USA Today Nov. 30, 1995 2D). She said it was devastating to her at the time but in the end it "forced me to be a survivor." Dr. Ilya Prigogine won the Nobel Prize for his work on "Dissipative Structures" that showed the emotional system was like a bone in that it healed stronger at the break point. His work offers proof that what doesn't kill you truly does make you stronger. He wrote, "Psychological suffering, anxiety, and collapse can lead to new emotional, intellectual, and spiritual strengths – confusion and death can lead to new scientific ideas" (Prigogine 1984).

It is almost a given that John F. Kennedy would never have become President had he not been so afflicted with physical problems. Kennedy received the last rites of the Catholic Church three times by age 35. Due to a long list of infirmities, back problems, malaria, Addison's disease, numerous cases of STD's, Kennedy believed he would be dead by forty. He had to achieve everything in just a few years and was a man on a mission seldom witnessed in ordinary mortals. Senator George Smathers advised him to slow down but Kennedy told him, "I can't. The drugs are going to finish me off by the time I'm 45. The point is that you've got to live every day like it's your last day on earth. That's what I'm doing" (Russell p. 95). Had Kennedy been less sickly, it is unlikely he would have achieved what he did. His mortality probably impacted his need for instant sexual gratification.

A similar epiphany occurred early for Albert Camus. At age fifteen the Algerian born philosopher was diagnosed with TB. In 1930 such a diagnosis was an automatic death sentence. Camus used his affliction as a motivator. He embarked on a life with unabated passion. Like Kennedy, he feared not living to fulfill his destiny as can be seen in his words, "Sleeping is a waste. I have a mad and avid thirst for everything. I'm in a hurry to live a lot, with lots of experiences" (Todd p. 49).

CRISES LEADING TO CREATIVITY. Carl Jung was already a practicing psychotherapist when he entered a state of dementia just after his break with Freud. Freud described this as his "psychotic period." Anthony Storr (1996 p. 91) described it a period of "creative illness." It was during this time that he produced virtually every innovative concept of his long life including: Collective Unconscious (Archetypes), Synchronicities (there are no accidents), Syzygy (Anima & Animus), Personality Types (extraversion & introversion), Individuation (holism), and Active Imagination (Introspection). Jung wrote, "everything essential was decided" during those years when "I was pursuing my inner images." He wrote:

> *These were the most important years in my life. It all began then; the later details are only supplements and clarifications of the material that burst forth from the unconscious, and at first swamped me.* (Hannah p. 127)

SYBARITIC GENIUS

TABLE 9 - BEHAVIORAL DATA ON PASSIONATE GENIUS

3 FEMALES - 11 MALES; 7 EUROPEANS & 7 AMERICANS

SUBJECTS	BIRTH ORDER	Slf-Empl. parent	Formal Educ.	MOVES TRAVEL	CRISES/ TRAUM	TYPE A A OR B	BIG T'S LITT t's	RELIG/ SPIRTL	CHARM	HIGH MACHS
		FATHER	HS/COLL	5 Moves	DEATH	A, B, A+	RISKER	DOGMA		
MALES										
BABE RUTH	1ST	YES	HS	ORPH	DEATH	A+++	T+++	CATH	CH+++	NO
ALBERT CAMUS	1ST	YES	MA	MOVES	DEATH	A+	T++	ATH	CH+++	NO
CHARLIE CHAPLIN	1ST	YES	3RD	ORPH	DEATH	A+++	T+	NONE	CH+	MCH+
LARRY ELLISON	ONLY	YES	HS	ADOPT	ADOPT	A+++	T+++	AGN	CH+	MCH+
BUCKY FULLER	2ND	YES	HS	MOVES	DEATH	A+++	T+++	BUDH	CH+++	NO
HOWARD HUGHES	ONLY	YES	11TH	BRDG	DEATH	A+++	T+++	PROT	CH+	MCH+
CARL JUNG	1ST	YES	MD	MOVES	NO	A+++	T	BUDH	CH+++	MCH
JOHN F. KENNEDY	MID	YES	BA	BRDG	DEATH	A+	T+++	CATH	CH+++	MCH+
PABLO PICASSO	1ST	YES	5TH	MOVES	DEATH	A+	T+++	ATH	CH+++	MCH+
BERTRAND RUSSELL	1ST	YES	PHD	BRDG	DEATH	A+	T++	ATH	CH+	NO
OSCAR WILDE	MID	YES	BA	BRDG	DEATH	A+	T+++	CATH	CH+++	NO
MALES (11)	1ST = 7 / 64%	Y = 11 / 100%	COLL = 5 / 45% / GRD = 3	M/TR=9 / 82%	CR =10 / 91% / DTH=9	A =11 / 100% / A+++=6	T = 11 / 100% / T+++7	RL = 4 / 36% / AGN=5	CH=11 / 100% / CH+++7	M = 6 / 55% / M+=5
FEMALES										
COLETTE	1ST	NO	8TH	NO	NO	A+++	T+++	ATH	CH+++	MCH+
ISADORA DUNCAN	LAST	YES	5TH	MOVES	DEATH	A+++	T+++	ATH	CH+++	NO
MADONNA	MID	NO	HS	NO	DEATH	A+++	T+++	AGN	CH+++	MCH+
FEMALES (3)	1ST = 1 / 33%	YES = 1 / 33%	COLL = 0 / -	M/TR = 1 / 33%	CR =2 / 67% / DTH= 2	A =3 / 100% / A+++=3	T = 3 / 100% / T+++3	REL= 0 / - / AGN=3	CH = 3 / 100% / C+++3	M = 2 / 67% / M+=2
GRAND TOTALS (14)	1ST = 8 / 57%	YES = 12 / 86%	COLL = 5 / 36% / GRD= 3	M/TR=10 / 71%	CR =12 / 86% / DTH=11	A = 15 / 79% / A++=9	T = 14 / 100% / T++10	REL = 4 / 29% / AGN=8	CH=14 / 100% / C+++10	MCH=8 / 57% / M+=7

Table 9 shows that 86 percent of these subjects faced some great trauma in their lives. For some it was the death of a parent or sibling as was the case of Picasso's sister, Hughes parents, and Madonna's mother. For Kennedy it was a sickly childhood and early adulthood when he didn't think he had long to live. With Ruth and Chaplin it was internment in a reform school and Ellison being adopted and never knowing his parents. Isadora Duncan didn't know her father and gave validation to this concept of crisis and creativity with her statement, "I was the most courageous when there was nothing to eat. I gained the technique which enabled me afterwards to face ferocious managers" (Duncan p. 20). Larry Ellison said it differently but with the same intent, "I think my dad had a wonderful effect on me. If fire doesn't destroy you, you're tempered by it. Thanks Dad" (Wilson p. 23). When Picasso's sister Conchita was diagnosed with a life-threatening disease he made a Faustian pact with God to save her. He promised to lay down his brush and never paint again if she were saved. She died a horrible death and the teen became a painter with a vengeance, one dedicated to destruction of all that was sacred. His bargain had been made in hell, since he didn't want to quit painting, and when his sister died he turned into a nihilistic artist.

MAGNETISM IS MAGIC. Image isn't everything. It is the only thing. These individuals were charmers. They had flare and used it to open doors that otherwise would have remained closed. Effective communications skill is the defining element of all leaders and crucial to success in any venue. The ability to communicate through the written and spoken word is essential and all of these subjects were more capable than most. Colette was called "hypnotizing and possessing a powerful seductive aura" (Thurman p. 297). The closest friend of Isadora Duncan said, "No religious experience ever moved believers to a higher ecstasy than Isadora's dance" (Desti 17). Ellison's ex-wife called him "electric." Columnist Rowland Evans said of Jack Kennedy, "Jack was simply the most appealing human being I ever met." Coco Channel didn't like Picasso but said, "I was swept up by a passion for him." Biographers described Carl Jung as possessing "majesty and a certainty that he was right." Oscar Wilde was dashing and magnetic.

CHEMISTRY, BEAUTY, STYLE, OR SENSUALITY?

What makes for a seductive personality? Some define it as chemistry between two people. Many studies have shown that beauty wins out in the race for business or the hand of a damsel. Isadora Duncan wrote, "I enthusiastically believed that it was only upon awakening the *will* for beauty that one could obtain beauty" (Duncan p. 174).

SYBARITIC GENIUS

The grand style of Oscar Wilde could be disarming as were the beautiful eyes of JFK. Sensuality was a powerful tool for Colette, Chaplin and Camus. Hughes was a dashing raconteur with power. Ellison had style and Madonna was provocatively sensuous. Adda Quinn, Larry Ellison's first wife, admitted that she didn't understand him, but said, "He was the most fascinating man I'd ever met in my life. He's beyond anything I've ever experienced (Wilson p. 39). His third Barbara Boothe told biographer Wilson, "I've never met anyone like him." When queried about not remarrying she responded, "Once you've gone vertical in a fighter jet, who wants to chug along in a biplane" (Wilson p. 155).

GRANDEUR, STYLE & GRACE. The sheer eloquence of Oscar Wilde was captivating. Both men and women melted in his presence. He was a 6' 3" and dressed elegantly. He walked into a room as if he owned it adorned in top hat, pearl cane, white gloves and satin or velvet coat. Those not enraptured by his appearance were by his wit. One British critic said, "He was the most brilliant talker I have ever encountered." George Bernard Shaw wrote, "If I craved for entertaining conversation by a first-class raconteur I should choose Oscar Wilde." Wilde was so used to using his grandeur to win over audiences he actually believed he would be able to defend himself before the courts and come away unscathed. He was wrong. The British court system was not quite so captivated by his pomposity and haughtiness as the salons. His charm made him but in the end destroyed him.

SPIRITUALISM/RELIGIOUS BELIEF

The majority of these subjects had a mystical spirituality about them, even the ardent atheists. Colette was into séances as was Carl Jung and Charlie Chaplin. Most were superstitious and Carl Jung, a highly trained scientist, used horoscopes in his psychotherapy and his research. Eight of the subjects, including all three females, were either agnostic or atheistic. The most rabid anti-Christs were those most steeped in religious dogma at an early age. Jung's father was a Bishop while Picasso and Camus were christened Roman Catholic. Bertrand Russell grew up in a Puritan home. His grandmother forced him to pray seven days a week and the rigor caused him to rebel by his mid-teens. Picasso, Jung, and Camus lost their faith before age twenty-one. Colette and Ellison never had any faith except in themselves. The most religious were Hughes and Kennedy and neither one allowed faith to interfere with their life.

TYPE A'S & PASSION

Passion pervaded these subjects like few others in history. One of the traits that exacerbated it was their Type A behavior. Such people are in a hurry to get through life and confuse self-worth with achievement. Consequently, such people must be the best in all things or feel inadequate. The women were all super Type A personalities while only six of the men were so off-the-wall. Type A's are impossible to live or work with. Type b's are able to relax and smell the roses and make better mates. These subjects seldom even saw the roses let alone smelled them. All had a propensity to live life in the fast lane and seldom found time to enjoy the fruits of their success.

SENSUALITY. Isadora was the personification of sensuality. When she walked on stage without shoes in a sheer lace gown she was mesmerizing especially in a period when people went swimming in full-length pantaloons. She was enchanting and sensuous and soon became the darling of the European artistic set. She had set out to marry dance with philosophy and the Greek Classics with music to set the tone. For her dance was a metaphysical and ethereal experience of the artist for the audience, a sensuous movement through time and space immersed in Wagnerian power and Nietzschean philosophy. Isadora spoke of working herself into "state of ecstasy" prior to going on stage. Her dedication to going within to find that "central inner force" or *will* she described as "That presence of a mighty power within me and reaches out through all my body, trying to find an outlet" (Duncan p. 24):

> *The dance of the future will have to become a high religious art as it was with the Greeks. For art which is not religious is not art, is mere merchandise. I feel the presence of a mighty power within me which listens to the music and then reaches out through all my body, trying to find an outlet for this listening. I was seeking and finally discovered the central spring of all movement, the crater of motor power.*

MACHIAVELLIAN PASSION

The term High-Mach is used by behavioral psychologists to describe those individuals who are insidious in their use of people. High Mach's use people and almost always make decisions based on the ends justifying the means. Just over half of these subjects were so inclined. Consider Jack Kennedy inviting Lyndon Johnson to be his vice presidential running mate when he detested everything Johnson stood for. But Johnson was critical to carrying the South in Kennedy's run for the White House.

Picasso was probably the most Machiavellian. He said, "Every time I change wives I should burn the last one. That way I'd be rid of them and they wouldn't be around to complicate my existence." Howard Hughes was a close second. He bribed FDR's son, Nixon's brother, and financed the Bay of Pigs invasion. He manipulated tax shelters and paid virtually no Federal Income Tax on billions in profits. His Spruce Goose airplane was merely a public relations stunt of mammoth proportions. It worked and Hughes Aircraft is still the largest satellite and space contractor in America. Why? Because Hughes was the man who built the largest airplane ever and the image gave him an edge over the competition. Power was his passion and he used both to his own ends.

Few women in history have been more Machiavellian than Colette and Madonna. Both used and abused friends, managers, lovers, associates, and other entertainers in their trek to the top. Charlie Chaplin had a similar propensity. His constant battles with women kept Hollywood lawyers busy defending his nefarious schemes and paternities suits.

DARING & CHUTZPAH

People on the edge have a unique appeal. They are exciting and draw followers who are inclined to further down those perilous roads than when following a wimp. The fearless go where the timorous fear and those with a boring existence see them as exhilarating and will go for the thrill if only for a one-time fling. It is not surprising to find a young female turned on when Larry Ellison asks her to accompany him on a spin around San Francisco Bay in his fighter jet. It was not too different for the young women of Manhattan who succumbed to the charms of the Bambino when he pulled up next to them in a flashy new sports car and asked them to join him for a drink. The sheer audacity of Colette and Isadora Duncan brought them fame and fortune that would otherwise have gone to someone with more talent.

Larry Ellison is a man who lives on the edge in all things. He is not happy if not in some life-threatening venture in the air, in business, on the open ocean, climbing a mountain, or in his personal affairs. The founder of Oracle broke his neck body-surfing in Hawaii on his fiftieth birthday and in 1990 when his company was close to disaster – he had lost a billion dollars – he told a reporter, "It's exciting, it's a rush man." Such swagger is often appealing to the women he dates in Silicon Valley. Madonna has a similar misanthropic appeal. She uses shock to succeed, and many of her fans don't dare miss one of her concerts for fear of missing one of her outlandish acts.

PASSIONATE RISK-TAKERS. All these individuals lived right on the precipice, but had the sense not to fall over. All were willing to lose big to win big. The Bambino said it best. "I swing big and I miss big. I live life as big as I can." Such a daring mentality led him to hold many strikeout records in his career. It also led him to hold equally as many homerun records. A similar penchant for danger led an ageing Colette to take up Alpine skiing a sport not known for the timorous. High risk defined their lives. It made them great and often came near to destroying them. Daring to challenge the system destroyed Wilde and caused Chaplin to lose his passport. Duncan and Camus both died in sports car accidents and Kennedy died due to his daring.

WHAT IS THE DERIVATION OF ARDOR?

Success is a function of identifying a dream or passion and pursuing it with great fervor. Find a dream and pursue it with ardor and the world becomes far simpler, and success is there for the taking. Passion can have many fathers. Dr. Prigogine in his Dissipative Structures work described it as breakdown leading to breakthrough. Alfred Adler saw it as overcompensation for insecurity. Csikszentmihalyi labeled it a "flow state" optimized through practice and focus. Frank Farley defined it as an overdose of testosterone. Joseph Campbell said, "Just follow your bliss." Freud called it the "Pleasure Principle." Students of nature over nurture admonish us to choose our parents very carefully. Others would argue that bipolar afflictions are manifested in hyper-energy, sexuality, and high performance. Gestaltist Abraham Maslow believed it was a transitional process ending with self-actualization. This author believes ardor emanates from a vision that is so strong it keeps you awake, interferes with your favorite pastime, and dominates every waking thought. It is a dream that cannot be extinguished rendering all else in your life as meaningless. A vision so strong it permeates your very being to the detriment of health and welfare. In the parlance of entrepreneurship, *If you are not willing to bet all you have for your idea or project then you are not sufficiently committed to make it a success.* In the production of ham and eggs you would say the chicken is dedicated, but the pig committed.

COMMITTED FERVOR. Passion is an internal energy capable of fueling action. But it must be directed at a creed, philosophy or cause. The dream is the goal. The passion is the fuel necessary to reach that goal. Passion fueled Alexander's dream of conquering the world, Joan of Arc's victories, Mother Teresa's battle against the ill and poor, Napoleon and Hitler's drive to power, and Maria Montessori's school of "social engineering." Passion was the defining factor in the huge success of these subjects. It kept them awake at night but armed them with energy incarnate the next morning. It is what led

Oscar Wilde to sacrifice family, career, and his true love Bossie. The essence of passion is why Howard Hughes risked his life continuously as a test pilot rather than leave such a perilous task to a hired gun. It made Isadora Duncan an ex-patriot, Carl Jung psychotic, and Bucky Fuller consider suicide.

True success without passion is an oxymoron. One can have some success or big success for a short period without intense fervor. But to get to the top and stay there one must have passion without compromise. Is there a big downside? Huge! But that is the price of eminence. Passion and success are inextricably intertwined in life and love. Mediocrity reigns supreme where passion is absent but eminence reigns supreme where passion dominates. A good life is possible without it, but a great life is only possible with it. Once you have climbed the mountain being a spectator is not sufficient. Enlightenment only exists in the so-called zone, that surreal place where ethereal brilliance is found and one will work without pay.

Success, vitality and passion are one. Get excited over your game or don't play. Get excited over your entrepreneurial venture or get a job. Get excited with your mate or find a new one. Get excited over your religion or start your own. Get excited about living or stop. Get a life or get strife. Get passionate and you will get what you want no matter the roadblocks. Will it be easy? No! But passionate failure is preferable to an indifferent success. Those without problems are those without action, and such a life is not worth living.

DR. GENE'S LAWS OF PASSION

In the digital world at the millennium our leaders would have us believe that numbers are more important than the quality of life, and our minds are inferior to the bottom-line. Nothing could be further from the truth. Listening closely to our heart and gut is far more important than some budget personally or professionally. Dreams, not numbers, are the panacea of productivity. Find your hot button or dream and pursue it, as it is the key to happiness. All success emanates from the heart not the head. Passion is the panacea of success and ardor is the armor. It wards off illness and can even intervene for a longer and more productive life. Zeal is the elixir that drives us and makes us whole. And be sure to ignore all those experts who know all the reasons why you should pursue their path. Enthusiasm emanates from that inner fire that makes life worth living. It makes us walk faster, work harder, and enjoy the journey more. Even when not successful we are glad we took the trip if it is our trip. Passion is that inner ardor manifested in exterior drive. Just don't confuse it with emotion or romance. They are different.

Dr. Gene's Laws of Passion!

1. PURSUE A VISION – NEVER NEEDS!
Why? Because labors of love are not work but play; fatigue is virtually
non-existent in play or passionate pursuits

2. FOLLOW YOUR BLISS; NOT ANOTHERS!
Live your own agenda, not someone else's. Pursue a philosophy of
pleasure never money; and life will be bountiful!

3. ITS OK TO BE DIFFERENT – WE ALL ARE!
All paradigm shifts are born in the fringe; embrace your uniqueness and
be the best you can be despite traditional venues. Abnormal success
demands abnormal people functioning abnormally.

4. OPTIMISM & ESTEEM ARE FUEL FOR PASSION!
Believe and the world will follow you even if you are deluded.

5. MAGNETISM IS MAGICAL!
The eminent are enthusiastic communicators. They mesmerize verbally
and non-verbally by getting excited about something.

6. LIFE ON-THE-EDGE IS FAR MORE INTERESTING!
The passionate find danger interesting not threatening; find a risk you
can manage and go for it as there are no big wins without big risks

7. PASSION TRANSCENDS RELATIONSHIPS!
Choose your battles because you cannot fight and win two at once; no one
can successfully serve two masters on the trek to the top

8. PASSION LEADS FROM PERSISTENCE TO SUCCESS!
Passionate people persevere. They never give up and consequently never
fail, they live longer, have less illness, and are highly productive

TABLE 11

ADDENDUM ON PASSIONATE PERSONALITIES

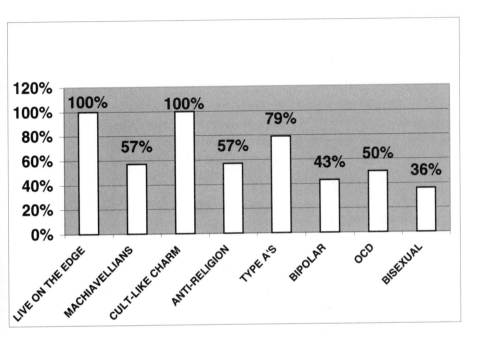

PASSION SELF-ASSESSMENT

SOURCE: SCAT Competitive Anxiety Test for Adults; Landrum's Passion & Performance research

Choose a number 1-5 (with 1 the lowest & 5 the highest) in terms of the degree to which you believe the question describes you and how you feel about the issue. Don't confuse passion with emotion or romance; passion is an external manifestation of inner drives.

1. Physical beauty excites me and is a distraction — 1 2 3 4 5

2. For a 30 minute rendezvous with my favorite film star I would stand up my mother — 1 2 3 4 5

3. I have been described by friends as aggressive and competitive — 1 2 3 4 5

4. Having power is of more important than having security — 1 2 3 4 5

5. Being told I will not succeed in a new venture is more motivating than discouraging — 1 2 3 4 5

6. When I find myself in a non-stimulating environment I find a more exciting one — 1 2 3 4 5

7. I am often described as highly enthusiastic and energetic — 1 2 3 4 5

8. Prior to any competition I worry a lot about my performance — 1 2 3 4 5

9. Given a choice, I will usually take the more glamorous road than the safer one — 1 2 3 4 5

10. Prior to a big trip I have trouble sleeping — 1 2 3 4 5

11. Excelling is far more important than building valued relationships — 1 2 3 4 5

12. Rules are made to break and I am inclined to break them if the rewards are sufficient 1 2 3 4 5

13. I tend to choke up and sometimes cry in emotionally charged stories and movies — 1 2 3 4 5

14. If sufficiently excited I am able to consummate a relationship regardless of location — 1 2 3 4 5

15. I prefer candlelight and wine to a smorgasbord — 1 2 3 4 5

16. Even if fatigued I would give up sleep to opt for an exciting new adventure — 1 2 3 4 5

17. Clothes are very important to me; the more provocative the better — 1 2 3 4 5

18. Sensual poems and letters are more important than a nice dinner — 1 2 3 4 5

19. Behavior is a function of the venue not the rules — 1 2 3 4 5

20 Sexual fantasies are an important part of my life — 1 2 3 4 5

SCORING TABLE (TOTAL SCORE)

90 – 100	SUPER PASSIONATE	80 – 89 PASSIONATE
65 – 79	NORMAL LEVEL OF ARDOR	50 – 64 AUSTERE
20 – 40	ASCETIC	> 20 DEAD BUT NOT AWARE OF IT

REFERENCES ON SEXUALITY

Baumeister, Roy & Smart, Laura. (1996) American Psychological Association, Psychological Review Vol. 103. "Relation of Threatened Egotism to Violence and Aggression: The Dark Side of High Self-Esteem. Pg. 5-29.

Brodie, Mathew. (1987). The Creative Personality: A Rankian Analysis of Ernest Hemingway. UMI, Ann Arbor, MI

Farley, Frank. (May 1986). Psychology Today, "Type T Personality" pg. 46-52

Fortune (May 10, 1999 pgs. 67-80). "Addicted to Sex in Corporate America"

Franzini, Louis & Grossberg, John. (1995). Eccentric & Bizarre Behaviors. John Wiley & Sons, N.Y.,N.Y.

Gornick, Vivian & Moran, Barbara. (1971). Women in Sexist Society - Studies in Power & Powerlessness. New American Library, N.Y., N.Y.

Grant, Michael. (1972). Cleopatra. Barnes & Noble, N. Y., N. Y.

Hill, Napoleon. (1960). Think & Grow Rich. Fawcett Crest, N. Y., N. Y.

Hutchison, Michael. (1990). The Anatomy of Sex & Power. Morrow, N.Y., N.Y.

Jamison, Kay. (1994). Touched with Fire. The Free Press, N.Y., N.Y.

Martens, Rainer, Vealey, Robin, & Burton, Damon. (1990). Competitive Anxiety in Sport. Human Kinetics Books, Champaigne, Ilinois

Mayo Clinic (Oct. 1999). Web Site OCD – Are You Obsessed With Sex?

Peele, Stanton & Brodsky, Archie. (1975). Love & Addiction, Signet Books, N. Y.,

Peterson, Karen S. (9-14-98 pg. 6D). USA Today "Power, Sex, Risk"

Pickover, Clifford (1998). Strange Brains and Genius, William Morrow, N. Y., N. Y.

Reich, Wilhelm. (1973). The Function of Orgasm, Condor, N.Y., N. Y.

Storr, Anthony. (1996). A Study of Gurus: Saints, Sinners & Madmen – Feet of Clay. Free Press, N. Y., N. Y.

SYBARITIC GENIUS

GENERAL REFERNCES

Adler, Alfred. (1979). Superiority and Social Interest. Norton & Co. N.Y., N.Y.

Boorstin, Daniel. (1992). The Creators. Random House, N.Y., N.Y.

Branden, Nathaniel. (1994). Six Pillars of Self Esteem. Bantam, New York, N.Y.

Campbell, Joseph. (1971). The Portable Jung. Pneguin Books, N. Y., N. Y.

Cheney, Margaret. (1981). Tesla - Man Out of Time. Barnes & Noble, N.Y., N.Y.

Clark, Barbara. (1988). Growing Up Gifted. Merrill Publishing, Columbus, Ohio

Conger, Jay. (1989). The Charismatic Leader, Jossey-Bass San Francisco, CA.

Csikszentmihalyi, Mihaly. (1990). FLOW. Harper-Collins, N.Y., N.Y.

Csikszentmihalyi, Mihaly. (1996). Creativity – Flow and the Psychology of Discovery & Invention. Harper-Collins, N.Y., N.Y.

Frankl, Victor. (1959). In Search of Meaning. Pockey Books, N.Y., N.Y.

Gardner, Howard. (1997). Extraordinary Minds. Basic Books, N. Y., N. Y.

Gardner, Howard. (1983). Framing Minds - The Theory of Multiple Intelligences. Basic Books - Harper, N.Y., N.Y.

Gardner, Howard. (1993) Creating MInds. Basic Books - Harper, N.Y., N.Y.

Gay, Peter. (1993). Freud – The Life For Our Time. Doubleday, N. Y., N. Y.

Ghislin, Brewster. (1952). The Creative Process. Berkeley Press, Berkeley, Ca.

Gilder, George. (1984). Spirit of Enterprise, Simon & Schuster, N. Y., N. Y.

Gilligan, Carol. (1982). In a Different Voice: Psychological Theory & Women's Development. Harvard University Press, Boston.

Goleman, Daniel. (1995). Emotional Intelligence, Bantam, N.Y., N.Y.

Hart, Michael. (1978). The 100 - A Ranking Influential Persons in History. Citadel Publishing, N.Y., N.Y.

Heatherton & Weinberger. (1993). Can Personality Change?. American Psychological Ass., Washington, D.C.

266

SYBARITIC GENIUS

Hershman D. & Lieb, J. (1994) A Brotherhood of Tyrants - Manic Depression and Absolute Power. [Hitler &Napoleon] Prometheus Books, Buffalo, N.Y.

Hershmann, D. & Lieb, J. (1988). The Key to Genius - Manic Depression and the Creative Life. Prometheus Books, Buffalo, N.Y, N.Y.

Hirsh, Sandra & Kummerow, Jean. (1989). Life Types. Warner, N.Y., N.Y.

Horn, Thelma. (1992). Sport Psychology, Human Kinetics Publishers, Miami, FL

Hunt, Morton. (1993). The Story of Psychology, Doubleday, N. Y., N. Y.

Johnson, Robert. (1986). Inner Work Harper, San Francisco, CA

Keirsey, David. (1987). Portraits of Temperament. Prometheus, Del Mar, Ca.

Keirsey, D. & Bates, M. (1984). Please Understand Me. Prometheus, Del Mar, Ca.

Klein, Burton. (1977). Dynamic Economics, Boston, Ma.

Landrum, Gene. (2000). Literary Genius. Genie-Vision Books, Naples, Fl

Landrum, Gene. (1999). Eight Keys to Greatness, Prometheus Books, Buffalo, N.Y.

Landrum, Gene. (1997). Profiles of Black Success. Prometheus, Buffalo, N.Y.,

Landrum, Gene. (1996). Profiles of Power & Success. Prometheus, Buffalo, N.Y., .

Landrum, Gene. (1994). Profiles of Female Genius. Prometheus, Buffalo, N.Y.,

Landrum, Gene. (1993). Profiles of Genius. Prometheus, Buffalo, N.Y, N.Y.

Landrum, Gene. (1991). The Innovator Personality UMI Dissertation Service, Ann Arbor, Michigan

Leman, Kenneth. (1985). The Birth Order Book. Dell Publishing, N.Y., N.Y.

Ludwig, Arnold. (1995). The Price of Greatness, Guilford Press, N. Y., N. Y.

Ornstein, Robert. (1972). The Psychology of Consciousness. Penguin. N.Y.

Pohlman, Livia. (First Quarter 1996). The Journal of Creative Behavior, "Creativity, Gender and the Family: A Study of Creative Writers"

Prigogine, Ilya & Stengers, Isabelle. (1984). Order Out of Chaos. Bantam, N.Y.

Rosenzweig, Mark. (1971). Biopsychology of Development, Academic Press, NY

267

Simonton, Dean Keith. (1994). Greatness. The Guilford Press, N. Y., N.Y.

Sternberg. Robert. (1996). Successful Intelligence. Simon & Schuster, N.Y., N.Y.

Storr, Anthony. (1996). Feet of Clay – A Study of Gurus. Free Press, N. Y., N.Y.

Storr, Anthony. (1993). The Dynamics of Creation. Ballantine, N.Y., N.Y.

Sulloway, Frank. (1996). Born to Rebel – Birth Order, Family Dynamics, & Creative Lives. Pantheon Books, N.Y., N. Y.

Walker, Harris. (2000). The Physics of Consciousness. Perseus Books, N. Y., N. Y.

Weeks, David & James, Jamie. (1995). Eccentrics: A Study of Sanity & Strangeness, Villards, N. Y., N. Y.

Wilson, Anton. (1990). Quantum Psychology, Falcon Press, Phoenix, AR

Zubov, V. P., (1968). Leonardo da Vinci. Barnes & Noble, New York, N.Y.

SUBJECT REFERENCES

ALBERT CAMUS

Camus, Albert. (1951). The Rebel. Vintage Books, New York, N. Y.

Literary Review (1990); "Camus the Outsider" page 225

Reiter, Joseph. 1995 Grolier Electronic Publications. "Albert Camus"

Solomon, Robert. 1995 Grolier Electronic Publications. "Existentialism"

Todd, Olivier. (1997). Albert Camus – A Life. Alfred Knopf, New York, N.Y.

World Literature Criticism. Pg. 384-385, "Albert Camus"

CHARLES CHAPLIN

A&E Biography Series (May 10, 1998). Documentary on "Charlie Chaplin's Life"

Chaplin, Charles. (1964). My Autobiography Simon & Schuster, N. Y., N. Y.

Milton, Joyce. (1996). Tramp – The Life of Charlie Chaplin, Da Capo Press, N. Y.,

Time. (June 8, 1998). "The 100/Most Influential Comedian – Charlie Chaplin"

SYBARITIC GENIUS

Wallace, Irving, Wallace, Amy, Wallechinsky, David, Wallace, Sylvia (1993). The Secret Sex Lives of Famous People. Chaplin, pgs 91-95, Dosrset Press, NY

COLETTE – SIDONIE GABRIELLE JUDITH THURMAN

Francis, Claude & Gontier, Fernande. (1998). Creating Colette – From Ingenue to Libertine, Steerforth Press, Vermont

Gallant, Mavis. (Oct. 17, 1999). New York Times Book Review p[g 12-14 "The Pursuit of Pleasure"

Thurman, Judith. (1999). Secrets of the Flesh. Alfred A. Knopf, N. Y., N.Y.

Wallace, Irving, Wallace, Amy, Wallechinsky, David, Wallace, Sylvia (1993). The Secret Sex Lives of Famous People. Colette pgs 102-104, Dosrset Press, NY

ISADORA DUNCAN

Desti, Mary. (1929). The Life of Isadora Duncan. Horace Liveright, N.Y., N.Y.

Duncan, Isadora. (1927). Isadora Duncan - My Life. Liveright, N.Y., N.Y.

Schneider, Ilya Ilyich. (1968). Isadora Duncan. De Capo Press, N.Y., N.Y.

Steegmuller, Francis. (1974). Your Isadora - The Love Story of Isadora Duncan & Gordon Craig. Random House, N.Y., N.Y.

Wallace, Irving, Wallace, Amy, Wallechinsky, David, Wallace, Sylvia (1993). The Secret Sex Lives of Famous People. Duncan pgs 131-133 Dosrset Press, NY

LARRY ELLISON

Benjamin, Matthew. (March 30, 2000 pg. 1). Investors Business Daily, "Ellison, Oracle ready for High Noon, Duel in the Sun with Web Gunslingers"

Consol, Mike. (Jan. 13, 1997). San Francisco Business Times, "The Grand Obsessions of Larry Ellison", Web site: www.amcity.com/san

Forbes (Oct. 11, 1999 pg 200). "Kings of the Code – Larry Ellsion"

Lardner, James. (1-18-99 Vol. 126 pg 38). U. S. News & World Report, "Corporate Evel Kneivel – Larry Ellison's Next Daring Stunt: taking on Microsoft"

Marchetti, Michelle. (June 2000). Sales & Marketing Management, "Master of the Online Universe?" p. 52

Seligman, Jean & Gideonse, Ted. (1-11-99, Vol. 133 pg. 68). Newsweek, "A Sail Down Under Becomes a Storm from Hell"

SYBARITIC GENIUS

Shah, Rawn. (Jan. 1988 NC World). Ncworldmag. Com. "Larry Ellison: The Man, The Myth, The Misses"

Wilson, Mike. (1997). The Difference Between God and Larry Ellison – God Doesn't think he's Larry Ellison William-Morrow, N. Y., N. Y.

BUCKMINSTER FULLER

Baldwin, J. (1996). Bucky Works – Fuller's Ideas for Today, Wiley, N. Y., N. Y.

BFI Institute. (Oct. 1999 WWW-bfi@aol.com). "R. Buckminster Fuller"

Fuller, Buckminster. (1981). Critical Path, St. Martin's Press, N. Y., N. Y.

Hatch, Alden. (1974). Buckminster Fuller, Crown Publishing, N. Y., N. Y.

HOWARD HUGHES

Bartlett, Donald & Steele, James. (1979). Empire - The Life, Legend and Madness of Howard Hughes. W.W.   Norton & Co., N.Y., N.Y.

Dietrich, Noah. (1972). The Amazing Mr. Hughes. Fawcett. Greenwich, Conn.

Higham, Charles. (1993). Howard Hughes. G.P. Putnam & Sons, N.Y., N.Y.

Wallace, Irving, Wallace, Amy, Wallechinsky, David, Wallace, Sylvia (1993). The Secret Sex Lives of Famous People Hughes pgs 225-228, Dosrset Press, NY

CARL JUNG

Hannah, Barbara. (1997). Jung, Chiron Publications, Wilmette, Ill.

Jung, Carl. (1976). The Portable Jung. "The Stages of Life" Penguin, N.Y., N.Y.

Noll, Richard. (1997). The Aryan Christ, Random House, N. Y., N.Y.

Storr, Anthony. (1983). The Essential Jung. MJF Books, N.Y., N.Y.

Storr, Anthony. (1987). The Female & Male Jung. MJF Books, N.Y., N.Y.

Storr, Anthony. (1993). The Dynamics of Creation. Ballantine, N.Y., N.Y.

VanerPost, Laurens. (1975). Jung & The Story of Our Time, Random House, NY

Wallace, Irving, Wallace, Amy, Wallechinsky, David, Wallace, Sylvia (1993). The Secret Sex Lives of Famous People. Jung pgs 244-247, Dosrset Press, NY

SYBARITIC GENIUS

JOHN F. KENNEDY

Guiles, Fred L. (1969). Norma Jean. Bantam, N.Y., N.Y.

Lacayo, Richard. (Nov. 17, 1997). Time. "Smashin Camelot", pg 41-48, V150

Hamilton, Nigel. (1992). JFK- Reckless Youth. Random House, N. Y., N. Y.

Hersch. Seymour M. (1997). The Dark Side of Camelot. Little, Brown & Co. NY

Reeves, Thomas. C. (1997). A Question of Character Prima, Rockland, CA

Wallace, Irving, Wallace, Amy, Wallechinsky, David, Wallace, Sylvia (1993). The
   Secret Sex Lives of Famous People. Kennedy pgs 250-253, Dosrset PressNY

MADONNA – LOUISE VERONICA CICCONE

Anderson, Christopher. (1991). Madonna" Dell, Publishing, N.Y., N.Y.

Bego, Mark. (1992). Madonna - Blonde Ambition. Harmony Books, N.Y.

Greenberg, Keith. (1986). Madonna. Lerner Publications. Minn., Minn.

Meisel, Steven. (November 1992). Glamour " Sex Tips from Madonna". pg 186.

Meisel, Steven. (October 1992). Vanity Fair. "Madonna in Wonderland" pg 206.

Sessume, Kevin. (April 1990). "White Heat". Vanity Fair. pg 143

Sexton, Adam. (1993). Desperately Seeking Madonna. Dell Books, N.Y., N.Y.

Schifrin, Mathew & Newcomb, Peter. (Oct. 1, 1990). Forbes pg 162, "A brain for sin
   and a bod for business"

Thompson, Douglas. (1992). Madonna , Leisure Books, NY

PABLO PICASSO (RUIZ)

Gardner, Howard. (1993). Creating Minds. Harper Collins. N.Y., N.Y.

Gilot, Francoise & Lake, Carlton. (1964). Life with Picasso. McGraw Hill, N.Y.

Huffington, Arianna. (1988). Picasso - Creator & Destroyer. Avon Books, N.Y

Obrian, Patrick. (1976). Picasso. Norton & Co., N.Y., N.Y.

Wallace, Irving, Wallace, Amy, Wallechinsky, David, Wallace, Sylvia (1993). The
   Secret Sex Lives of Famous People. Picasso pgs 356-359, Dosrset Press, NY

SYBARITIC GENIUS

BERTRAND RUSSELL

Russell, Bertrand. (1967). The Autobiography of Bertrand Russell – Vol. 1, Little, Brown & Co., Boston, Ma

Russell, Bertrand. (1987). Ethics, Sex, & Marriage, Prometheus, Buffalo, N.Y.

Wallace, Irving, Wallace, Amy, Wallechinsky, David, Wallace, Sylvia (1993). The Secret Sex Lives of Famous People. Russell, pg 384, Dosrset Press, N.Y

GEORGE HERMAN (BABE) RUTH

Barra, Allen. (July 7, 1999). WSJ, "Baseball's Best Hitters" Sports Section

Blum, Ronald. (Dec. 11, 1999). Naples Daily News, "It's nearly unanimous: The Babe is the best" pg. 2C

Brady, Erik. (Feb. 3, 1995). USA Today, "Legend keeps going" pb. C-1

Creamer, Robert. (1974). BABE, Penguin Books, N. Y., N. Y.

Herzog, Brad. (1995). The Sports 100. "Babe Ruth pg 17, McMillan & Co., NY

MacCambridge, Michael. (1999). ESPN – Sports Century, Hyperion – ESPN Books, New York, N.Y. Babe Ruth pg. 80-91

Wallace, Irving, Wallace, Amy, Wallechinsky, David, Wallace, Sylvia (1993). The Secret Sex Lives of Famous People. Ruth, pgs 390, Dosrset Press, NY

OSCAR WILDE

Ellman, Richard. (1988). Oscar Wilde, Alfred A. Knopf, N. Y., N. Y.

Melmoth, Sebastian. Contemporary Authors, Vol. 119 "Oscar Wilde pg. 403-414

Robot Wisdom Press (Oct. 1999). "Oscar Wilde's 1895 Martyrdom"

Rowse, A.L. (1995). Homosexuals in History, pg 164-169, B&N Books, NY

Schmidgall. Gary. (1994). The Stranger Wilde, Penguin Group, N.Y., N. Y.

Wallace, Irving, Wallace, Amy, Wallechinsky, David, Wallace, Sylvia (1993). The Secret Sex Lives of Famous People. Wilde pgs 471 Dosrset Press, NY

INDEX

INDEX

INDEX